SU XIAOKANG

A Memoir of Misfortune

Su Xiaokang was born in 1949 in China's Zhejiang province. An investigative reporter who made a name for himself during the 1980s for tackling many sensitive subjects, he is best known as co-author of a six-part television series, *River Elegy* (1988), which caused widespread debate about political reform and China's future. It was this brief period of intellectual effervescence that ultimately led to the Tiananmen Square Massacre on June 4, 1989. Named number five on the government's wanted list, Su Xiaokang was smuggled to Hong Kong and then Paris before settling in 1990 in Princeton, New Jersey.

ABOUT THE TRANSLATOR
Zhu Hong, formerly of the Chinese Academy of Social Sciences, is currently Visiting Professor at Boston University.

A MEMOIR OF MISFORTUNE

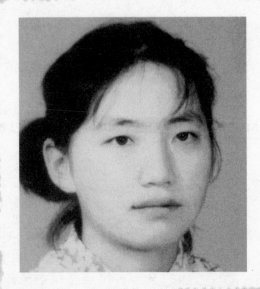

FU LI DURING THE CULTURAL
REVOLUTION, AROUND THIRTEEN
OR FOURTEEN YEARS OLD

A Memoir
of Misfortune

Su Xiaokang

TRANSLATED FROM THE CHINESE
BY ZHU HONG

Vintage Books
A Division of Random House, Inc.
New York

FIRST VINTAGE BOOKS EDITION JULY 2002

The Library of Congress has cataloged the Knopf edition as follows:
Su, Hsiao-k'ang, 1949–
[Li hun li chieh tzu hsü. English]
A memoir of misfortune / by Su Xiaokang; translated
from the Chinese by Zhu Hong.—1st American ed.
p. cm.
ISBN 0-375-41039-2
1. Su, Hsiao-k'ang, 1949– 2. Authors, Chinese—
20th century—Biography. I. Chu, Hung. II. Title.
PL2904.H654 Z46513 2001
895.1'85203—dc21
[B] 00-062001

Vintage ISBN: 0-375-70919-3

Book design by Iris Weinstein

www.vintagebooks.com

Printed in the United States of America
10 9 8 7 6 5 4 3 2

This book is dedicated to Fu Li's parents,
Mr. Fu Boling and Ms. Wang Jingjuan

CONTENTS

FOREWORD

The New England summer was heavy with fruit, the fragrance of their juices clinging to the air. Everything was ripe to bursting. The rich North American foliage lulled me into indolence. It was a pleasurable indolence—perhaps "impotence" in trendy terms, actually an overdose of indulgence—vastly different from the feeling of desolation that the arid plains of China, stretching out from the other end of the earth, inspire in me.

The contrast was especially striking during the summer months, with mowers humming in the dazzling sun as immigrant workers cut the lawns. At first the noise pounded mercilessly into my ears, but later I could nap through it undisturbed. The raw pungency of juices wrung from the piles of mangled grass, however, would still make me dizzy; I was more used to the odorless austerity of crackling wheat stalks on North China's yellow plains. Nor could I stand that nondescript blend of exhaust and perfume cloying the air in European cities.

When I arrived in Princeton, New Jersey, from Europe in 1990, I had felt so intoxicated by the fragrance of cut grass and the chirpings of the summer nights that I could hardly sleep. It was just a few days to my forty-first birthday. I sat up late that first night and asked myself, Have I reached the stage of "beyond confusion"?[1]

> I hope you can see this letter on the day of your forty-first birthday. Our son and I are celebrating here [in Beijing]; you must feel it right where you are. I hope we will celebrate your next birthday together. Our son says that our wish will surely come true.

Fu Li's letter was written in pencil, the writing light, the words burning. Later, a photograph was smuggled out: sparkling candles cast a glow over a loaded dinner table while disjointed shadows reflecting on the glass tabletop conjured up a vision of maimed felicity. She had planted a smile on her face for the camera as she finished lighting the candles, the burnt match still held between her fingers. Our son meanwhile stood behind her, his

---

[1]Confucius said, "Since the age of fifteen, I have devoted myself to study; since thirty, I have been well established; since forty, I have understood many things and have no longer been confused; since fifty, I have known my heaven-sent duty; since sixty, I have been able to distinguish right and wrong in other people's words; and since seventy, I have been able to do what I intend freely without breaking the rules." *Analects of Confucius* (Beijing: Sinolingua, 1994), page 14.

mouth pursed, his downcast eyes fixed on the table. The picture stayed at my bedside thereafter, sole comfort for the hollowness within me.

Three years later, in 1993, reunited with my wife and son, I decided to take a summer trip, with no end in view other than to travel aimlessly across North America. This was for me a step forward. Up to now, the ends I had relentlessly pursued had been grandiose indeed—the study of the decline of civilizations and the rise and fall of nation-states,[2] for one; and on a lesser scale, "enlightenment" and rousing the masses or creating shock effects for fame and achievement. These goals had pushed me on and on, right up to getting myself driven out of my country. Only then did it dawn on me that all those strivings were nothing more than chasing after will-o'-the-wisps. Hence the feeling of hollowness.

[2]A reference to the script for the six-part TV documentary *Deathsong of the River* by Su Xiaokang, introduced, translated, and annotated by Richard W. Bodman and Pin P. Wan, Cornell East Asia Papers 1991, now commonly referred to as *River Elegy.* According to Bodman's introduction, it is "one of the more creative, maverick, and controversial works to emerge from China since the founding of the People's Republic of China in 1949. In proclaiming the death of traditional Chinese civilization, this 1988 TV documentary series set off a debate comparable in nature to the Death of God controversy in the West—for technically atheist China has many worshipers at the altar of national greatness—and with all the intensity and invective of a religious war. Yet the Death of God in the West did not produce a single auto-da-fé, while the makers of this film series have had to face the full wrath of a modern inquisition."

A MEMOIR OF MISFORTUNE

SU XIAOKANG, FU LI, AND SU DAN
AT NIAGARA FALLS ON THE DAY
OF THE ACCIDENT

Chapter One

A BLACK HOLE

Fu Li and I, with our son Su Dan squeezed between us, were in the backseat of a '93 Dodge rental. I was dozing, thanks to a bunch of Chinese students in Buffalo who had kept me up the night before. It was my own damn fault, of course, with my "elegy" of the "yellow civilization" and all the rest of it. I had been badgered with questions on the subject all the way from one end of the world to the other, and in Buffalo, the night before, the discussion had lasted into the small hours. Mind you, to bemoan the fate of the "yellow civilization" under the night skies of North America— that in itself was a form of self-indulgence, an exercise in words—at least until Fu Li walked into the room.

"Su Xiaokang, you are driving tomorrow. Time to break it up."

That was Fu Li's style: no mincing of words, no room for saving face. Her goal in life had always been clear-cut—to be a doctor. But in China even the unenviable job of seeing a hundred patients every day had been taken away from her as one of the side effects of my being on the wanted list. In the United States, she had struggled through the exams needed to qualify as a registered nurse. The exams were now over, and I was dragging her off to see the country.

Fu Li was dressed in a loose-fitting cotton top and shorts, but she was not relaxed. Even half asleep, I could feel the tension in her as she sat on the other side of Su Dan. She had always lived life as if it were filled with pitfalls, while I was perfectly relaxed. For a period of several years I had actually let fame and fortune go to my head, which Fu Li had found intolerable. Fu Li is the sort of person that folks in her home province of Henan refer to as "women with heads held high and men with downcast eyes"—that is, people who do not conform to their prescribed roles. Fu Li always held herself upright, the expression on her face calm and collected. My own infantile attempts at sophistication, added to my general inability to say no—what is called the "amiable ear"—had always roused in her a kind of loving resentment, and she would call me a good-for-nothing.

I had taken my wife and son on this kind of aimless roving several times before. Once, with a group of five or six people, we drove down to Virginia to see where the early English colonists first landed. When we stopped at a restaurant on our way, I picked up my courage and tried to order in English. One young woman giggled, and Fu

Li exploded. "What's so funny? His English is not as good as yours? So what? Isn't it just a matter of your being a few years younger?" She got up and walked out, leaving the girl, Chai Ling, with a flea in her ear.

On another occasion, we went up north to Montreal and then to Toronto and saw Niagara Falls from the Canadian side. Now we had been to see Niagara Falls again, but from the American side, as if there were some strange affinity between its raging turbulence and something in ourselves.

Within the Falls area, Route 90 on the U.S.-Canadian border, though not wide, is neatly divided down the middle by grass dividers. It has an air of tranquillity typical of the East Coast, nothing like the superhighways of the West Coast, where, rather than driving, one seems helplessly propelled forward by a frenzy of speed. Anyway, there we were. It was three or four o'clock in the afternoon and there was very little traffic on the road. The sky was a wash of blue and I dozed off and on, oblivious to Fu Li's tenseness.

I knew Fu Li had doubts about the driver. This was one of the differences between us. Ever since landing in this nation of cars, I had never hesitated to entrust this hundred-plus pounds of whatever I'm made of to whomever it might be at the wheel, driving at whatever chosen speed. I was like one of the eight hundred million Chinese who put themselves into the hands of Mao Zedong to be experimented with during the Great Leap Forward and the Cultural Revolution, without bothering their heads about possible disastrous consequences.

My trust had always been given cheaply: I would gladly entrust my safety, my reputation, and my honor to my friends to do with what they liked, as if they were honoring me and giving me "face." Fu Li could never stand this side of me, and we had had many rows about it after we got married. She had never stayed in the West before, but she was by nature a very private person and always drew a line between herself and the rest of the world. During our aimless driving about after her arrival here, she always avoided riding in other people's cars. She did not trust other people's driving, just as she did not trust other people's morals or other people's consciences. But on this occasion she had no choice. I had spent the previous night holding forth and had driven all morning; in the afternoon I was burnt out and had given the wheel to someone else. Fu Li probably had been worrying about this since the night before.

Route 90 was so smooth and the traffic so light, it seemed the Dodge had the road to itself. The Falls area was immersed in the serenity of the summer afternoon. The world had never been so genial. On these open roads, driving was child's play. What was there to worry about? I finally fell sound asleep. The last thing I felt before I departed into slumberland was eleven-year-old Su Dan's little head resting on my shoulder. I now say "departed" because at the time I did not realize that this interval in slumberland (I am not even sure for how long) was a threshold, an entry into another world. Fu Li took leave of me across this threshold, and I did not even give her a parting glance. She had not slept and had not gotten over her tension. Later I realized that people who can sleep through a high-speed car trip must be people like me who are incorrigibly credulous and trusting. So far, the world had treated me well. I do not understand why suddenly, on a quiet highway near Niagara Falls, it changed face without warning.

Seven days and seven nights later, I woke up to a gray misty world similar to one I had woken up in after a raging fever during my early childhood in the city of Hangzhou: a gray mist accompanied by the smell of antiseptic. Shadowy human shapes flitted before me. They said, "You were in a coma for three days, and then you were raving for three days." Their voices seemed to come from some cavernous depth and made a buzzing sound. Could I walk? I couldn't feel my right leg, and my hipbone hurt excruciatingly.

What happened? Where were Fu Li and Su Dan?

The car had flipped over a short distance west of Buffalo, and all three of us were found unconscious. Fu Li and I were taken to Lake Erie County Hospital, while Su Dan was taken to Children's Hospital in Buffalo. He had regained consciousness the next day and was safe in Princeton with a friend.

Somebody came for me and put a pair of crutches in my hands, and I hobbled after him into another room. There was a single bed in the room, surrounded by a network of colorful tubes and gadgets. A figure lay on the bed, hair spread untidily on the pillow, mouth covered by a strange-looking mask. This was not an apparition. The shape under the white cotton sheet was unmistakable. I would know it if it were burnt to ashes: Fu Li. I had a dim memory of her all tensed up in the car when my world was still intact. Now she was lying here, not only totally relaxed but not knowing where her soul was hovering.

I realized that something bad had happened to my beloved. It is a dreadful thing, this unbearable shock of realization that flashes through the brain and drains it. The brain breathes, and it can asphyxiate. The world had given me three such shocks during my life thus far. First, when I was sixteen years old, Father stood with his back against the light of the window. I could not see his face. I only heard his voice tell me, "Your maternal grandfather has been executed by the government." This meant I was a "damned cur" one generation removed, not one of the five categories of "red offspring." The second time, I was forty years old. In a darkened room, poring over a pencil scrawl on a piece of paper, I made out the words saying that I was fifth on the government's most-wanted list. The third shock came when I was overseas. My cousin called and sobbed over the phone, "Second Aunt has passed away." Her second aunt was my mother. Always during those moments my mind would at first go blank and then realize in a flash that my world had changed. But July 19, 1993, was different. This time my world collapsed.

I had fallen asleep and, asleep, had passed through a disaster, the details of which I will never know. It was a dream without memory, blacking out the most fateful moment of my life, leaving me nothing with which to go on. I had no choice but to accept other people's versions of what happened. The car flipped over because the driver, a woman, was fumbling for the windshield wiper. Did it rain? How can one be thrown off the highway for lack of a windshield wiper? The police report stated that when the car went off the highway and flipped over, it landed on its right side, where Fu Li was sitting. Another version had it that both Fu Li and I were thrown out of the car and knocked unconscious. I was sleeping and did not wake up even when my world crashed. Yet a third version held that Fu Li, awake, stretched over from the backseat to help the driver control the car, which had gone insane; that she was struggling in an upright position, and when the crash came her head hit the windshield. This was the cruelest version, and I could not bear to hear it.

Lying in my hospital bed, I tried but could not piece

together anything that had occurred in the hours after the crash. I felt frustrated, having my life described to me by others. I felt as if the day of my birth as told by my mother was the only kind of information that was trustworthy.

Come to think of it, however, isn't it true that the Chinese are always having the "unexpected" in their lives interpreted for them by others, and isn't this especially true of my generation, which seems to have grown up through a series of "unexpected" events? For instance, in 1971 Lin Biao tried to "defect" and his plane crashed in the desert.[1] At the time the whole country seemed to have gone into a state of shock, and everyone waited for Premier Zhou Enlai and company to offer a proper version of what had happened. At the same time, we did not trust this official version and were always hungry for alternate ones. Again, in 1989 in Tiananmen, there was another crash. How many died? Who gave the orders to shoot? The world would not accept the version offered by the Chinese leadership but could not come up with a version of its own. Why didn't the students retreat? one

[1] A reference to the September 13 incident of 1971, whereby Lin Biao, Mao Zedong's designated heir, was said to have plotted the "571 Project" to assassinate Mao and seize power. When the plan went wrong, Lin Biao left hastily with his wife, son, and close followers in a Trident jet but crashed in Mongolia. All aboard were reported dead.

might ask. The so-called student leaders at Tiananmen Square each have their own versions. Whom should we believe?

About the car crash of July 19, I accepted only two facts. One was that Fu Li was in a coma. The other was that the police report stated the driver could not drive. By then I had lost even the capacity for anger. From that day onward, the world turned upside down and swallowed me up.

"In a Land Far Far Away"

On August 12, 1993, Fu Li opened her eyes. From then on, she stared silently at nothing for days on end.

Had she lost the power of speech? Was she brain-damaged? Paralyzed? Would she become a vegetable? The moment she opened her eyes, she had to fit into one or another of these categories. It seemed there is a wide range of definitions for the state of existence between non-living and non-dying.

She did not appear to notice the people who came to see her. However, when our son was brought to the hospital from Princeton one afternoon, the minute his loud voice was heard from the corridor, a shiver went through her whole body and her eyes turned this way and that, trying to locate the sound. Yet when our son entered the room and bent over her, calling "Mummy!" she looked at him dumbly, without uttering a word.

I marked this day as the day of her awakening and wrote in my diary, "Fu Li has regained consciousness."

I wondered if she recognized me. My one way of checking was to hold her tremulous right hand every day and try to register its every squeeze, as well as each twitch of her leg. I firmly believe that it was her way of responding to me, the only way she could.

Suddenly one day, a tear welled up in her right eye and lingered over her cheek. I wiped her cheek and cried uncontrollably, turning to the window to hide my tears. Suddenly I felt a tapping of her right hand on my left. I turned around and saw her face contorted intensely. In desperation she tried to tap me again. I suddenly understood what she was saying: "You mustn't cry, mustn't cry."

Only when vocal communication failed did I realize the importance of speech. I tried another kind of language and whispered a song into her ear. I remembered a lullaby, "Little Swallow," that she used to sing our son to sleep. Now I was singing it to wake her up.

Here is a woman with whom I shared life for more than a decade, and now I have to see her reduced to this. Was this kind of life worth living? I had thrust this life upon her. These days, during changing time, when I saw her limp body being turned this way and that by the nurse, all I could do was stand aside and weep. "I am a good-for-nothing," I would tell her, over and over again. This was the first time I ever saw myself in this way.

It was impossible even to "hold hands and shed silent tears,"[2] for her face was totally devoid of expression. She had never been the expressive type, never put on feminine airs. Now out of her coma, she remained gazing in front of her, her face placid and detached as it had always been. It held the essence of the look of hers that I had always loved best. When I first saw her with that expression on her face, on the bare yellow plains at the other end of the world, my heart had told me, She is the one. We both belonged to that generation when the aging leaders sowed wild oats while we in the bloom of youth were repressed. We first had our hormones diluted with cheap idealism; following that, in the years of "opening up," we were poisoned by greed and driven by brute appetite.

Love had always eluded us; without a miracle one would never encounter the real thing. But our miracle came in her hometown in Henan province in 1979. At the time I was on the editorial staff of a daily paper; Fu Li was a medical student at a local professional school of medicine. It seemed she was determined not to go with the tide. Already twenty-six years old, she still refused to date the young men hovering around her. Her mother,

---

[2]Stock phrase in classical Chinese romances.

onetime editor-in-chief of a daily paper, was anxious for her to marry and mentioned the matter to an old acquaintance—who happened to be my boss. Thus, she and I met.

To this day, I do not know why she bothered to show up. She walked in, tall and slender in a light blue skirt, gave me a look, and sat down. My boss and I did most of the talking; demurely, she put in a word now and then. She had a mole on the left side of her chin, similar to the one on Mao Zedong's chin, supposedly a mark of great-ness, not a beauty spot, which traditionally should be above the lips. Later I asked her about it. She smiled and told me a mole was just an abnormal growth on the skin and, if hers had not been on her face, she would have had it surgically removed. At the time I was thirty and had just emerged from a disastrous love affair into which I had thrown myself recklessly with a youthful ardor akin to religious fervor. I felt drained and defeated, with no hope of finding anyone else. But the day I met her, I felt as if I had walked into a refreshingly cool morning. It must be the kind of feeling described by Eileen Chang[3]: "To meet the one among ten thousand, to meet in ten

[3]Chinese writer (1920–1995), born in Shanghai, left China in the early 1950s and settled in the United States. A prolific writer, Eileen Chang is best known for her short stories, the novels *The Rouge of the North* and *The Rice-Sprout Song* (both recently reissued by the Univer-sity of California Press), and other works of fiction, many of which have been translated into English.

thousand years, not a moment too early nor a moment too late, right on the dot of time. It is beyond words." After marrying me after a minimum of romance, she later told me that the minute she saw me, she knew I was the one.

She also told me that once she had made up her mind she invited her close friends to meet me, her peers who were already married and had children. She lured me to her place under some pretext and put me on display. Her friends looked me over and unanimously voted against me. They said I was a worthless scribbler and barely matched her in height. (Among the people of Henan, tallness is one of the basic requirements of the eligible bachelor.) But Fu Li said she liked me for my temperament and air of a literary man. So she married the worthless scribbler.

From the hospital window I could see the housing projects of Buffalo's inner city. The Lake Erie County Hospital, over ten stories high, stands right in the middle of them. I often pushed Fu Li's wheelchair down the corridor of the hospital ward; through the window at the end of the hall, we would gaze beneath us at the the dumb desolation of the projects in the stillness of the setting sun. Life suddenly stood still, frozen, in the summer dusk. Even the lushness of North America would wither before our eyes. How did the two of us find ourselves here? Where are we, anyway?

On another occasion, a familiar melody suddenly

broke the silence of her room, sending a thrill through me. It came from the tape recorder at Fu Li's bedside, singing a song: "In a land far far away, there's a sweet sweet girl." The glow of the setting sun settled itself on Fu Li, now tied to her wheelchair, her head secured between two supports, the head once held high now drooping if unsupported. Thus we let time slip by, as the strains of the song drifted around us. The tape was a gift from Kang Hua, a Ph.D. candidate in physics at Buffalo University. It was at his place that we had talked away half the night on the eve of the accident.

I do not know whether Fu Li could hear the once-familiar song or whether she could hear me when I sang "Little Swallow" between sobs. But I found myself lost in the melody, hearing in it a primitive beat, a universal appeal. It reminded me of the forlorn situation of Fu Li and myself, and our helplessness as human creatures cast on this earth. I said to her, "I escaped in the late spring of 1989, and we were torn apart for two whole years. Now, in the blazing summer of 1993, we were only parted for a week, but it is like a parting for life." This is how the song moves me, making it my own particular song of "Far Far Away," and brings tears to my eyes every time I hear it.

I am not talking about music, I am concerned only with how the song affected me. Actually, "In a Land Far Far Away" was originally a folk song of love from rural northwest China[4] recovered by the musician Wang Luobin. During the fifties, it was on everyone's lips, virtually becoming our national anthem, a political symbol of "national solidarity." In fact it had been so politicized that, during the dark period of the sixties,[5] the genuine ring of the song was totally lost. I had always disliked politicized love songs, the most repulsive being "The East Is Red,"[6] which was originally a love song from Northwest China. Our thoughts have been so inured to these fakes, we have lost the capacity to enjoy the flavor of genuine love songs.

But that evening my soul was transported by the strains of the song, as if I had had a glimpse of heaven. Only in the depths of pain, perhaps, can one be so blessed. Without being conscious of it at the time, I was

---

[4]Northwest China covers a wide area, but here it refers to the base area centered around Yan'an, Shaanxi province, where Mao Zedong set up his power base in the middle 1930s. The folk culture of this area had a deep influence in the forming of the communist literary tradition.

[5]Referring to the Cultural Revolution, launched in 1966.

[6]
> *The east is red,*
> *the sun rises,*
> *Mao Zedong appears in China,*
> *he seeks the good of the people,*
> *he is the savior of the people.*

Sung day in, day out, on every occasion, big and small, by the largest population on earth for the longest period of time.

able to hear that song in its pristine rhapsody; it gripped my heart and flooded my soul. For a moment, I felt that Fu Li and I were back in the misty heights of Mount Lu during our honeymoon trip in 1979. We took the boat from Wuhan to Jiujiang city and from there headed up the mountain to find ourselves the only occupants of a little guest house wreathed in mists at the peak. We were in raptures. After leaving Mount Lu, we took the train and at dusk found ourselves in the town of Tai'an on the outskirts of Mount Tai, right on time to celebrate the Moon Festival. Fu Li said, "Come on, let's climb the mountain!" and off we went. In the darkness of the night, we set out from the north gate of Daiyue Temple, the temple guarding Mount Tai, and started up. The first leg of the climb, from the Daizong Gate to the Dai tip, was reputedly composed of seven thousand stone steps. Her ponytail swinging behind her back, Fu Li charged ahead, never stopping to rest, and arrived at the Double-Pine Pavilion before daybreak. Obviously impressed, a group of young Latino men at the other side of the Heavenly Ladder decided to race us. Thus as we climbed the dangerously steep stairs, sometimes Fu Li and I left the tourist group behind and sometimes they outstripped us. Racing each other from either side of the Heavenly Ladder, we reached the Southern Gate of Heaven, covering another 1,594 steps for this last leg of the climb. This was the proverbial Eighteen Steep Windings, Eighteen Slow Windings, and

Eighteen Windings neither Steep nor Slow. On the last stages of the Eighteen Steep Windings, one of the young Latinos flopped down on the ground from exhaustion and started throwing up. I stopped to catch my breath for a moment and went over to see whether he was okay. Panting for breath, he pointed to Fu Li and said to me in broken Chinese, "Your . . . girlfriend . . . is beautiful!" I was off guard and didn't catch his words at first, then realized that he was smitten by Fu Li. What he did not know was that she was already twenty-eight years old. As I turned back, I regretted not telling him that she was my wife. We waited for sunrise at the peak. It was cloudy and the sun did not show herself, but we were blissfully happy anyway.

During the Moon Festival of 1991, Fu Li had been in the United States barely a month. One night after a party, she wrote this in her diary. I came across it by chance after the car accident.

It is the Moon Festival, and the first time in three years that we celebrated it together. Twelve years ago today, Xiaokang and I got married and went to Mount Lu and Mount Tai. I can't believe that time has passed so quickly. Just now Xiaokang said to me, "Look, you are getting old. Remember how that young foreigner admired you at Mount Tai?" I replied, "It's so depressing to hear you say so." But it's true, I am getting old, with nothing to my name. It breaks my heart.

When I am with Fu Li, I am lifted into heaven; away from her all I have is worldliness, but I never realized it at the time when I was catapulted into celebrity. And now, I am again able to have a glimpse of heaven because "in a land far far away," there are only the two of us together, she seriously wounded, and that land far away is a new stage in our lives. I watch helplessly as our son grows up on his own. He is no longer what we conventionally consider a Chinese and will not be moved by a song like "In a Land Far Far Away." After that evening, I often played that song, repeating it again and again, ruminating through its melody on what I have lost and what I have gained—making a set of accounts one might say. I will never forgive my own recklessness. Recklessness seems to be the most destructive factor in my makeup. Fu Li fought against my recklessness all through our married life, but she lost the battle, in a series of grave misfortunes.

Take this last calamity, for instance, which was outrageous beyond belief. After Fu Li's accident, the driver admitted that she had never driven on a main highway before. Yet I had given the car over to her without a thought and dived into the backseat to catch some sleep.

For the last ten years, I myself was like a crazy old car, careening recklessly among the potholes of China's dangerous political highway, on more than one occasion almost running out of control. Back then Fu Li was at my side, desperately trying to hold me in check, until the spring of 1989, when the car of my fortunes turned upside down. Here in the United States, it was Fu Li who was hurt most seriously, with a cerebral hemorrhage, broken ribs, and punctured lungs.

The pattern of our lives seemed to be that Fu Li would first try to keep me in check and, failing that, would fall into the trap that I had laid.

For instance, I always picked sensitive subjects on which to report, making myself a thorn in the side of the people at the CCCP[7] Propaganda Department and the Ministry of Security. Fu Li would give me a mild rap on the shoulder. "Take it easy, our son Su Dan is still a baby." When *River Elegy* was caught up in controversy, she reminded me not to jump into the fray. But she began to dislike my literary buddies and gave them the cold shoulder whenever they crashed in without warning. She had no trust in the kind of things they were dabbling in.

When the students started their actions in Tiananmen, Fu Li watched me closely. She asked for leave at the hospital where she was working and followed me wherever

[7]Central Committee of the Chinese Communist Party.

I went. One day Yan Jiaqi[8] came over and asked me to join him in Tiananmen Square for a declaration. Fu Li held my sleeve and followed me all the way to the square. Carried here and there in the swirling crowd, she would give the sleeve a tug now and then, reminding me to keep a check on my tongue. Suddenly there was a call for a march and demonstration. The few so-called intellectual elites were caught unprepared, at a loss over how to introduce themselves to the crowd. After all, they couldn't very well repeat the antics of the Cultural Revolution and parade themselves in dunce caps with a board hanging down their necks, could they? In the midst of our perplexity, Huang Shunxing of Taiwan showed up wearing a cloth band slantwise from shoulder to waist with his name and title—HUANG SHUNXING REP-RESENTATIVE TO THE NATIONAL PEOPLE'S CONGRESS—written for all the world to see. It was the answer to our prayers, but where were we to find cloth bands in the square? Huang's was probably brought over from Taiwan where it had seen long service, and obviously he had kept it around, foreseeing that sooner or later it would come in handy. For lack of cloth bands we had to make do with paper. "Fine doings!" Fu Li snorted

---

[8]At the time, head of the Institute of Political Studies at the Chinese Academy of Social Science, Beijing, and an advocate for political reform. On the wanted list after June Fourth, he is now in the United States.

when she saw me sporting a paper band advertising SU XIAOKANG, AUTHOR OF RIVER ELEGY. However, she followed me up onto a truck, and thus we paraded up and down the Avenue of Eternal Peace. When we got home, she spat out, "Very nice, you got your moment of glory. All videotaped by the security. From now on you're not going anywhere!" She meant exactly what she said: She stayed home, guarding the door, in case I was dragged out again.

Some individuals would not take no for an answer, my writer friend Zheng Yi being one. He came for the "May 16 Declaration" that I was supposed to have drafted. It was a declaration on behalf of the intellectuals of Beijing in support of the students. But I had barely written a word before I dropped it to take part in a new TV program. Zheng Yi was baffled and exploded.

"Fuck! Doing TV *now,* in these times?"

"That's his job," Fu Li countered.

"Job! Anyone can write a fucking TV script! This is the turning point of history! Everyone has to account for his performance!"

Fu Li exploded in turn. "You go ahead and make history. Leave Xiaokang alone, he hasn't got the makings."

Following that sparring, Dai Qing came over to ask me to join her in Tiananmen Square to advise the students. Fu Li wouldn't allow me to budge. Dai Qing started begging. "Dear little sister"—Dai Qing's family name was also Fu and she was older than Fu Li—"please give me face just this once." Fu Li wouldn't let go; she held me tightly by the hand all the way to the door.

Then she gave up.

As a result, I went to the square.

As a result, I was accused of "counterrevolutionary incendiarism" by the Communist Party.

I ran off to save my own skin, leaving Fu Li behind. By then everyone was heading south, so she also headed south and reached Guangzhou (Canton), on the southernmost tip of the mainland. But she couldn't bear to leave our son, so she turned around and returned to Beijing. By then, she was prepared to join me in the trap I had set for myself.

As a result, she is lying here, with a cerebral hemorrhage, punctured lungs, an incision in her throat for oxygen, and two tubes down her nostrils for medication and nutritional fluids.

These alien objects were intrusions in the sensitive parts of her being. The minute she returned to consciousness, she fought them. So her right hand, which was not paralyzed, was tied to the bedpost. Within a few minutes, she freed her hand and again started tugging at the gadgets. So the nurse tied her fingers together one by one before tying the hand to the bedpost.

What followed was a repeated pattern of her fingers struggling through the layers of gauze to pull out the tubes in her nose. The nurse was furious and shouted at me, "She's making it worse for herself. Do you know how painful it is to insert the esophagus tube?"

I could not bear to watch every time her tube was reinserted. That combination of courage and mad determination on her part, that stubborn resistance to any forced manipulation, was a quintessential expression of her innermost character.

I had never before realized what kind of a woman I had married.

Every morning as I rushed to the hospital, what first met my eye was invariably the sight of bloody marks where she had chewed her mouth in frustration. I would see her sitting in her wheelchair as she let the nurse fix her hair, twisting it into whatever shape she liked.

Letters from Fu Li

The first letter, which someone carried by hand to Paris, was not dated. It was probably the spring of 1990. At the time I was shuttling between Paris, Taipei, and the United States, feeling very good about myself, while she was trapped and miserable.

Someone is leaving, and will bring this letter to you, though I am not sure whether you will see it. Your letter made me full of anxiety. I worry about your health. A few days ago, a friend who had seen you in Paris stopped by and described your situation abroad, which made me worry all the more. I cannot imagine how you manage day by day.

As to the folks at home, there is nothing to worry about. Your parents are not affected, they are in good health, and your father goes to work every day, though I do not know where. Neither are your sister or brother affected. In July [1989] the local security asked your brother for your whereabouts, and they were very civil. During the summer when your whereabouts were unknown, our home was searched, but the people were also very civil. My mother's life has not been affected, either.

One chilly morning on May 20, 1989, almost on the eve of the bloody onslaught, Li Peng[9] proclaimed martial law. I feared the worst and hastily left the group working on the sequel to River Elegy. *I scuttled here and there, not daring to go home, not knowing where to hide. Fu Li searched for me far and wide. When she finally found me, she did not waste words. She entrusted Su Dan to her younger sister and, holding me by the hand, dragged me to the Beijing railway station. We left for Zhengzhou city in her native Henan*

[9]Prime minister of China during June 4, 1989.

province, to take refuge with her mother. The train was crowded with students who had been to Beijing to take part in the hunger strike. Some of them actually recognized me, but Fu Li avoided them, giving me no chance to show off. She left me in Zhengzhou and headed straight back to Beijing, an eight-hour train ride, first laying down the law about my seeing anybody. Two weeks later, she held our son in her arms through a night of terror as the Avenue of Eternal Peace was strewn with bloody corpses. But at the break of dawn she still went to work at the hospital. Her hospital was located on Chongwenmen Avenue, running parallel to the Avenue of Eternal Peace. One side of the high-rise in-patients' ward had been splattered with bullets the night before. The military police started looking for the "wanted" from door to door. Fu Li figured I might not be safe in her mother's place. For the second time, she left our son with her sister and went south, trying to negotiate a safe hiding place for me. So engrossed was she that she did not even know of the secret directive for my arrest. When she first heard of the "wanted" list, she still did not imagine that I was among the wanted, though by then she had figured out that no one would risk helping her. She worried about me and she worried about our son. On her return, she dared not stop midway in Zhengzhou but flew right back to Beijing.

My mother's health is okay. She worries about me and came to Beijing last November. Seeing that I was all right, she was relieved and headed back.

Things are okay here with me and Su Dan. The child is somewhat affected by the event, but not too darkly. I approach things from the positive side, telling him that his father is a good man, that sometimes good people are wrongly blamed, but that everything will be cleared up eventually. He does not doubt this for a minute and thus has no sense of inferiority. He will be fine.

The police showed up at the hospital where Fu Li was working. They brought her to the security office. Then they made her sit in the middle of a circle while seven or eight men questioned her on her movements after June Fourth. In July they came again, this time to notify her of a search of our apartment. She said, "Fine. But it must be during my son's absence." The whole hospital, doctors and nurses and staff, all witnessed the scene as Fu Li was taken away by the police.

Su Dan's grades are okay. He doesn't put enough effort into his studies, always looking for fun, but he has no serious problems. I often criticize him, but never because I am in a bad mood myself and want to take it out on somebody. He has an enormous appetite and is a bit overweight, I am helping him reduce. As for myself, everything is fine. Swings in mood are inevitable, but it all depends on the situation at your end. If your situation remains stable, so will my mood. Physically I am also holding up;

nowadays I am really careful about preserving my health. In the daytime I study English, and every Wednesday night I attend classes in Chinese medicine, learning basic skills such as massage and acupuncture. Who knows, someday they may come in handy.

My own assessment of the situation is this: first, the possibility of your returning in the near future is nil, so the only way to reunite is for us to exit; second, my chance of leaving the country through regular channels is very slim, but it is worth a try, as only through regular channels can I take Su Dan with me; third, I have no hope of applying for study abroad, so I do not let this fact affect my spirits and do not suffer any disappointment on that count; fourth, I am prepared to be denied the right to join you for many many years. I will carry on as usual and bring up our son. Let your heart rest at ease on that count.

What worries me is your situation. I think that in the first place you should let go of your sense of mission; just sit back and be content to survive as an ordinary man. Only by surviving can you achieve something or write something. Put aside other people's hopes in you, ignore their expectations. Just be yourself, live according to your own wishes. Perhaps your life will be better. A man cannot sail through life having everything his way, so it is important to keep up your spirits when things do not go as you would like. I can understand you. Try not to drink too much. Take care of yourself and live regularly on a daily basis. If you find it too hard to be on your own, find someone; I won't blame you. But whatever you do, the most important thing is to create an environment wherein you can lead a normal life. Also, don't go on buying toys for Su Dan. I have money, enough to last me and our son for many years. Don't worry. As to your own income, I advise you to make some long-term plans. A good friend will be leaving in a few days and I will send you some supplies.

The second letter is also undated. By then I had settled down in Princeton. A good friend of hers was coming out as a spouse, and through her Fu Li sent me clothes and medicine. There was a stack of photographs in the envelope, one of Fu Li standing in front of the bookcase in our Beijing home. Dressed in a red woolen sweater, she stood with her arms crossed, looking very composed, but the expression on her face was forlorn.

I really do not know the particulars of your circumstances, cannot put myself in your shoes, and do not have much advice to give you. But somehow I sense that you are under extreme psychological pressure. I feel that in the first place you should just be yourself and try to live according to your own inclinations.

With too much sense of your responsibilities and no ability to fulfill them, life will be very burdensome. In your literary circles, wasn't there a saying about how everyone has his turn in the spotlight? That is a perfect description of your situation. A man cannot be on a pinnacle all his life, nor can his writings. If every composition is a work of genius, then the world will be exploding with works of genius and writers of genius, as a result of which there will be no more writers and no more works of genius. If every hill is the highest peak, there will be no more peaks. I never expected you to be a celebrity, and I don't care one whit what others expect of you. Relax, use this chance abroad to learn something, read what interests you. The situation at home is still pretty tense; attacks have increased. I really think there is not much hope for this country; nobody can fix it. The population is too big, too uneducated, and now everything is at a standstill. Who can tell what the future holds?

As to the problem hanging over those of you out there, I'm afraid we won't see an early solution. Don't be fooled by the release of several individuals. They're far from thoroughly cleared, just out on bail and living in pure misery. They say that even though you people out there are suffering in exile, you're better off than they are. As for yourself, I don't think you'd be released, even on bail, if you were caught. The police are pursuing your case on two counts: the first is the connection between *River Elegy* and Zhao Ziyang,[10] the second is your going to Tiananmen to speak to the students. As to the first, they have ended up with nothing substantial. On the second issue, the organizer, Dai Qing, has not yet been released, but from the material I have been able to get hold of, it seems they can't build up a major case against her. From the way the people who are handling her case are talking, you can tell that the episode of going to Tiananmen is not a major issue. Which means to say they know you have nothing to do with politics, but they still won't let you off the hook. Do not delude yourself with false hopes.

Of course I am not saying that you should throw yourself into politics just because of the hopeless situation. I think you should consider the roads open to you. Above all, never become a "professional revolutionary." Learn English, find a job, and cut your links with the clique you are currently involved in. Your strength is still in your pen, but do not rush things. The day will come when we can all settle down. Most people feel that it will be decades before

[10]Secretary-General of the Party, generally regarded as sympathetic to political reform, he had to step down in the aftermath of June Fourth.

our country can enjoy real stability. So in terms of the future, you must be prepared to settle abroad. Even if you need to come back for the sake of your "identity," our family still needs a place abroad as a last refuge. I hope that you will be able to hold out under any circumstances and face life and the future in a spirit of optimism. Our day will come.

Fu Li left home and came to a foreign land to join me. What's the point of babbling about "concern for the nation and concern for the people" if I cannot even protect a woman who has given up everything for my sake? That the Almighty decided to punish me by hurting her is more than I can bear; I beg the Almighty on my knees to kill me instead. I was never a man destined for good fortune, but it turned out that I married the best wife in the world. What is the meaning of all this?

There is a destiny in men's lives. Apart from us mainlanders who have been brainwashed into a ruthless atheism, is there anyone in the world who does not harbor a fearful respect for a power beyond themselves? Since 1985, I had been basking in worldly gain and glory. In the years 1988 and 1989, so-called mediums had sent me warning signals, not to mention Fu Li's anxiety on my account. I ignored them all, being totally wrapped up in myself, but in her eyes I was more immature than the students.

When I luckily escaped the pursuit and arrests following June Fourth, I actually wallowed in self-
congratulation, deluded fool that I was. As the shots rang
out in Tiananmen, I left my mother-in-law's home in
Zhengzhou and started on my hundred-day life on the
run. A group of people whom I had never met came to
my rescue. Casually, they walked me out of a city where
the WANTED list was posted on every street corner and
where the police had conducted a meticulous door-to-
door search. Equally cool, these people escorted me onto
an island in the sea, an island where every incoming ferry
was searched and questioned. Following that, we crossed
a bay that was crisscrossed by patrol boats and the opposite shore sealed off with gun emplacements. Finally, late
one night I stood in Shatin under the windows of a high-
rise building, gazing at the glittering lights of the Hong
Kong racetrack, and my heart was actually filled with
self-glory. How could this be other than the hand of
Heaven steering me?

But the same hand that steered me to safety thrust me
in deeper trouble. As in the previous case, I had been
warned but had ignored the signals. Was this not fate?
The sweet was followed by the bitter, giving me a taste of
the whole range of human emotions.

*I am looking again at the picture of Fu Li in her red woolen
sweater, arms crossed, the expression on her face forlorn, as I
continue the letter that was brought me by hand.*

My life here is very smooth, believe me. Colleagues at the hospital are friendly, no one picks on me, and I have enough to live on. Don't worry. I feel low now and then, but how can I help it? However, these moods come and go. A while ago, you told me to apply for permission to go abroad, and I started the proceedings. But to this day I have not received your affidavit of financial sponsorship or acceptance into a school for Su Dan. Have I been misinformed, or have you run into difficulties? There's no way to discuss this over the phone. But I want you to know where I stand: Su Dan and I have no problems staying here on our own. The reason for trying to leave is to join you, because in such adversity it is better to have family with you than to cope on your own. Whether we should try to leave earlier or otherwise is up to you, depending on circumstances on your side. Think it over carefully and give me an answer as soon as you can, so that I will be prepared. As to the methods of exit, I insist on leaving through legal channels; I will start the application process only when everything for a legal exit is in place, because only then can I take our son with me. I do not consider for a moment other, irregular, ways of exit. Also, if it is within your means, try to lodge an appeal for family reunion through "humane" channels. You have got yourself entangled in this mess; it's hard to get out of it. Face the fact that this society of ours does not respect the individual, so don't indulge in wishful thinking. Actually, you have always held illusions regarding China.

I have no illusions whatever. My letters to you were mostly written for police inspection. After you left, many former friends were afraid to contact me. Some, however, offered to use contacts with the higher-ups to get me out. I refused. I also warn you to be careful when speaking to people you don't know. Never mention anything you heard from me; that's dangerous. During this past year since you have been abroad, you have gradually lost your vigilance toward the situation here. Actually we are still in danger. Any hints in your letters, if detected, mean trouble for me. People change, you know; you can never tell what they are capable of. How I wish you could go back to writing freely on any subject you liked! But above all, extricate yourself from politics. Even if it is not possible, still you must keep a grip on yourself. Another thing is, don't let whatever steps you take hinge on my situation. If in our telephone conversations you keep talking like that, it will just encourage them to keep me here to control your movements abroad. It will actually hurt my cause. Remember, they can't really do anything to me. In a word, let your decisions rest on your judgment of your own situation. This letter has been dragging on for three days. Such an opportunity! I just put down whatever pops up in my head.

I have been thinking and thinking since you left, and I decided that just sitting around and waiting is not the solution. I want to be self-supporting under any circumstances; perhaps this is one of the differences between me and the other "fugitive" wives left behind. I think it is better for my spirits too to be trying to do something instead of just sitting back and waiting. Of course separation is painful, how can it not be, unless our marriage is on the rocks? Your letter tells me to just wait patiently. I do not understand what you mean. Do you mean I should not do anything, but just live day by day? Do explain what you mean when you write next.

I asked a cousin to issue Fu Li an invitation, and I also sent her an I-20 form. She followed the application procedures step by step, and soon sent me another letter.

After my trip to my mother's place for the Spring Festival, I returned and went straight to the Public Security for my application. The answer was speedy: I am classified as one who would "constitute a danger to national security" if allowed to leave the country, and I was told to forget it. Besides, there are documents, I was told, specifying that family members of "traitors" and people on the WANTED list cannot be allowed to leave the country. I asked which organization had issued the documents. Were they for internal circulation or open to the public? I was told that they are internal documents from the State Council. I further asked whether this conforms to civil rights ensured by the Constitution, and whether this is in keeping with Party policy. The answer is, This is necessary for national security. From then on, they stopped talking any sense. We always overestimate these people, making them out as better than they are.

Finally I made two requests. I said, I cannot do anything to counter your documents, but for my own sake and that of the child, can I leave the country with my child if I annul my marriage? The answer: "Your marriage does not look like it's being annulled, is it? And even if it is, the answer is still no." Then I said, Okay, if I am to be tied down to the marriage all my life, so be it, but my child is innocent. He is not yet of age, he would not be a threat to national security. But the answer was still no.

I appealed to an international human rights organization, and luckily Fu Li was included in a list of people that the U.S. government negotiated with China to have released. And so at the end of the summer of 1991, Fu Li was allowed to leave the country with our son. Child in hand, she crossed thousands of miles to be with me, and I was blessed with the joy of family life for two years. And then, things were so ordered that I was made to fall asleep in a car on a highway so I would wake up to see my wife lying in an emergency room like a vegetable, and to hear the doctor tell me that she is hemorrhaging into the brain.

Is this fate? I asked myself as I stood in the huge hospital building. It looked like a factory where patients were parts and pieces of the machinery. People like me who write "uplifting" prose use the word "fate" with the highest frequency, but we always use the word to question the country or the nation, uttering it so grandiloquently and so glibly. There was even a section on "fate" in my TV series *River Elegy.* But when it is my turn to ask about my own fate, the heavens have already collapsed around me.

I suddenly remembered the first calamity that had struck Fu Li and me. She had conceived a pair of twins but had only been able to keep one. Twelve years later the second calamity; she was allowed to travel thousands of miles to reunite with me in the United States, only to be struck down. It is senseless. Aside from the punishment of heaven, there is no other explanation. Fu Li was a naturally cautious person, always weighing pros and cons before taking a step. After losing that other son, she was even more fearful of some unforeseen disaster, but it happened anyway.

It occurred to me for the first time that Fu Li was most unfortunate in marrying me. There seem to be unforeseen calamities in my life, but, my fate being "tough," my calamities were transferred to this woman who is my wife. Why are things ordered like this?

I was always running into scrapes, but I never gave them a thought, never learned caution. Not even Fu Li could deal with my recklessness. That day in the lounge of the hospital, I suddenly remembered I had been warned of this calamity.

It was the summer of 1991. I was working on a TV movie in Taipei and at night was often dragged by friends to the Yinlu Teahouse, where we drank wine and listened to music and songs sung in the local dialect. After several visits, I learned that the owner was actually a fortune-teller. There were some among our group who dabbled in stocks and would consult him on their luck. One day they egged him on to tell my fortune. I can't tell whether he knew anything about my background. He asked my date and hour of birth and said, "The gentleman has just passed through a great calamity, is that right? Well, not to mince words, there is another one coming."

"When?"

"When you are around forty-five. It is probably something like a traffic accident."

Nobody took this warning seriously, treating it as a joke. I didn't give it a thought myself. The fortune-teller was probably the only one who was in earnest. But when the accident happened, I was forty-five by the lunar calendar.

If I used a wet napkin to wipe the dead skin and dried blood clots off her lips, Fu Li stretched her mouth to meet the wetness of the tissue. Her throat gurgled dryly. Sometimes she coughed or sighed or even made a sound like "ouch." Her punctured lungs had become infected, and she had lost the ability to swallow. Giving her water through a feeding tube was out of the question. It was equally impossible to quench her thirst through the nose tubes. She was being tormented by thirst and could not say it; she could not even make a gesture because her hands were tied.

As I wiped her with the wet napkin, I kept saying to her, We shouldn't have left your hometown of Zhengzhou. If we hadn't moved to Beijing, I wouldn't have earned that bit of fame and wouldn't have gotten into so much trouble. Today we would be sitting with your mother and sister and brother, leading our quiet lives, making hot dumplings for the Spring Festival. "Or," I said, "I should have waited for you in Paris, we wouldn't have driven anywhere, in someone else's car; the metro is superb, and you would have loved the rich cultural heritage of Paris and the ease of living." She opened her eyes, her face placid and relaxed, just listening. Sometimes she would be restless, trying to turn her body this way and that; we turned her over—ah, her buttocks were red and infected. Once when we did this and our faces were close against each other, her right hand clung to my head, trying to press it against her face in a show of endearment, while her bandaged hand patted my face softly as if saying, Don't be sad.

In the afternoon, I would sit in the ground-floor lounge, waiting to take her to her physical therapy session. One day in the middle of September, the news broadcast suddenly announced that Wei Jingsheng, after fifteen years in prison, was being released. It was part of China's bid for the Olympic Games. I should have gone to prison, I thought to myself. Avoiding the calamity of prison only called up another calamity. If I were in prison in Beijing, Fu Li would come for jail visits with Su Dan. But now our roles are changed; she is in prison, while I bring Su Dan to see her, though he cannot understand the nuances of the situation. As my thoughts wandered here and there, I seemed to understand for the first time that I was but a mediocre creature, mistaken by the world for what I was not, and only with the collapse of my world could I be freed from that imposture. But I have never acted with evil intent; why was I being punished thus? I was scared out of my wits by the prospect of prison. Was I being punished for that by having my wife turned into a wreck?

As I wake up this morning, I see a naked back protruding out of the other sleeping bag, lying exposed on the floor. It's Su Dan, turned virtually motherless in the blink of an eye. Only then am I aware, with a wisp of sadness, of the existence of my son. When Children's Hospital found that both parents of this Chinese boy were still unconscious, they planned to follow regulations and take him to an orphanage. Fortunately a friend, Su Wei, rushed over from Princeton to keep him for us, pretending to be his uncle. At the time, Fu Li was still unconscious, and for seven days I was stuck in a hospital bed, unable to walk. I drifted in and out of consciousness, hallucinating that I had taken Su Dan with me back to the apartment of Kang Hua, the man with whom we spent the evening before the accident, and that I had been lying on the floor at his place for a whole month.

Su Dan was still asleep. I crawled over and said to him softly, "Daddy is leaving."

He turned over, raised his head, and asked, "When are you coming back?"

"Seven tonight."

"Try to come back early, Daddy."

Every morning I left him lying on the floor. Kang Hua

would come pick me up at a fixed hour and drive me to the hospital, and I would always ask him to stop by a flower shop to get Fu Li a rose. In all our dozen years of marriage, I had never given Fu Li roses. At the time in China, it was not the thing to do. But now I wanted to give her a rose every day.

That morning, I got up exceptionally early and walked out in a daze. Buffalo, bordering Canada, was wrapped in the shadow of autumn, especially bleak on a deserted morning like this. All alone, I walked aimlessly about in the woods, until I found myself at the edge of a shimmering lake. As I stood by the water, my heart was filled with tender sweetness. I felt uplifted, as if I had reached a wonderful fulfillment. But immediately I was seized by a fearful shivering and rushed off. I don't know how long I had been walking about until I reached a highway. There was no traffic and I stood there on the highway all alone, with one thought only—how to end it all.

I don't know how I left the highway. Perhaps it was the memory of Fu Li lying unconscious in the emergency room, perhaps it was the vision of Su Dan's naked shoulders on the floor that pulled me back. All I remember is the thought that flashed through my mind, but I did not know how to describe it. Only later, while reading an interpretation of Dostoyevsky, did I accidentally come across the perfect description of my state of mind at the time, of "hope forever gone, only life left behind, and there is a long life to go through. You cannot die, even though you do not want to live."[11]

I had loved Dostoyevsky ever since I was young and had enjoyed reading *The Idiot.* I was quite dejected when I could not find volume II after finishing volume I. My father told me to read *The Brothers Karamazov,* but I couldn't finish it. Later I realized it was because I could not understand the soul-searching nature of Dostoyevsky's prose. But now a few words on Dostoyevsky could light up my soul. I wrote in my diary:

> In all my readings of the last ten months, this passage is closest to my heart: unprecedented despair and devastation with no words of comfort, no ways of displacement nor means of release. Everything gained in life irretrievably lost, with not a single straw to hold on to; this is probably what I had never realized before—the rootlessness of the individual soul.

All I can remember of that time by the lake was that it was a day in early September, 1993. But on that morning I suddenly saw the abyss of existence, the bottomless black hole extending under my feet. The experience of

[11]See Lev Shestov: *Dostoevsky and Nietzsche: Philosophy of Tragedy* (1924), quoted from Liu Xiaofeng: *Truth Crucified* (Beijing: Sanlian Joint Publishing, 1991).

that morning cut my life into two. The first half, carrying with it the burden of my youthful strivings and worldly gains, had drifted away into meaninglessness. What was left was the second half, an empty mortal coil, a wandering ghost in a huge black hole.

Hitherto I had never had an impulse toward death but only a desire for life. Often, the more terror life held, the more I wanted to live. In my fugitive life following June Fourth, I had once hidden for nearly fifty days in a darkened room. I felt I was going mad, but I still clung to life. Only when living means unbroken fear does one have the impulse to give up. I suppose that is the black hole. Perhaps it is only when man faces this black hole that he can begin to question what existence is about and realize that living needs courage, ask himself whether his life is a failure and question whether it was worthwhile.

Lost forever was the tender sweetness that wrapped itself around me by the lake that morning. I have faced this black hole, faced a broken-down existence that was mine alone. The fact of Fu Li lying there unconscious condemned me to utter defeat and reduced my life to absolute meaninglessness. Saying that man can control his own destiny sounds to me like a hideous joke. My friends and I had thought of ourselves as somebodies, had been so cocky about fixing our country, our nation, our society, our civilization, all sick to the core, yet when we have to face alone the calamity of an individual or a family, our world collapses beneath us and we have nothing to hold on to.

One of the co-writers of the script for *River Elegy,* Yuan Zhiming, was quoted as saying that we have been chased out of China at the risk of our lives; he meant that "we have gained the freedom of a heaven, but lost the earth beneath our feet." I myself, however, beg to disagree. His saying about losing the earth seems to echo the concept of "earth fixation" that he himself had condemned in his script. When I myself was reduced to crying to heaven and earth in absolute despair, there was nothing to gain or lose; there was no distinction between sky and earth.

Soon after the accident, Chen ShuPing with her husband, Professor YingShih Yu, took the train from Princeton to Buffalo.

As she entered the hospital room, Chen carried a soft toy rabbit, holding a baby rabbit to its breast, which she laid softly at the top of Fu Li's bed. Fu Li was still bound to her wheelchair, unable to raise her head, and could only tap her friend with her right foot. "She was greeting me," Chen told me later.

I followed Professor Yu to the second-floor cafeteria and started crying the minute we sat down. "I want to take her home to China," I said. He took out cigarettes, handed me one, and, seeing that I refused, lighted one himself as he answered, "You think they will be so kind as to let you in?"

I had made a brief stop in Paris in the early spring of 1993. Mlle. Tan Xuemei, a professor of Chinese literature at the Seventh University of France and a good friend of ours, had mentioned a new book by García Márquez: Strange Pilgrims: Twelve Stories. *She had translated an article on the book, but by the time her translation reached me by post, Fu Li's accident had happened.*

Her translation reads:

It is quite obvious even from the theme that *Twelve Stories* hovers between the fantastic and the cryptic. Known for his *Hundred Years of Solitude* and *The Autumn of the Patriarch,* García Márquez in this new work again incorporates the Latin-American tradition into his own unique style. Márquez's own writing life began with legends, but he is now drawing inspiration from reminiscences of his exile in France, Barcelona, and Italy. Yet his own distinctive style remains.

In his introduction to *Twelve Stories,* García Márquez mentions that these stories acquired form twenty years ago and then were left to brew. They were gradually forgotten and sprang to life again during his exile in Europe. The "geological" method of composition, typical of his style, highlights one outstanding incident and piles over it layers and layers of memory, achieving a final effect with the realistic precision of the earth's crust. One of the stories involves a figure who haunts the halls of the Vatican, dragging the corpse of his daughter. Another describes a young Colombian woman honeymooning in Europe, and how she dies from loss of blood from a prick on her finger. In a third story, a group of children on holiday in Sicily plot to kill their obnoxious housekeeper. The stories seem unearthly and yet earthy. They are uniformly about rootless people trying to break out of their stifling "continental rationalism" but only able to escape through absurdity, magic, insanity, or death itself.

Chapter Two
THE TWINS

W hat a piece of work is a man! . . . the paragon of animals!"[1] But what makes man unique? Engels has it that man can produce tools of production, while other creatures cannot. He goes on to say that only thus is man capable of labor, which is a prerequisite for speech. I would deduce that the basic distinction between man and other animals is the ability to form words. So much for what remains of my materialistic worldview. Thus I am always deeply saddened by the expressions of dread on the faces of victims of head injuries who cannot speak. I think it shows their fear of losing their human status.

Among Fu Li's fellow head-injury patients, there was a white man who retained his powerful build and handsome features but had lost the power of speech. During

[1]*Hamlet,* act II, scene ii, lines 316ff.

family visits, he would wave his hands and feet about, trying to express himself to his ten-year-old daughter, while his wife stood apart in the farthest corner of the corridor with her face averted, as if she could not bear to face a husband deprived of words.

Another kind of situation is even scarier. Once Fu Li and I were sitting in the hospital cafeteria, silently facing each other. Suddenly there was a sound of scratching metal, but on listening closely, it sounded like English. I turned and saw two old ladies sitting nearby, chatting animatedly. It couldn't be those two, I thought to myself, but trying to trace the sound—good heavens!—I found that it was indeed one of the old ladies. She sounded like the robot in *Star Wars,* but the sound was emerging from a live, wrinkled, human face. It sent chills down my spine. There was a electro-larynx attached to her throat, and with every movement of her mouth it issued a sharp, unearthly, mechanical English, sounding as if the era of the electronic robot had arrived.

There are gradations in the loss of speech. Failure in enunciation can be remedied by technology, as in the case of the old lady. There are also electronic devices: The patient's speech is converted into digital words that form themselves into sentences. The most serious problem is not deafness or dumbness but the inability of the brain to organize language. By the time a human being has lost this unique power, the claim to be "the paragon of animals," he or she is beyond all help from any technology. Fu Li's serious brain damage was to the language area in the frontal area, the doctor told me tactfully. "I think she has definitely lost her second language"—meaning English. "As to her native language, I don't know Chinese, so I can't tell."

It was a well of despair that I dared not look in too closely. Fu Li's instinctive reaction after regaining consciousness was to try to read Chinese characters. She would look at each one carefully, scrutinizing every ideograph but unable to pronounce them out loud. Then she tried to write the Chinese characters, starting like children do with the Chinese written strokes for "one," "two," "three," "four," and so on. She would draw the lines painstakingly like a child and then pass her right hand lovingly over my hand up to my shoulder and then to my neck, all the while looking at me serenely, as if begging me to understand that she really couldn't do any better. When reduced to such a state, any little improvement seemed nothing short of a miracle.

One afternoon I was waiting for her as she was having her physical therapy when a hospital aide rushed out of the room, waving a piece of paper at me, telling me excitedly that Fu Li had just written this. I saw a few barely discernible letters, one that obviously stood for the word "Li," the "Li" in her own name. My tears flowed uncontrollably.

. . .

I t finally happened. It was around two o'clock in the afternoon, and Su Dan and I were wheeling her to the cafeteria. As we returned to the table with some hamburgers, she leaned over, grabbed me by the collar, and drew me to her lips. I heard her say clearly, "Does Mother know?" and then she muttered something indistinctly. I moved closer to her, but all I could make out was something like "I want to leave, I don't want to be here."

What a coincidence! The day she started to talk was the nineteenth of September, exactly two months after the accident.

I was delirious with happiness. Granted, coming out of the crash alive was a great piece of luck; now this was another. I phoned everyone I knew with the good news, including the person who had caused the accident.

At the news, Chen ShuPing said that the first words Fu Li uttered were out of the ordinary.

I suppose she was remarking on the fact that the first thing Fu Li struggled to say was to inquire after her mother. This after all may be a true manifestation of the supremacy of the human being.

After using all her energy to ask after her mother, Fu Li drifted into another world, a world that we who live on the surface of consciousness could not penetrate. I had celebrated prematurely. After those first words, her speech became less and less clear until it was almost impossible to make out anything she uttered.

Wandering in a Foreign Land

Fu Li had lost her memory, and everything that had been part of her real world had faded away. She kept mumbling that she was lying in the New Crossroads Hospital, the one closest to where we had lived in Beijing. Gradually she didn't even recognize me and would struggle to ask me, "Why doesn't Xiaokang come?"

Where had her soul drifted to?

The Fu family in the ancient city of Zhengzhou were already blessed with one son and one daughter when, in the year 1952, they had another girl, Li. She didn't seem likely to survive, so the mother handed the dying infant to a woman named Huang, saying, "Try to raise her like your own; if she can't make it, more's the pity." The woman Huang, who had never married, took away a sickly bag of bones and brought back a chubby little girl.

"Let me keep Chubby, it's fated," she said, and thus Huang stayed with the Fus and was their housekeeper for more than a decade. Addressed as Auntie Huang, the housekeeper had greater authority over the children than their mother. It goes without saying that this second daughter, nicknamed Chubby, was Huang's favorite.

Chubby was a little firebrand, whom no one dared to bully, and also something of a tomboy—climbing trees, raiding birds' nests, fighting with the boys—and she got away with it all with Auntie Huang staunchly behind her. When the Cultural Revolution started in 1966, however, the so-called revolutionary masses chased off everyone working as household help in the homes of cadres, and Auntie Huang was forced to leave. Like all teenagers at the time, Chubby was sent down to the countryside. By the time she returned, a tall slim young woman, poor childless Auntie Huang was already bedridden. Fu Li cooked for her, fed her, and changed her right up to the time of her death.

"Yesterday Auntie Huang came and asked, What's happened to you, Chubby? And I told her, I am wandering in a foreign land. She said, Why not go home? I asked her, Where is my home? I have no idea. Besides, they won't have me, seeing the state I'm in." This is what Fu Li said to me later, as she lay in the hospital.

I had never met her Auntie Huang. All I remember is that when we were first dating and Fu Li was still a student in medical school, I had gone with her to a wretched-looking tenement. She made me wait outside while she went in with towels, stockings, and other supplies that she pulled out of a bag. After a while she came out red-eyed and said, "Let's go, I've washed and changed her." Which is how I knew that she had gone to see her nursemaid. At the time I was very surprised. It struck me that I too had had nursemaids when I was little, but I had even forgotten their names.

There was a deep bond of affection between Fu Li and

her Auntie Huang, the one who had kept her alive. She held a place in the deepest recesses of her consciousness, without any dividing line between this world and the next. When memory is lost, past events are not really wiped out but are cut up into fragments for lack of an organizing system. When one tries to pick them up again, it seems there is still a rough pecking order. Lost in the timeless, placeless void of enveloping fear, Fu Li reached out for her first savior.

Later she began to talk about the father she had lost when she was seven years old, saying, "Father is lying in bed and throwing up." Her father had suffered from a form of brain disease and died in his thirties.

At the hospital, if she asked me, "How do you find out that I'm here?" I would know that she had wandered off the night before and had been communicating with people not of this world. Thus we would chat about people who were gone as if they were still around and feel perfectly at ease.

To her the real world was dead. There was a great deal of snow that winter, and once I was late. I found her in the hall among a lot of handicapped and mentally retarded people. Seeing me she asked calmly, "Have you come to take away my corpse?"

The same second hand-delivered letter from 1990, a photograph of her in a red woolen sweater, arms crossed, the expression on her face forlorn.

To tell you the truth, I don't understand you any-more—to see no future ahead, that is terrible. As for me, you would never imagine, but I have gone back to keeping a wide circle of friends, as I used to do before we got married. Under present circum-stances, it is important for me to have a few good friends. So don't worry about my spirits.

Neither of us is responsible for the breakup of our family. Let's just hope the future will be better. I sometimes feel that, since marrying, I have rarely enjoyed any days of peace and quiet. You used to complain that I had made overly high intellectual demands on our marriage. Actually, what I feel is that you don't have a clue as to what family life is about, or perhaps you are not interested. There is no way to make up; I am left with regrets only. When-ever I remember the past, I want to cry. I can't exactly lay my finger on what it is, but I'm sad, as if there's a wound that is hurting. Do you understand? Do you have similar feelings? Separated as we are at opposite ends of the world, I really want to say something cheerful, but then to whom else can I pour out my sadness if not to you? Now that I've gotten it off my chest, forget about it, don't take it too seriously. So long as you know that you have the most faithful wife in the world, that's enough for me. Your letters and phone calls are getting rarer. I suppose you are busy. You were always the busy one and I was always the one to give way. A lifetime like this is more than I can bear. If everything is more important than me, then why marry?

Three years after writing this, she did not recognize me as Su Xiaokang. She and I actually carried on the following dialogue, she lying in the hospital, supported between six mattresses, when I came to visit.

"Who am I?" I asked her, according to the doctor's directions.

"My husband."

"And what are you to me?"

"I am your wife."

Lying in bed one day, she said to me dreamily, "Why doesn't Xiaokang write?"

"Where is he?" I countered.

"He has gone to Gansu province."

Why Gansu, I have no idea.

I heard that you are disheartened, smoking and drinking heavily. I am so worried. You must remember you are a father and a husband. If this kind of dissipation leads to illness, how are you going to discharge your responsibilities to us? All I want is for you to lead an ordinary life and not think too much about things beyond your control. The tide of history cannot be changed by a few individuals. Besides, I always feel that there are many factors inherent in a society that cause change, and individual efforts do not make much difference. Take it easy and lead a regular life; so long as things are going smoothly on your side, I will feel easy here. Your last letter said that you were sick. I worried for days without being able to contact you. It was pure mental torture. So I sometimes think perhaps it is better for you to find someone. I just can't imagine how you manage on your own. As to your income, don't squander it, think long-term. It is not the socialist big bowl where you are. I have some savings which will last me quite a while. Our son is well.

Lying in the hospital, she said to me, "Yesterday I dreamed of you and Su Dan trying to escape."

"Why escape?" I asked.

"The police were after you. You hid in a village called Fox Run[2] and the police surrounded you."

Yesterday I measured Su Dan, height four foot three, weight 60 jin.[3] He said, "When Papa comes back, perhaps I'll be taller than him." His grades are okay, but he buries himself in comics the minute he comes home. His two bookcases are stuffed with

[2]The apartment complex in West Windsor, New Jersey, where the Su family was living at the time.
[3]Unit of weight equal to 0.5 kilogram, or roughly 1.1 pounds.

comics. He knows a thing or two, though. According to him, I am dumbest, you are next, while he is the smartest.

Always fearful of losing this son, Fu Li was in the grip of a primitive fear from the moment he was born. As for me, I can never forget the night at the Greyhound station in Buffalo ten weeks after our car accident.

Once Fu Li had regained consciousness, she was to be moved from Buffalo to a hospital in New Jersey, and the arrangement was to transport her in a medical emergency plane. It was very small, similar to the kind of private planes that Americans fly for sport. It had space for the patient to lie down and two seats, one for the pilot and one for me.

What about Su Dan? Friends in Princeton wanted to drive up to get him, but he said, "No, I want to travel alone by bus." Greyhound? My eyes nearly popped out of my head. I had only traveled by Greyhound once, and that was with friends. And Su Dan was only eleven years old. But he decided to travel by bus from Buffalo to New Jersey. It was a whole night's trip, and no one could be with him.

The transfer was scheduled for the next day. There was no time for deliberation. At half past eleven that same night, there was a Greyhound bound for New York. A Chinese student, Sun Dake, drove me and Su Dan to the station. I poured out warnings and advice and admonitions ad nauseam. A leather carryall slung over his shoulder, Su Dan stood there silently, a serious expression on his little face, nodding now and then at my words. Then I turned to the driver and begged him to watch out for him.

The bus started off at midnight with a handful of passengers, leaving the station in pitch darkness. Suddenly I was seized with a sense of danger and regretted letting him go. I shouted, "Dake, follow that bus!"

We tailed the Greyhound through the empty streets of Buffalo. I kept begging Dake, "Faster, faster, keep going!" as tears blurred my eyes. Will Fu Li approve of what I have done? I asked myself. How could I let go of my son like that? Supposing he is lost forever? Dake followed that bus for a long time, until I calmed down and said, "Well, let him go!"

Su Dan really left us for good that night. Gone was the little boy who expected to have everything done for him, from his daily food on the table to the daily change of clothes, even to have his earwax removed for him if it felt itchy. All he had to do was to dash into his mother's arms. Now in a flash, that little boy was gone.

Later he told me that when he heard the doctors and nurses in the children's hospital say that his mother was still unconscious and probably wouldn't make it, he had cried secretly. This accident had robbed him of everything. There had been no one to lean on except his mother; Father was a flitting shadow, here one day and gone the next. Besides, he was in a strange country and did not know the language well. Su Dan had indeed started off on his own, crossing from one state to another in the dark.

The next day as I flew with Fu Li, I crouched at the window to have a better look at the route that our son had traveled alone the night before. He was indeed gone.

Fu Li's next letter is dated March 3, 1990:

Your letter has arrived. When Su Dan found there was no message for him, he fumed for a whole afternoon. In revenge he has refused to write you a word. I hope that next time you will be a better father.

In two weeks, it will be his birthday. He will be disappointed if he does not get a letter from you before his birthday. The child has gone through a psychological change, I have no idea how it will affect his future development. He has a deep sense of solitude, which shows itself in refusing to socialize with other kids. Especially if another kid mentions his father, he asks him to leave.

I suggested that we have a few friends over for his birthday, but he only wants Yuan Zhiming's daughter Xianxian, saying that everybody else has their father with them, why would they want to come here? A few days ago, there was a prize-giving cere-

mony broadcast live on television. He sat unmoving
in front of the TV, telling me that there might be a
prize for his father. I don't know what to say. Poor
Su Dan.

Twice every week, Chen ShuPing would take the train
to Buffalo and then a taxi to visit someone who had completely forgotten her. For a long time, Fu Li would
address her as Doctor Zhou. Next to myself, Chen was Fu
Li's most frequent visitor in her pitiful condition.

After transferring to JFK Hospital in New Jersey, Fu
Li was still unable to swallow. The doctor was concerned
that the nasal tube, in place since the accident, might
cause infection and decided to insert a tube directly into
her stomach. On the morning of the operation, Chen
ShuPing went to be with her.

"Before the operation, my mother must sign her con-
sent, please get my mother, please," Fu Li begged.

"Where is your mother?"

"Right across from the hospital, in her office in the
Provincial Bureau of Public Health. You can give her a
call."

Chen ShuPing was perplexed. Later I explained that Fu
Li had at one time been an intern in the Henan Provincial
Hospital, which was indeed across from the Provincial
Bureau of Public Health, where her mother had at one
time been the vice-director. Her soul was obviously still in

China. But suddenly one day, she pointed to Chen and told the American doctor who was giving her physical therapy, "Her husband is a celebrity."

That night, Chen ShuPing phoned me and said, "Finally Fu Li has returned from China and is back in New Jersey."

Obviously, the two women had a very special line of communication.

October of 1993 had a golden glow, but Fu Li was still in a state of timelessness and spacelessness. The psychiatrist told me that a person who has nothing in time and space to hold on to is in a perpetual state of fear. Once, after a visit to the hospital, Chen ShuPing phoned me to ask, "How many children did you have with Fu Li?"

"Only Su Dan. Is anything the matter?"

"Well, today Fu Li said she had lost two vaginas. I think she means children."

I was struck dumb. *Two* children lost? Su Dan's twin brother had died at birth. But that was Fu Li's only confinement, I explained to Chen over the phone.

"There's another one lost, according to her."

Which one could that be?

"Has Fu Li ever had an abortion?"

Oh, why had it never occurred to me! It seems that men are not aware of life at this level. Yes, three years after giving birth to Su Dan, she had an abortion. It is the common lot of all second pregnancies under China's one-child policy. But she did not tell me until afterward. I was enraged. "How could you just go and do it?" She retorted, "What's the use of telling you? We're not allowed to have it anyway. Pity I don't know whether it's a boy or a girl." She was sad as she said it, and then the mood passed.

To us, that unknown life was a misunderstanding, a frustration we could not afford to dwell on. Like a flash of lightning in the sky, it had come and gone without leaving a trace.

But that day those lost children came back to haunt us.

My routine was to have supper with her, help with her arm and leg exercises, massage her neck, and then leave. She would usually turn her face to the wall daily in the gesture of a last farewell that always made me sad. But one day, soon after Chen had asked me about those children and as I was saying goodbye as usual, she suddenly turned to me beseechingly.

"They'll be coming in a minute. What shall I say to them?"

"Who's coming?"

"Su Dan and his elder brother, with the little one between them."

In a timeless, spaceless, memoryless state, her consciousness had gone back to Auntie Huang; this I could understand. Common sense told me that this long-dead nurse must be buried in the deepest recesses of her memory, much deeper than her birth mother. But why were these two dead infants coming back?

"What does Su Dan's elder brother look like?"

"Exactly like Su Dan."

"How old?"

"Eleven." It was Su Dan's age when he first arrived in the United States.

"What about the little one?"

"I don't know."

"Is it a boy or a girl?"

"I can't see clearly."

"Why are they coming?"

"They say they are coming to keep me company. But how can I explain to them?"

It is true. How can we explain to them? Fu Li asked me, and I asked myself. Do we have to answer to them, these lives that were created through us? Is it the responsibility of any living person? In the past we could fob off the question by claiming that they do not exist. But now they are coming to look for their mother. No matter how weird the circumstances, it goes to show that these flesh-and-blood creations from the body of the mother are forever tugging at her heartstrings, whether in dream or in reality.

O ne day in spring, 1994, I drove Su Dan from the hospital to the university library to take out some books.

Suddenly he asked, "Why are there so many babies around here?"

"Where?"

"Near the church. Look at all those tiny little grave-stones."

I looked to the left and saw a cemetery dotted with elaborately carved markers, a familiar sight in American small towns. What startled me was the fact that Su Dan knew they were infants' graves. And my thoughts immediately went to those little beings, like the child that Fu Li and I had lost.

Fu Li became pregnant in the second year of our marriage. At the time we had not planned to start a family. She had just graduated from medical school and was hoping to work in a pediatric clinic. Her job assignment didn't work out the way she wanted, and she was running around making a last-ditch effort to straighten things out. During the first few months of her pregnancy, she did not suffer from morning sickness; on the contrary, she had an enormous appetite. Once we were assailed by a mouth-watering fragrance from our neighbor. I discovered that they were stewing wild rabbit, and Fu Li asked me to go and beg a few mouthfuls. Aren't you afraid our child will be born hare-lipped? I joked. And she had said, I am past caring, at least for now.

Entering into the fifth and sixth months of her pregnancy, Fu Li was enormous. On the bus when people got up to give her a seat, she could not fit into it. We were bemused, but the doctor who first examined her listened to the baby's heartbeat and could find nothing wrong.

And then they missed the heartbeat, and then they found it again. Better get a sonogram, we were advised.

I remember it to this day. I went home for lunch and Fu Li rushed into my arms.

"Guess what happened? It's twins!"

And that explained why she was so big. I was not surprised. It was in my mother's genes. My third aunt, my mother's young sister, had had twins.

Fu Li now began preparations in earnest. Her girlfriends helped her, and the little gowns and blankets were all made in pairs. To this day I remember a red-and-white flowered pattern that they used.

Close to the due date, she had another sonogram. I saw two little heads both facing downward. It was like their first photo together.

Fu Li finally went into labor and entered the Henan Provincial Hospital, where she had worked as an intern. As if she had a premonition, she stated on arrival that she was twenty-nine years old and could not possibly give birth to twins on her first confinement and demanded a cesarean delivery. But the obstetrician brushed her words away as a lame excuse to avoid the pains of labor and insisted she go through natural childbirth.

She was wheeled in and out of the delivery room several times. From the corridor where I was waiting, I could hear her again demanding a cesarean. Once she caught sight of me and cried out, "Su Xiaokang, don't believe them. Go find someone. Time is running out for our babies!"

Poor Fu Li was totally helpless and isolated, and I was shut out of the delivery room, unable to take action. Worst of all was the fact that I had no premonition of disaster. It just seemed to be a difficult birth. By dusk of that day, March 17, 1981, a nurse discovered that Fu Li's water had broken. At the same time, Fu Li's mother arrived with an experienced obstetrician, so finally Fu Li was wheeled into the operating room for a cesarean section.

I sat on the steps outside the operating room and waited.

The door opened and two nurses came out, each holding a bundle. The one in front bent to look into the bundle as she walked; the one behind kept her eyes ahead, as if unaware of having anything in her hands. I rushed up to them, only to have the news thrust at me. The second nurse made a slight movement as if to keep me away from the bundle and said icily, "Only one made it." My legs gave way and I collapsed.

When Fu Li and our two sons were in the throes of the struggle of life and death, I was totally oblivious to what they were going through. It was only when the struggle was over and the death sentence pronounced that pain overtook me. It seemed I was fated always to suffer the regret of the might-have-beens. After my initial obtuseness to impending disaster, the agony that followed virtually tore me apart.

The first baby was asphyxiated so this one, according to their order of appearance, would be the younger brother. Seeing that he was born with a brother but had to go through life without one, we named him Su Dan,[4] not having foreseen, however, that people would confuse it with the kingdom of Sudan, as if we had given birth to a prince.

I said to Su Dan, "It's not everybody who can have a gravestone after death. Your brother doesn't."

"Where is he now?"

For the first time I told him the story of how his brother was buried.

I was the only parent who saw that son of ours. That March day in 1981, when I walked into the nurse's station of the obstetrics department, he was lying in a cardboard box in the corner of the room, spending his first night in this world all alone. A nurse walked over, opened the box, and showed him to me. He did not even have a scrap of clothing to cover his nakedness, although his mother had prepared his baby clothes and his little blankets of red-and-white flowered patterns. He was well formed, a full five jin, not a whit less than his brother. Long black hair covered his brow, almost reaching to his

[4]*Dan* means "single" in Chinese.

cheekbones on either side; his hair was wet, as if he had sweated profusely in the fight for life the night before. I put my hand to his forehead; it was soft to my touch. I did not have the courage to hold my dead son in my arms.

A few minutes later I was standing on the steps of the hospital with the body of my son in a cardboard box. It weighed on my hands, as if it were a live thing. A wave of desolation swept over me: Where on earth would I find a spot to bury my son? The nurse at the obstetrics department had told me they would leave him to the cleaners to dispose of as garbage or use for dissection; it was the usual practice on the mainland in pursuit of the one-child policy. Countless mothers who did not have a quota for childbirth were forced to abort and the fetuses were dealt with in this way. "I don't have the heart to do it to him; see how well formed he is," the nurse whispered to me as she handed me the box.

A friend of mine came over to be with me. He said, "If you know his burial place, it will be an unending source of anguish all your life."

"Why?" asked Su Dan. "Why shouldn't you know? Look at all those little gravestones in the churchyard."

I could not make him understand why China did not have churchyards, though it would be a lame excuse. Neither could I make him understand why China is now a land with not enough space to bury its dead. All I said was that my friend and I left with his brother in a box and walked toward the countryside north of the hospital. After walking a long way, we finally met a group of peasants. I explained why we were there, and an old man spoke up.

"Twins, did you say? Then the method of burial is different. A branch must be placed at his side."

"Why?" my friend asked.

"He will be lonely down there. With a branch to keep him company, he will not miss his twin. . . . You just listen to me, I know what I'm talking about."

With tears streaming down my face, I shook out all the cash in my wallet and gave it to him. Then I put down the box with my son in it and fled.

"How can you be sure they buried my brother?" Su Dan found something unsatisfactory in the way I had handled the matter.

"Where do you think he is, then?" I asked.

"I have the feeling that he is alive somewhere," Su Dan said.

They were single-cell twins and the spitting image of each other. Perhaps there was a mysterious telepathy between them, who knows? As far as I was concerned, this son of mine is still somewhere on this earth. My lasting regret is that I do not know where. Sometimes the thought of him wraps itself around my heart and gives me solace; sometimes the thought of him is a dull pain I do not dare to linger over. Cut off from the joy of sharing family life with him, the hurt is somewhat softened by illusory encounters that flit in and out of my consciousness, totally outside my control. For four years after he was gone, I cannot count the number of times I would jump on my bicycle on an impulse and dash off to the countryside north of the hospital. Distraught, I sometimes felt that I would surely come across a little mound and my son would be lying there. At other times I wanted to believe that my son was right before me: that little boy collecting cow dung on the dusty roadside, perhaps.

In 1985, I was assigned to Beijing and left Henan for good. Su Dan was four years old, and Fu Li wanted me to take him to Beijing and put him in a nursery. The morning before leaving, I crept to the countryside for a last farewell. My links with this ancient central plain of Henan were to be snapped once and for all, but a filmy thread of remembrance will always tug at my heart and appear in my dreams.

Two years later, I wrote the script for *River Elegy*. When the hell-raising controversy over the TV series had finally blown over, I suddenly realized that my thoughts had never consciously gone back to my dead son during the writing though I had named the work *He Shang*. According to the precise definition of the term, *shang* means untimely death at an early age without being gathered into the ancestral burial place.

The Rag Doll

I often ask myself, At the Last Judgment—if it comes—who should answer to God for those lost children: our son who died at birth and the one that died before birth, and the countless other little children whose lives were extinguished in the darkness of their mothers' wombs across the land of China? I suppose modern men are not oppressed by such fears, because they do not retain memories of those unlived lives. To them, obviously, commemoration only pertains to those who have lived an earthly life. But through Fu Li I discovered that people are just fooling themselves. It seems that any spark of life that has throbbed in its mother's womb, even though it never sees the light of day, still lives in the unconscious of its mother. Fathers here are irrelevant.

Our two children came looking for their mother, not to settle accounts but to be at her side during her suffering, even though this mother had not been able to ensure their right to life. To a normal person, the scene of brain-damaged patients at the rehabilitation center attached to JFK Hospital, where Fu Li now stayed, was sheer bedlam, ranging from stony stillness to lunatic frenzy. Nights were worse: screams, cries, talking in sleep—the sounds echoed in the darkened building. Who knows how many shattered lives were communicating with each other in this dreamlike state or locked in fierce contention?

As for myself, I would leave after dark with a heavy heart, sadder than four years ago when I escaped by way of the southernmost tip of the mainland, leaving Fu Li to the mercies of Li Peng[5] and company. Back home, after fixing supper for Su Dan, I would throw myself on the bed, sick at heart. I knew it was time for the two children to appear to Fu Li.

The elder is always holding the little one by the hand. Every day after I leave they approach Fu Li's bedside and spend the night talking to her.

The next morning when I got over to the hospital, the first question I asked her would be, "Did they come last night?"

"Yes, we chatted."

"About what?"

"I don't remember. . . . Anyway, the minute they arrive, all the other shadows disappear."

"What do you call them?"

"The big one, I call him Baobao; the little one was not named. I don't know whether it's a boy or a girl."

Back when we were expecting the twins, Fu Li had already named them Baobao and Beibei[6] but only Beibei

---

[5]See chapter 1, note 9.
[6]*Baobei* is Chinese for "treasure."

was spared us, and to this day Su Dan's pet name is
Beibei. Fu Li had been unconscious when she was
wheeled out of the operating room. The next day when
she regained consciousness, she only asked after "the living one" and has cherished him ever since.

I had been puzzled that she never mentioned the other
baby. She later told me what had happened. She finally
had her cesarean birth the evening of March 17. Lying on
the bed, she was aware that the firstborn was silent and
did not respond to stimulation. She knew in her heart
that it was Baobao and she said a last goodbye to him.
Then she heard a cry, loud and forceful, and she knew it
was Beibei; "Then my heart gave a thump and I fainted
away." She only told this story once and never referred to
it again. During those years when I mourned for Baobao,
sometimes she would say, "I understand. You have seen
him." What surprised me was the fact that she could now
remember a name from more than ten years ago, a name
she had never uttered. But she was not going to give the
aborted little one a name; better to let it remain name-
less. Perhaps the human unconscious is not as chaotic as
Freud described.

Gradually only Baobao came to her; the little one disappeared. The little one's life span was shorter, and stayed
for a briefer time in Fu Li's subconscious. Such is the
inexorable ordered pattern of life itself. Finally, Baobao
also stopped coming. Fu Li was alarmed; every time I was
about to leave she would ask me to bring back Baobao.

Failing that, she asked for Beibei to keep her company at night. That being impossible, she took her roommate, an elderly black woman, for Su Dan and would worry about the way the nurse changed her.

One day as I was going to visit as usual, I absentmindedly walked into a store without really knowing what I was looking for. Suddenly my eye was caught by a rag doll, perched on top of a galaxy of women's clothes—a chubby little boy in a white suit and a little black hat with red trimming. That's it! I bought the rag doll and put him at the head of Fu Li's bed, and she would hold him every night in her sleep.

Today the doll, named Baobao, sits in Su Dan's room, by now an established member of our family. Once I accidentally came across a label sewed to the doll's wrist with the name of the brand, I think, and the information that the doll was made from parachute material, a fine and lasting synthetic fiber. It was also marked MADE IN CHINA. To me, he flew over from China to be with us.

The twins born to Fu Li and me seemed to have been naturally meant to be one for her and one for me. Su Dan is every inch his mother's child, from looks to temperament. I figured that if the other had not died prematurely he would have taken after me. I'm not jealous, but I can't help noticing that Su Dan loves his mother to the very marrow of his being, while just sparing a particle of love for his father. I don't blame him;

ever since infancy, there was only Mama to rely on, while Father flitted in and out and disappeared altogether after 1989. When the police came to search their home, it was Mama who dealt with them while the TV said that Father was a great villain. At the time he was only nine years old. What had he made of it? I have no idea.

Su Dan had been briefly separated from his mother when he was four. I took him, and we said goodbye at the Qingdao railway station to Fu Li, who stood on the platform and cried uncontrollably. Ever since he was born, she was the irreplaceable nurturer in his life; neither the hired nurse nor the day-care teachers nor his grandparents—and much less me—could understand him. He was a happy-go-lucky little fellow, the picture of innocence, calling for his mummy for everything, even to wipe his bottom. He had once wandered away from the day-care place, crossed several blocks, and hid in a little wood to watch the shadow of his mother in the window of the hospital where she was working. But when he was four, Fu Li had a chance for further study, so I took him away to Beijing for a year.

To soften the pain of separation, the three of us went first on a tour to the seaside resorts of Dalian and Qingdao and then parted at the Qingdao railway station, Fu Li going southward back to Zhengzhou while I took Su Dan to Beijing. In Beijing, Su Dan continually asked me to walk the streets in search of his mother. I did not know that, in day care, he used to hold his poopoo until he was home. Once he overdid it, and I had to take him to the hospital to be disimpacted. Only Fu Li knew his oddities and let him have his way without any confrontations.

In 1989, after I left, Fu Li also wanted to leave, to escape the continual harassment of the police, but she couldn't bear to leave her son behind. Every day he waited at the gate of his school for his mother to fetch him. If his mother did not show up, he would probably have stood there and waited forever.

After the accident, he realized that his mother would not be there for him anymore. One day he said to me, "Father, when we are back in Princeton, please let me go and learn karate." At the moment we were in a McDonald's in Buffalo near his mother's hospital. It was in the inner city, surrounded by rotting slums. My mind was preoccupied with other things and I said, Yes, of course. It is hard to know what kids are thinking. Why karate? Later I realized it was one of the first things the lone immigrant child turns to when faced with the reality of America. He knew instinctively that there would be no one to protect him. Su Dan's link with his mother was not only part of his birthright, it was further strengthened during the days of terror he shared with his mother in Beijing. When we first arrived in the United States, black and Latino kids not only hit him on the school bus, they sometimes came to the house to beat him up. Su Dan was like a little chick, trying to hide under the wings of the mother hen. It was a pattern in Asian immigrant families; the parents were so busy making a living that they did not see what their kids were up against.

For Su Dan the first thing to do was to learn to protect himself. It was essential to his self-esteem, especially as a little boy. If children cannot deal with bullies, they will shrink within themselves and fear all competition. I had been talking on about "culture," but it was only through Su Dan that I first glimpsed the youth culture of America, the worship of the top dog that is so deeply rooted in American secular life. We adults just didn't have a clue. After Fu Li's accident, Su Dan's teacher called. Su Dan was quite smart, he told me, but he was concerned that the accident would affect the boy's studies. I said there was nothing I could do about it. To my surprise, the teacher called again soon afterward to say that Su Dan was in a fight. A white boy in an upper grade had heard that Su Dan was practicing karate and wanted to test him. He began by insulting Su Dan. Su Dan said, "Apologize," but before the other boy could react, Su Dan punched him and put him down. When the school punished both boys, Su Dan said it was not fair.

Without my noticing it, my son was gradually changing into another person. I was frantically trying to save Fu Li and had no time for him. He survived on instant noodles, sandwiches, and hot dogs. All the clothes on his back were castoffs. His winter coat of down was brought over from Beijing. He was the worst-dressed boy in the school but his grades jumped. He was not afraid of anybody, nor did he rely on anybody. Insensitive to other people's feelings, refusing to say the right thing, he was totally self-absorbed. It worried me, but remembering the harshness of the world, I realized it had not been easy for the boy. He is stronger than I am.

After Fu Li regained consciousness, she would always cry at the thought of Su Dan, full of guilt at not doing her duty by him. He had lost an elder brother at birth and now just missed being left an orphan. Fu Li could not accept the fact that Su Dan had already left his childhood behind.

Chapter Three
ON THE PLATEAU

It was October 1993, three months after the accident.

Charles Wei-hsun Fu, professor of theology at Temple University, had come from Philadelphia to see me. "Regret and self-reproach are futile, and religion is no escape," he said, standing slim and tall, flaunting a head of brilliant white hair. No one had ever come to the point so bluntly. He added, "You have no alternative but to acknowledge the fact. Cry if you want to. Think of your guilt day and night and try to do something to alleviate her pain. Later, when you have put all this behind you, you may think back and ask yourself: Was I worthy of taking on the guilt? Ah, well, it's too early to talk about that now."

Dr. Fu had just recovered from a life-threatening illness himself a year ago. He talked as if he were lecturing in a classroom, going through the points one by one, and I took down everything point by point without understanding a word of what he said, especially what he meant by "worthy of taking on the guilt." He said they were Dostoyevsky's words. Later on he sent me his book, *Death with Dignity and Life with Dignity.* Reading it was like carrying on a conversation with him on the question of death.

True, I couldn't bear the guilt and had been playing with the idea of running away—it is my habitual way of dealing with problems. I had sneaked away to Shanghai for a few days at the outbreak of the Tiananmen movement. When Zhao Ziyang, then Secretary-General of the Communist Party, tried to mediate and the situation showed signs of calming down, I returned to Beijing. But how could I have known that, once in Beijing, I would be even more deeply entangled? When martial law was proclaimed, I did not wait for the bloodbath in Tiananmen before I took to my heels. After arriving in Paris, I published an article that began with the words: "I am probably the topmost coward of the '89 democracy movement, what Beijingers call a good-for-nothing bum." In my present predicament, my escape instinct surfaced again, and I was looking for an ostensible excuse to take French leave. Sorting through my own conflicting inclinations, one thought emerged: Cornell, the quiet grove of academe on a hilltop, the jadelike lakes nestled among the hills Fu Li had loved. In my self-absorption, I began to entertain visions of Hu Shih[1] rowing on the lake.

Fu Li had been most insistent that I should study. It was an issue I had always tried to evade, while she always kept after me. She would say that not to study while in exile abroad was absolutely self-destructive. Actually, during that summer of 1993, we had visited Cornell with study in mind and had stopped at Buffalo on our way back only to revisit Niagara Falls when the accident happened. I chose Cornell because the English translation of *River Elegy* was published by Cornell and translated by Professor Richard Bodman, a Cornell graduate then teaching Chinese at St. Olaf College, Minnesota.

Now that Fu Li was plunged in darkness, the idea of going to study at Cornell seized me again and I started applying frantically. Professor Edward Gunn of the East Asian department there had invited me over for an interview, and Professor Bodman had made reservations for me at a hotel nearby.

[1]Hu Shih (1891–1962), poet and scholar, studied at Cornell and Columbia. On his return to China, Hu Shih was an important influence on the May Fourth movement of 1919 (see chapter 7, note 28). He was dean of Peking University in 1932 and president in 1936. During World War II, he was China's ambassador to the United States and later librarian at Princeton University.

Now, in the depths of winter, Zhang Langlang[2] was driving me back to Buffalo from Cornell. After the accident, there was an interval when I was incapable of driving. Langlang had just returned from Beijing and volunteered to be my personal driver for a while. He kept me company in the hospital during the day and amused Fu Li with his jokes. She would laugh until the wheelchair she was sitting in shook under her. At night, Langlang slept in a bedroll on my carpeted floor. This had been going on for two weeks. The two of us had left Fu Li behind to go to Cornell, hoping to be away only two days and one night. Langlang was driving back nonstop, afraid that Fu Li might be anxious. I dozed off and on in my seat. Suddenly I heard him gasp. His hands let go the wheel to grip his heart while the car wobbled.

"What is it?" I asked in alarm.

"No big deal. Let's get off the road and take a break." And he stopped the car and rested for about ten minutes, leaning against the wheel.

"Wow, that was close," Langlang said, as he sat up again.

Zhang Langlang had come out of ten years in prison during the Cultural Revolution with a heart condition and had to be fitted with a pacemaker. He always referred

[2]Writer and art critic, imprisoned for ten years during the Cultural Revolution, currently in the United States.

to himself as "a mindless, heartless good-for-nothing." He came to keep me company during these dark winter hours, uttering no words of comfort, holding back the jokes, just staying quietly by my side. Once, as he drove me back from the hospital, he turned on the tape recorder and the strains of "In a Land Far Far Away" drifted through the car. It brought tears to my eyes, and Langlang stopped the car and waited in silence until my fit of crying was over.

Cornell was out of the question, of course. But now that the whole affair is over, it amazes me that no one tried to stop me while the fever was on me, including Professor Bodman, who had helped me fill out the application forms and tried to convince Cornell that my English would pass muster if I went through a crash course. Professors YingShih Yu and Perry Link of Princeton had both written recommendations for me, while Professor Gunn had even made inquires about medical insurance for Fu Li. Everyone saw I was trying to escape, but no one could bear to spell it out for me. Chen Shu-Ping even said, "Go. Just look at it as being an acolyte in a temple. Fu Li will be pleased. She has always wanted you to study."

The day after I returned from that trip to Cornell, an early morning call from the hospital informed us that Fu Li had fallen and hurt her head as she tried to get up on her own. We were in the car in a flash. As we raced toward the hospital, Langlang kept muttering, Let's hope it's not serious. I thought to myself, Perhaps she felt I was running away and had got out of bed to try to hold me back.

Images of the lakes of Cornell lingered in my imagination for the longest time, and I practiced English assiduously for the Test of English as a Foreign Language (TOEFL). At an unconscious level, I was trying to deny the reality of my wife's disability. This denial even tried to justify itself on the basis of Fu Li's disappointed wishes for me, by claiming that going off to study would give her satisfaction. It meant I could not face her squarely, a paralyzed woman.

It took me a long time to be aware of my superficiality, in spite of Professor Charles Wei-hsun Fu's attempt to enlighten me. One day in October three years after our last conversation, he left this world. I learned of the news half a month after the event when I came across an old newspaper. He was a specialist in the study of death; few people knew more about death than he did, and I don't mean just commonplace knowledge, experience, or beliefs. Unfortunately, he had to experience death personally as part of his study. He is gone. His death deeply shook my confidence in this branch of study. Of course I am aware that death is death and learning is learning, but still the death of a man who had discussed death with me was unnerving.

A Little Path

Ninety-three—not Victor Hugo's novel but a year in my own life. The merging of warm air from Mexico and cold air off the East Coast caused the biggest snowstorm in seventy years. New Jersey became a frozen world; the superhighway was like a sheet of glass, and every morning I had to break through a coating of ice over the car. Su Dan thought it was fun and tried to help by kicking at the trunk, so that to this day the car bears the dents of his boots. I hated the year 1993. Often I had to coax my car through the snow, not knowing where I was heading. At night, the only thing that gave me some warmth was a song:

> *"A little path, winding on and on,*
> *Leading farther and farther into the mists. . . ."*

Sung by a Russian mezzosoprano, it was popular during World War II. On the mainland, there are few people of my generation who do not know this song. The first stanza ends with "I want to be with my lover on the battlefront." The next stanza ends with "I want to save my lover from the battlefront." The tune is sorrowful and hesitant, steeped in a typical Russian melancholy. I let it disentangle my moods as the car bumped along in the snow. Where was my own little path?

At least there is a little path now, and not the abyss that was yawning under me. To help Fu Li grow up for a second time—that is my little path. The old Fu Li, standing up straight, head held high, knowing her own mind, taking care of every detail: There she is, standing at the other end of the path. I must go to the end to get her back. "Winding on and on" describes my mood perfectly. I can't see the end of the little path; it's lost in mists.

I had to face up to my guilt, but the first bitter pill I had to swallow was the fact that the woman on whom I had totally relied was gone. Married men are not necessarily mature. Take me, for instance, throwing my weight around in the outside world, but, once back home, I was just like a child and relied on my wife to run our life. The son whom she bore seemed to be a baby brother or a toy to me, something to play with. I had decided that she was not supposed to meddle with outside affairs, only to maintain the home and give me face. But the moment she was gone, everything was sucked out of my life.

As early as the summer of 1993, when Fu Li was still in intensive care in Buffalo, I told Chen ShuPing over the phone, "Fu Li will probably turn into my daughter." I had said it vaguely, without knowing what I was saying because I had never really been a father. The truth dawned on me later when Su Dan said, "I feel that the mother I used to know is gone." Saying which, he ran into his room. I finally realized that I was on my own.

I dread thinking back to that bitter winter of 1993. A little-girl Fu Li made her appearance at that time. She would wait for me every day at the nurses' station, asking them now and again, "Why isn't my husband here yet?" They would ignore her. One day when she saw me coming, she said I was her elder brother. She said it quickly, in a low voice, as if being naughty. I was shocked. Then, for the next couple of days, she told me, "Xiaokang is not here." To this day I feel that she was not as confused as she seemed, but just preferred that the person who was taking care of her to be not her husband but a brother. It was a strange beginning.

Every evening before I left the hospital, she would make me take the clothes and stockings that she needed for the next day and put them on her bed; she would stuff the stockings under her pillow and hold tight to her nightclothes like a little girl preparing to spend a long night under a stranger's roof. That done, she would signal to me that I could go. This familiar scene was repeated night after night without leaving me touched in any particular way, until suddenly one night I realized that she had indeed become a little girl. The minute I realized this, I was overcome with guilt at not having been a good husband. I was in a turmoil of conflicting feelings—sweet, sour, bitter, and spicy spilling out in a strange mixture. Back home a son was waiting for me to make dinner without waiting for Mother anymore. So there we were, the two of us, with four chopsticks between us but nothing to say.

Gradually I quieted down and accepted the fact that Fu Li was a little girl. There were good moments too. Once she said she dreamed that she could walk and had joined a marathon, marching through the snow in her boots. For a moment she seemed as excited as a little girl.

But mostly she was sad. She had lost touch with home for too long, she said. Sometimes she would lie in bed and cry, saying, Look at me, no mother, no father, and this is how I end up. She said she wanted to go back to China. She kept begging me to take her back to China. If we can't go by car, she said, we can drive to an airport, get a ticket, and fly there.

Christmas arrived, and she became more anxious and kept saying, Spring Festival is coming, Mother will be anxious if we don't show up for the Eve of Spring Festival. Christmas Eve at the hospital was exciting. I bought some Chinese snacks and planned to spend the night with her away from her ward. Many people had come to see her. She was having her period, and by the end of the day she was dead tired. I helped her to a training room on the first floor, and made her lie down on a sofa in the room. Su Dan was left home alone with his Nintendo for company. That was how we spent our third Christmas Eve together in the West.

Fu Li dozed for a while, then woke up suddenly to ask, Why can't we just buy an airplane ticket and leave? I did not know what to say. Being uprooted from home was probably what dragged her back into her girlhood. Girls make their own homes after marriage and are not supposed to be running back to their parents, and this tradition is specially strong in her native Henan. Fu Li was very aware of this and had thrown herself wholeheartedly into building our little nest. She detached herself from the affairs of her mother's family and never ran back when she had troubles of her own; that would be loss of face. But now she was really at the end of her resources. Lying in a coma for a month had cut off what she had had of her life; she did not know where she was, only that her little nest was shattered. For a husband to pop up in her present rootless state was more than she could take in.

After staying in the training room for a while, she wanted to go back to her room to sleep. There was no Christmas for us.

I took her back to her room. There was a noisy party going on upstairs. In the corridor, an old woman who had a stroke was screaming in pain; another very overweight lady was shouting "Merry Christmas!" at the top of her voice. The noise woke Fu Li, who opened her eyes and asked, "Who's crying?" and then fell straight back to sleep. Her personal hell was not in her dreams.

At last the hospital quieted down, the main gate was

locked, and I left. On my way back, it was eerily quiet. All the cars were crawling along. The ice-crusted road lay wide and clear in front of me. A light snow drifted down slowly.

There was a frame hanging on the wall over each bed, filled with photos of members of the patients' families—for them, it was their only link with the world that had left them behind. They themselves might not be aware of the link, they were suffering from head injury, or stroke, or the consequences of a traffic accident. But the frame over the bed of Fu Li's roommate was filled with the photos not of people but of horses.

We had moved to the rehab center of JFK Hospital in November 1993, before the onset of the stormy winter weather. As we followed the nurse into the ward assigned to Fu Li, her roommate presented a shocking sight. She was obviously unconscious, her eyes were tightly shut and her mouth gaping open, as if she had no control over herself. She was a picture of acute suffering that engraved itself indelibly on the mind of the beholder. Although Fu Li was conscious, the world did not exist for her. I could not bear to take a second look at the woman who would be sharing her room. But I was intrigued by the photos in the picture frame. Why so many horses? I took a closer look, and they turned out to be pictures of the same horse, a handsome dark Arabian Thoroughbred. There was always a young woman in the pictures, leading the horse, feeding the horse. It was the roommate. You could tell she had been a beautiful woman.

How sad! One couldn't help feeling the pity of it. My own Fu Li too in her day, although not as beautiful, was also a sight to warm the eye, standing slim and tall, with a head of shiny black hair. All these things were more appreciated now that they were gone for good. It was only in the winter of 1993 that I truly understood the meaning of the line in Li Yu's poem: "Past events may only be mourned."[3] But the picture frame was a reminder: I went home and dug out hundreds of old photographs. I took a few that showed Fu Li at her best, threw in a snapshot of our son on his first day at school in the United States, and made a collage for the picture frame above her bed. That was Fu Li's link with the world.

Lying there she would gaze at the boy framed in the pictures. Suddenly one day she said, "Look at him, so healthy and good looking, and the mother paralyzed and ugly."

Several days passed by. Luckily, Fu Li was never bothered by the woman with the gaping mouth lying across from her in the same ward. In the afternoon, the young woman had many visitors, an old gentleman with a cellular phone in his hand—her father, very likely—and sev-

[3]Translation by Kang-i Sun Chang, see *The Evolution of Chinese Tz'u Poetry* (Princeton, N.J.: Princeton University Press, 1980), page 83.

eral fashionably dressed young women, probably her sisters. They showed up briefly every day, performing a perfunctory duty. Among the arrivals, one carelessly dressed man stuck out like a sore thumb among the genteel company. He always stayed on after the others had left, sometimes outstaying even me.

Finally, one day, Fu Li noticed her neighbor. "Why is her mouth always open? Is she alive?" And once, when I was there early, Fu Li greeted me by saying, "Do you know? After everybody is gone, the man keeps speaking to her." I observed him closely and saw that he was very handsome, but pale and disheveled.

One day before leaving he came over and asked, in a heavy Spanish accent, "What happened to your wife?"

"Car accident. And you . . . are her husband?"

"Yes. I am from Argentina."

"What happened to your wife?"

"Kicked by a horse. That horse."

And he pointed to the pictures on the wall. He added that his wife's family was formerly from Germany and had always kept horses.

On the way back, I was bemused. Kicked by a horse? That horse? And yet they still kept its picture and put it up over the head of the woman that he had kicked? Then I remembered that there was another picture in the frame, a picture of the young woman in church. I seemed to have a glimmer of understanding, without really understanding.

I observed the young woman and saw that the back of her head was missing. Later, when we got into a conversation, the Argentinian told me it happened when she was feeding the horse. It kicked and sent her flying through the air. She crashed against a wall, and the corner of the wall shaved off the back of her head. She had been lying like that for seven months without regaining consciousness. He would whisper into her ear day and night, trying to wake her, and he had kept it up for seven months. . . .

I had done the same for Fu Li, but only for twenty days or so. The contrast in our situations filled me with respect for him. Argentina, horse-racing, German descent: these disjointed images kept swimming in my head, but standing before me was a real man.

Every day the Argentinian stayed long after I was gone and kept calling his wife, trying to wake her. Fu Li became more and more frightened and had nightmares every night. In her confused state of mind, I don't know what she made of his words and his heavy accent. He was probably appealing to his wife's soul.

Finally I had no choice but to request a change of room. After a lot of hassle, the hospital decided to remove the other woman because Fu Li was now able to move about and should stay near the nurse's station. After the change the manager told me that the other couple was very nice, and he had hoped we could have gotten along.

The Argentinian man refused to speak to me after

moving out. If we crossed each other's paths, he would turn away. I know that he was hurt, and I am sorry. There is so much hurt in the world, why did it have to happen to him?

Mlle. Tan had succeeded in translating another segment of {Kundera's} "Conspiracy of Details" for my sake. The segment reads:

Still another great change in Andrei Bolkonsky's internal world: mortally wounded in the battle of Borodino, he lies on an operating table in a military encampment and is suddenly filled with a strange sense of peace and reconciliation, a sense of happiness, which will stay with him; this state of happiness is all the stranger (and all the more beautiful) for the enormous harshness of the scene, which is full of the hideously precise details of surgery in a time before anesthesia; and strangest of all about this strange state: it is provoked by an unexpected and illogical memory: When the doctor's assistant removed his clothes, "Andrei recalled his earliest, most remote childhood." And some lines further on: "After the agony he had been enduring, Prince Andrei enjoyed a blissful feeling such as he had not experienced for a long time. All the best and happiest moments of his life, especially those of early childhood—when he had been undressed and put to bed, and when his nurse had sung him lullabies and he had buried his head in the pillow and felt happy just to be alive—rose to his mind, not as something past, but as a present reality." Only later does Andrei recognize, on a nearby operating table, his rival, Anatol, Natasha's seducer, whose leg has just been cut off by a doctor. The usual reading of this scene: Wounded, Andrei sees his rival with his leg amputated; the sight fills him with immense pity for the man and for man in general. But Tolstoy knew that these sudden revelations are not due to causes so obvious and so logical. It was a curious fleeting image (the early-childhood memory of being undressed in the same way as the doctor's assistant was doing it) that touched everything off—his new metamorphosis, his new vision of things. A few seconds later, this miraculous detail has certainly been forgotten by Andrei himself just as it has probably been immediately forgotten by the majority of readers, who read novels as attentively and badly as they "read" their own lives.[4]

---

[4]See Milan Kundera, *Testaments Betrayed,* translated from the French by Linda Asher (New York: HarperCollins Publishers, 1993), pages 217–218.

Fu Li pined for home, like a little girl in the nursery. I was touched and one day asked my writer friend Zheng Yi to help me smuggle Fu Li out after lunch, when the nurses were busy with tidying up and weren't watching so closely. Once down the stairs, we got hold of a folding wheelchair. Wrapping her in a down coat, we got her out through the side door of the laundry room and put her in the car. This was Fu Li's first day home since the accident. She was all excitement as I helped her up the stairs—we were then still living on the second floor. After sitting for a while in the living room, she went to Su Dan's room and slid into his bed. "Just like a doghouse,"[5] she remarked sadly. After half an hour, we had to take her back. Going down the flight of stairs was a real challenge for Fu Li. Zheng Yi carried her down on his back. Zheng Yi and only Zheng Yi, I suppose, with his bull-like strength and perseverance, could have managed it.

As winter ended, Fu Li's nightmares became worse. She was moved to a single room, but the nightmares continued. She kept mumbling in her sleep, words like "It doesn't look real." Every time I arrived at the hospital, I would see her sitting alone at the window staring at the melting snow. The window faced a little wood, revealing a path in its midst.

[5]"Doghouse" is used to refer to messy interiors in Chinese, as is "pigsty" in English.

"Are they poplars?"

"Similar to the poplars of Zhengzhou, aren't they?"

"Let's hope so."

"Missing China?"

"China doesn't concern me. I miss home."

"Missing whom?"

"I only miss my mother. My mother was widowed young and raised us children all on her own. Now I begin to know what it's like."

From then on, I negotiated with Dr. Elie Elovic, Fu Li's attending physiatrist, for permission to take Fu Li home. He was a Jewish doctor with a bushy beard, a very jolly person who always said he wondered how Fu Li managed to recover so quickly.

Of course the doctor would not agree to release her from the hospital for weekends. And the reason was a shocker. He said Fu Li was recovering so quickly, it was almost a medical miracle. The insurance company also said that according to their information, the doctor's opinion had been that Fu Li was unlikely to move beyond the first stage of recovery for head injury—that if she were lucky, the first critical stage of recovery would take not months but years to complete—and yet Fu Li had recovered remarkably well in just a few months, completing the first stage of recovery by the end of winter after her accident in July. The doctor could not understand it. Of course he did not know that we had asked for help from Qigong master Yan Xin. (I never knew what secret cures Yan Xin had worked on Fu Li, but apart from our regular doctor in Western medicine, Qigong was the only cure we sought.) If it was not Yan Xin, it could only have been God himself who had effected this miracle.

Only then did I realize that I had given up on supernatural powers too rashly. I had been beaten down by pain and could not transcend. All the rituals of faith, whether the mediations of Qigong or the prayers of Christianity, had not been able to lift me up from pain. The Christians would tell me, "the only possibility of transcending the world is to die and be reborn." But I had no spiritual strength to overcome the fear of death. And thus I went through a hellish journey through the various illusions of supernatural omnipotence and miracles of the secular world. I had written in my diary:

When I woke up from the coma, I found the world collapsed around me. For the duration of a year, I knew only that the past was a blank, and I have nothing by which to foretell the future. In spite of myself, I hoped for a supernatural power to save Fu Li and me, and had even made some appeals to them. But at the end of a year, I finally realized that it was impossible for us to communicate with either God or Buddha. I had nothing to draw on except my own naked mortal coil, although its spirit and energy had dwindled to a breath.

The doctor had examined me three months after the accident and had diagnosed head injury, depression, and something else that I forgot.

Are clinically depressed people incapable of embracing faith, or is faith itself a sign of clinical depression? Fu Li's continuing nightmares made me guilty, exacerbated my own anxiety, and gave me hallucinations, plunging me deeper into depression. I had been with her all the way and matched her in all her abnormality. It is not that I indulged myself and gave way to grief, it is that I had no energy to come out of this black hole on my own.

The snow was melting, and before you know it, spring had crept on us.

Something else also crept on us unawares. On Sunday I took Su Dan with me to the hospital to see Fu Li, and the two of them had fun teasing each other. Su Dan made faces at her and Fu Li laughed and said, "This son is making faces at me, I don't want him anymore." It was the first time she laughed.

Back home, Su Dan said dully, "Mother keeps calling me Beibei in a hoarse voice." I looked at him, not knowing what he was talking about.

The next day, I told Fu Li that our friend Zheng Yi and his wife had a baby daughter. She said, "Indeed? I am good at giving birth to boys. I'm going to have more boys."

Every afternoon, she made me wheel her downstairs to call Su Dan. She would grasp the receiver with obvious effort and always say the same thing: "Your daddy is spending all his time with me and neglecting you. Accept my apologies."

A new role had revived in Fu Li. It began with her recognizing that she was in the United States. She said, "I always thought I had returned to China in 1991 and the car accident was a figment of my imagination. Now that people in this hospital have seen Su Dan, it proves that everything is real. We didn't return to China in 1991."

I suddenly realized that, owing to memory loss, Fu Li was cut off from a part of her past, including her personal life after 1989 and the two years she had been abroad, all wiped out as if deleted from a computer file. And in deleting the past, she had made an "attachment" to the file, a make-believe personal history. In this make-believe, Su Dan was replaced by his brother and Su Xiaokang was split into two, one of which was left behind in China. But now it seemed she was getting over the make-believe.

One day Fu Li said to her doctor in English, "My husband always speaks to me in Chinese," and then laughed, for the second time.

Once after I gave her dinner she suddenly asked me, "You're tired, aren't you? Why are you always coming to wait on me? Do you know what I think? I think that you don't like it, but you're afraid my mother would blame you, so you keep coming. Now that I am handicapped, do you still want me? You still do? Well, thank you."

The next day she asked my friend Su Wei, who came to see her, "What do you think will become of me and Xiaokang?"

When Su Wei told me of their conversation, I had mixed feelings. At least I was not mistaken for her brother anymore; at last she saw me as her husband. This might be the resumption of another role, but would the former Fu Li come back to me with the resumption of roles?

A few days later, as I was giving her her dinner, she said, "Just for the way you are giving me my dinner, I vow to repay you. If you are sick, I will serve you hand and foot and carry out your bedpans."

"Just get well, and don't mind anything else. Of course I'll take care of you. It's just a bit hard on Su Dan," and I couldn't keep from breaking down in tears again.

"Now that you're crying, I feel guilty," she answered, but she didn't cry.

That same night I couldn't help calling Chen ShuPing to say, "Fu Li is such a good person."

Yes, this painful recapture of our previous roles showed all the more that Fu Li is a pure-minded decent human being who had married me by mistake.

I wrote to Mlle. Tan in Paris:

As I observe Fu Li's resurrection, I begin to understand what it is to be a woman. From their bodies to their souls, women belong to a totally different category of being, entirely different from men, different in their subconsciousness, their illusions, as well as the cultural baggage that they carry. After Fu Li woke from her coma, for half a month she was unable to speak. Then her period, which had stopped for two months, returned. I think this marked the beginning of her resurrection. She tried desperately to embrace Su Dan and me with her right hand, which could move. Two days later, she spoke for the first time and could write out figures and the letters of the alphabet. Her consciousness returned. For the moment, her memory was weak, she still lived in illusions, full of the agony of her first confinement, the pain of abortion and sense of loss, and had even imagined that the son she had lost was suffering by her side in the hospital. For days on end, I would be in tears as I drove home. I would ask myself, How could my petty male ambitions compare to what she stands for?

On awakening, her subconscious obviously revived itself along the order of daughter—mother—wife; this is a gendered order, and also a cultural order. Her resurrection was achieved through her revived humanity. Her first thoughts were of her mother. Then of the safety and the hardships of her child. Wifeliness came last, which to her was something tacked on. Compared to her, what I have over and above is just something external to my humanity.

(Mlle. Tan's reply)

I cried as I read your letter. I understand you perfectly . . . everything will be all right. You and Fu Li are standing at the two ends of a horizon, stretching out your arms as you rush toward each other, Fu Li's black hair streaming behind her in the sea breeze. I am constantly reminded of your happy reunion two years ago, and I know I will again see Fu Li cutting your hair for you, and I will again be at your birthday dinner sharing the dumplings that Fu Li personally made for you.

After receiving your letter, I dialed dear old Mr. Xie Rongkang in the United States. He asked me about Fu Li, and I couldn't resist reading your letter to him over the phone. Somehow as I read out your letter I felt chilly all over, trembling in shock, choking with tears. . . . Xiaokang, you must hold out. When I put myself in your shoes, I realize how hard it is. I am also very concerned about Su Dan and his future. Remember, he woke up after the accident to find both parents in a coma. Think what a shock it must have been, especially when he was still in puberty. . . . I'm afraid the shock may affect him for life. You must give him all your particular love and care so that the wound might heal in time. What shall I mail him for a gift?

I just saw a Portuguese film, very feminist and very lyrical. As I left the theater and walked through the beautiful old lanes in the Latin Quarter, I hoped that next year at this time, you and Fu Li would be with me here and we would walk together.

The doctor could no longer withstand my importunings to take Fu Li home, but he requested two rehab doctors to inspect the state of my apartment before he would release her. That caught me totally unprepared. I was still on the second floor. So a friend nearby who lived on the first floor lent me his apartment, and after tidying up the place we made ready to receive the inspectors. The two rehab doctors came over, measured distances within the room, and shifted the furniture about to prevent all possible falls and scratches. I complied with all their requests with a flourish, but of course it was all a hoax. We often took advantage of naive Americans and even gave ourselves a pat on the back for being smart.

In January of 1994, Dr. Elovic finally agreed to let Fu Li go home for weekends. Three months later, Fu Li left the hospital for good and became an outpatient at the St. Lawrence Hospital nearby. The doctor thought I was foolish. No American would try to get a paralyzed family member out of the hospital; that meant that he or she would be tied down to nursing. But I really could not bear to witness Fu Li's misery in the hospital. I felt that at home she might have a sense of belonging that might help restore her memory.

I did not look at the problem from a clinical point of view; perhaps she should have stayed in the hospital although it was hell for her. I had never taken this path before. I was feeling my way in the dark, like Deng Xiaoping's "cross the river by feeling out the stones."[6] And, predictably, we came across a problem. The insurance company said that since Fu Li was well enough to go home, they were not paying the hospital bills of the previous couple of months, which amounted to close to one thousand dollars per day. Dr. Elovic could only smile helplessly.

After leaving the hospital, I put the memory of that place completely behind me, except for thinking sometimes of the Argentinian. Only by thinking of him did I realize that I was not the most unhappy of men. But it was precisely this man that I had hurt. A year later, we went back to the hospital for a checkup. At the end of the corridor, I saw the Argentinian pushing his wife's wheelchair, bending with his mouth to her ear.

---

[6]Famous saying of Deng Xiaoping regarding China's path to modernization.

Finding Our Bearings

I'm not even sure when the process started, but gradually I calmed down.

I remember the last time I cried, a year after the accident. It was a Monday, and the social worker from the rehab center told me there were five spots where Fu Li was suffering cerebral hemorrhage. I broke down, and so did Chen ShuPing. She explained to the social worker in English, "He never knew until now." I lost the impulse to cry. Only the melancholy tunes playing on the car radio gave me pain.

During this period, I exchanged some letters with Yuan Zhiming.

Su:

It seems that there really is a spiritual being deep down inside the human heart, something man himself is not aware of. I only came across it during my calamity. This spiritual being is beyond the control of human will or concept or rationality. It has its own mysterious dynamism; you can neither repress its sorrow nor overcome its restraint. My unawareness of this spirit is the long forty-year-plus story of my life. If man cannot even recognize this spirit in himself, what more is there to be said? Is this what you mean by spirituality in religious terms?

Yuan:

All men have "innate spirituality." The vanity of the earthly life and the true face of despair—no matter what shape it takes—can awaken that spirituality. But that is not enough. Only by the grace of God can that spirituality revive and assert itself. St. Augustine said, man's soul is restless until it meets God. Why? Because that spirituality comes from God.

Su:

I cannot recognize that innate spirituality of mine, nor do I know where to find God. During those stormy winter nights, I knelt in front of a wooden crucifix night after night, begging God to dispel her nightmares, begging God to enable me to share her nightmares. But after all that praying, I just slept through the night. As time passed, I realized that all I was doing was seeking solace for myself. It was my own heart groaning in the abyss of despair that wanted a miracle and found a transient peace in prayer. Fu Li was still tormented in the hell of her nightmares.

Yuan:

You ask where God is. Your soul knows where God is; your reason rebelliously asks for proof. Why are you still searching? Are you trying to rationalize the godliness that you have already touched? Are you trying to deconstruct the spirituality that is just awakened in you to fit into a rational system? Will you not be satisfied until you have reduced your spiritual link with God to worldly sensations?

Of course I could not get at what he was saying.

It seemed that, to Yuan Zhiming, the spirituality I discovered in myself was what God has planted in every man, though not awakened until he has turned Christian, and what obstructed the awakening was nothing but man's human nature and rationality. But first, I am not sure how much of my rationality was left to me after the accident, not to mention the question of how much rationality there is in man in general. And second, human nature is by definition human and easily reduced to beastliness, something we see all the time. As to ascending into godliness, I am very suspicious. If man regards himself as being endowed with godliness, it is very frightening; he will take on the role of God. It's enough to maintain human nature, the best that man can do.

But later, I found something I could understand. This spirituality is what the ancients call "a tiny space" or, more literally, "one's bearings." A line in a Tang poem reads, "This heart a tiny space, all the sorrow it can hold." Critics have commented that "sorrow is a living thing, it could spread out to fill the universe and it could retire into secrecy."[7] It too could be a link between heaven and man. A proof that man does have this "tiny space" is none other than the true self of Fu Li. The first time I saw her "self" was after a three-day trip to Chicago to seek help from Qigong. I had returned empty-handed to the hospital in Buffalo and sat down in front of her.

At the time Fu Li was tied to the wheelchair. Her head, held in a clasp, turned right and left aimlessly; her unfocused eyes swept over me now and then for half an hour without any sign of recognition. I waited moment by moment, waiting for something to happen. . . . She stopped her aimless motions and stared at me for a full five minutes; then suddenly her mouth twitched, her eyes focused, and a wave of sadness swept over her face, like a

[7]Quoted from Yu Biyun, *Interpretations of Tz'u Poetry from the Tang and Sung Dynasties* (Shanghai: Classical Writings Publishing House, 1985).

blush covering a young girl's cheek, and her whole body started shaking.

The memory of that moment will stay with me for a lifetime. She had lost her memory and could not recognize me in her timeless, spaceless state. But the other, essential "she" still had a faint recognition, and when I was away "she" looked for me; it seemed that "she" had been looking for me all the time I had been away.

From then on, Fu Li seemed to be always on the lookout for someone. During that period, when I kept her company in the hospital, talking to her as she dozed a little, she would suddenly sit up in shock and start anxiously looking for me even though I was sitting right next to her. I would show myself to her, and after a close look at me she would relax. The person looking for me anxiously was a Fu Li I had never known before in all our years of marriage. Fu Li was never demonstrative and never clung to me. She just kept to her own world and was never dazzled by the trendy. But the minute I took French leave, she was the kind of woman who would go to the end of the world to be with her man. She later told me that when martial law was proclaimed in Beijing, she went immediately to Guangzhou to look for me. Not finding me there, she flew back to Beijing. At that moment, she said, the world was pitch black for her.

She crossed the ocean to be with me and ended up a

wreck. And now she and I were sitting across from each other. She gazed at me, totally relaxed, but where was "she"? I did not know. In that "tiny space" it was not easy to find each other and communicate. That "tiny space" is a spot of spirituality that even the self cannot recognize—that is, not until one has exhausted the limits of human meaningfulness; only then does this light of spirituality show itself. Our old life was gone; we were started on a new life of healing. In addition there was Su Dan. Every morning as he left for school, he would say goodbye and ask, "Will you be here when I am back from school?"

Mlle. Tan sent over a tape. She wrote:

I hope that everything is going well. . . . I have taped several segments of adagio from Mahler's symphonies; the far-flung strains of the melody send one into a distant region of peace and calm, embodying a majestic air of transcendence. I hope they will bring you peace. Other movements in Mahler's symphonies express disquiet, even tortured feelings, and sometimes humor, all of which is hard to take in one breath, so I chose passages from the Fifth (my favorite), the Ninth, the First, the Third (on nature), the Fourth, and the Second (resurrection). The "Hymn to Resurrection" at the end of the Second is so beautiful, I think you will both enjoy it. I have translated for you the chorus from the original German; it is by the eighteenth-century religious and patriotic German poet Klopstock,[8] and Mahler set it to music.

> *Oh, trust, my heart, oh, trust:*
> *Nothing is lost to you!*
> *Yours is, yea, yours what you desired.*
> *Yours what you loved, what you fought for!*
>
> *Oh, trust, you were not born in vain,*
> *have not for nothing lived and suffered.*
>
> *What has arisen, that must perish,*
> *What has passed must rise again!*
> *Stop trembling! Prepare yourself!*
> *Prepare yourself to live!*
>
> *With wings which I have fought for . . .*
> *in hot love's striving I shall fly upward.*[9]

[8]Friedrich Gottlieb Klopstock, 1724–1803, religious poet, author of *The Messiah.*
[9]Quoted from 1969 Polydor International GmbH, Hamburg, texts provided by Mlle. Tan Xuemei.

The Plateau Syndrome

With the coming of spring in 1994, we reached a plateau.

Only through the term in English did I realize the horrifying implications. It refers to a stop in the process of healing: that is, the "plateau syndrome." A rehab specialist from the St. Lawrence Center near Princeton, a very energetic lady and former student of Dr. Elovic, had helped Fu Li exercise for three months. She was also knowledgeable in Chinese acupuncture. At the end of that period, she wrote to the insurance company, using the term "plateau" to describe Fu Li's condition. From then on, the company cut down payments for a lot of expenses. In a word, Fu Li was condemned to "life without parole." Medicine had exhausted its resources as far as she was concerned.

It seemed that both miracles and men's spirituality—if it exists—have their limits. Groping for three weeks of confusion about the implication of the term, I finally grasped it. After three years of being off cigarettes, I resumed smoking, quickly reaching the rate of one pack per day.

I would tie a band around Fu Li's waist and hold her, as one does a child, while she practiced walking. This is not like cancer, where the doctor will tell you how much time you have left. In this case they give you a bottomless hope. Brain cells once dead cannot be revived, but it is a medical hypothesis that they may be replaced by other brain cells. The rest of our lives will be dominated by this hypothesis, but I must hold on to it. I bought many appliances and helped Fu Li exercise over and over again every single day. Su Dan installed games in the computer for her, to train her reflexes, her power of concentration, and her resilience.

These are all part of so-called rehabilitation, but can a human being be reconstructed?

People in the West are hard to understand. On the one hand, they hold that man is created by God, that man cannot create man. On the other hand, they uphold science and tinker with man incessantly, from artifical limbs to organ transplants to chromosome research. Science fiction and film are full of supermen and utopian visions of creating the perfect man. The United States has a high rate of strokes and traffic accidents, but Americans have no concept of being disabled; everything can be fixed and the body can be extended by artificial means, so much so that sometimes you feel that they are dehumanized. But society is very considerate to the disabled, providing every convenience, displaying a deep spirit of humanity.

This is an illustration of the culture. Americans are so practical. If you are paralyzed, you are paralyzed; they just try to use every means to live as normal a life as possible, or they can choose to end their lives. But it is a different case with my "little girl." She is stuck in this calamity; the past is a blur and the future an illusory craving.

Every morning, the two of us would first listen to TOEFL recordings. Then I took two knitting needles, each with a bead stuck at the end, and waved them in front of her, training her ability to move her eyes on the same axis at the same time and to test her left-field vision. After that she read Tang poetry word by word, with stops after every word, I recorded it and played it back for her to correct her pronunciation. She sweated over every word but sometimes pronounced them very precisely. I also made her sing. She is the kind of person who never sang a tune in her life, but I coaxed her, saying, "I have heard you sing Su Dan to sleep." She said that was "Little swallow, in new clothes, come to visit, in the spring" and started to sing it. But she couldn't get the tune and ended up reciting the words. I would leave her and she would go on humming that song by herself until one day she finally got it right. Then I taped it and played it back to her.

After that, I would use all kinds of self-made instruments to help her exercise the muscles of her left arm and left leg. We would persist in the exercise until she would shake with exhaustion and then I would give her a massage or a hot bath for the muscles to relax. After lunch, we would sit down together, close our eyes, and practice Qigong meditation. And then she would have a nice long nap. In the afternoon, she would watch soap operas on TV, often chuckling over the funny parts. In the past we had found the jokes in soap operas hard to understand. But after her loss of speech, the doctor used English to train her speech ability, and somehow her understanding of the language became better than it was before the accident. From magazines she read extracts of the memoirs of Mao's personal doctor. She said, "How can a doctor expose his own patient?" I said, "If he didn't do that, how could we know about certain aspects of Mao?" But she insisted that doctors should be held to an ethical code; it was her steadfast belief.

The brain is a tricky thing, the main structure seems to be rebuilding while some of the minor components are not in place. For instance, Fu Li recovered her memory, her English was better than before, she could even talk to Americans on her own. But her perception of the world in general was very elementary, to say the least, with only a fractured sense of the past, including her own past, our past life together, and the world in general. Mistrusting everyone else, she concentrated all her caring love toward Su Dan. I doubt that she was aware of her own true state. Every day on going to bed at night she would say, "I'll start walking tomorrow."

Fu Li did not know she was on a plateau. She disliked all appliances, including canes and wheelchairs, as she tried to walk. I was close to her yet miles away from the internal tortures she was undergoing. We are so glib about the "connectedness" of two souls. One day in a mall she raised her cane from her wheelchair to hit me and then burst out crying. Only then did I realize that actually I am quite a stranger to her.

This is her temperament; from childhood on she refused to be a loser. Brain damage robbed her of all her previous sharpness, but the temperament is still there. I have really worried about this, as it comprises a psychological problem. Dale, a young girl with a degree in psychology who came over now and then to help Fu Li train her mind, told me that Fu Li's most precious gift was the will to live and not give way to despair. The fact that she would not accept her situation was the best psychological protection she could have. Dale said that when people sink into despair and break down, it's the end for them. It seems that a human being's instinct for life in a hopeless situation is a very subtle thing, and Fu Li's temperament was the saving of her, by now her only asset.

Fu Li was becoming quite greedy, always asking for snacks and even fighting with Su Dan over them. She was getting more picky, and I had fun seeking out novelties to meet her tastes. She loved snacking but didn't move about much so I called her "Fat Cat," while she countered by calling me "Mangy Dog." (It was true, I had lost a lot of weight.) We found out that, according to Western astrology, she was Taurus while I was Virgo. The inversion of roles made us double up with laughter and we ended up calling each other "little virgin" and "big bull." We did a lot of joking with each other, but no one can know the heartbreak of having to grow up again; even I could not know what really went on in her mind. The sight of her in the mall when I left her wheelchair in some corner and rushed to do some shopping was heartbreaking. She would peer around while trying to look unconcerned and then give a gasp of relief when she caught sight of me.

Once I went to Professor YingShih Yu's place for a chat, the first time I went on my own initiative in the five years that I have been in Princeton. Our chat lasted six hours, until Su Dan called from home and said, Mother is awake.

Professor Yu told me that many people were asking after me and said I shouldn't give up because of the accident. He advised me to look for something that would interest me and help raise myself out of the fix that I was caught in and not wallow in it. He said that only by transcending events could I clear my head and become more rational. Think long-term, he advised; perhaps this is something you have to live with all your life. Expect the worst, and you will not be beaten down by disappointment. Go and read from the lives of exceptional men in history to enrich yourself. Take the case of Chen Yingque, for instance, who concentrated his writings exclusively on his internal life during the agonizing years after 1949.

It turned out that I had called on Professor Yu precisely to seek enlightenment on the life of Chen

Yingque.[10] I had accidentally come upon his book on Chen Yingque published twenty years ago, a scholarly work of textual commentaries, called *Commentaries on Chen Yingque's Late Poetry and Prose.* Chen had started to write the unique *Unofficial Biography of Liu Rushi* in the year 1954, "glorifying 'femaleness' to such extremes . . . far outstripping the bounds of rational judgement."[11] This actually had to do with a slice of his private life: his deep regret at having disregarded his wife's advice to pack up and quit on the eve of 1949 and lead the life of a wandering exile. I have a pitiful knowledge of classical studies and could not understand Professor Yu's book. I still remember twenty years ago when I came across Chen Yingque's book on Liu Rushi in my father's bookcase and how I had been completely baffled by its erudition. Now, after the accident, I began to understand that the great master's feelings of "the jade spring brimming with tears, rather endure in secret than overflow in grief" was really

[10]Chen Yingque (1890–1969), Chinese historian. Chen was a respected scholar and professor of Chinese history who traveled widely in Japan, Europe, and the United States. In 1939 he was made a member of the Royal Academy but was prevented by the breakout of World War II to take up a teaching position at Oxford University. On the eve of 1949, he decided for personal reasons to stay on the mainland and settled in Lingnan University in Guangzhou.

[11]Quoted from YingShih Yu: *Commentaries on Chen Yingque's Late Poetry and Prose* (Taipei: Shibae Wenhua Publishing House, 2nd edition, 1986), pages 76–77.

communicating a universal feeling, although he had concealed his own feelings in an intricate code system, closed to the ordinary reader, which only a learned man like Professor Yu could decipher. And now with the publication of the book *The Last Twenty Years of Chen Yingque's Life* on the mainland, all Professor Yu's conjectures made nearly forty years ago, of Chen Yingque's sorrowful regret, were solidly validated. It is literally an academic miracle.

Although I could not read Chen Yingque's erudite book, yet the writer's "regret at disregarding his wife Madam Chen's advice and his admiration for her foresight" is something I could identify with in my own bottomless regret and guilt regarding Fu Li. What I was mired in was precisely my regret for disregarding Fu Li's repeated admonitions to me regarding my gullibility, my blindness, and my lack of judgment, which ultimately led to major disaster for myself and ended in hurting her so deeply. This is a lasting regret and guilt that will never heal. Many people said I was tormenting myself and having a breakdown; they did not understand that this kind of emotion is necessary to man, beyond the understanding of the outside observer. Looking at the issue rationally, regret is useless, but I know that when a man is reduced to such a pass, he has no other resort except regret. I never knew how much I had been destroyed; my thinking, my judgment, my power of self-questioning, my social abilities and behavior—everything seemed to have been reduced to nil.

In the preface to his own book, *Death with Dignity and Life with Dignity,* Professor Charles Wei-hsun Fu had referred to the protracted suffering of death described by Arnold Toynbee in an article "The Relation Between Life and Death." According to Professor Fu, the English historian had said that the death of one spouse in a marriage is a kind of "dyadic event" in which the one who is left behind is likely to die in spirit before he or she dies in body. Toynbee had said of himself that he would be content to precede his spouse in death, but that he would find it hard to imagine what would sustain him in life if his wife went first. This is exactly what I was going through: fear of being left behind and the feeling of having reached the limit of endurance. The almost inhumanly cruel sights that I was forced to witness in people in a brain-dead state, the fatalistic feeling of being forsaken when Fu Li was denied supernatural grace in spite of all my prayers and had to subject herself to the tinkerings of human "repair"—all this added to my feeling of forlornness. I was steeped in a sadness that wrapped itself around me day and night. It was as if the first half of my life were hanging in front of me like an inverted mirror, and every past enjoyment, every fleeting happiness, was now turned into a jab of pain, highlighting the desolation of the present.

Chapter Four

THE SEARCH FOR SALVATION

That day in the fall of 1993 when I sat weeping with Professor YingShih Yu in the cafeteria of the hospital in Buffalo, I had told him I would be going to Chicago to look up a Qigong master the next day.

"Go ahead," he said briefly. "ShuPing will be here with your wife, don't worry."

Two years later, Chen ShuPing told me she realized at the time that when a man is desperately appealing to heaven and earth, nothing can stop him.

By "heaven," she probably meant the heaven that Yuan Zhiming had found for himself, way before I was plunged into the black hole of despair. It was not "heaven" as understood by the Chinese people, but heaven of the West. At that moment, however, I was not overly concerned about which one. The ultimate question that nagged me was, If I had joined Yuan in discovering his "heaven," would I have been spared this disaster? Would I be saved from the black hole?

Yuan Zhiming and I are really two of a kind, like two grasshoppers strung on one string. After June Fourth, all the fugitives made off, each through his or her own secret channel. I found myself in Guangzhou in the blazing heat of summer. One day I was strolling downtown, disguised, as I thought, beyond recognition, when I felt a hand on my shoulder. Paralyzed with fear, I turned around to see—of all people—Yuan Zhiming.

"The minute we passed each other, I knew it was you," he said, as the two of us moved into a little restaurant.

This encounter was straight out of the blue. In our conversation, I felt that although he was not as frightened as I was, his despair was total. In the short time we shared, clinging to each other for support, he would fly into screaming hysterics every night, followed by violent convulsions, and only woke up when I shouted him down.

I had always thought that, being of peasant stock, Yuan's collapse was due to disillusionment over the Chinese Communist Party that had risen to power through peasant rebellion. As for myself, my disillusionment had long been completed during the Cultural Revolution. Later, our so-called circle of exiles reveled in the boundless horizons of life abroad in Paris and America and experienced something akin to what Lin Yutang[1] described as "heathen pleasures." But Yuan Zhiming often stayed alone in his room and cried, refusing food and drink.

Yuan's wife, Liu Lili, and Fu Li became friends in adversity after June Fourth. But by the time the two women arrived together in Princeton, Yuan had already converted to Christianity, one of the earliest converts among the exiles. That was something I found hard to understand. Alone, he decided to embrace the Cross, leaving us all behind. He invited us to his baptism ceremony. As I saw him being immersed in water, the thought, Will this really change him into a new man? flashed across my mind. It did. The self-confident, emotional Ph.D. candidate whose fate had been briefly linked to mine disappeared, transformed into an eloquent preacher, highly regarded among Chinese Christians in the United States.

At the time of Fu Li's accident, Yuan and his wife were in Jacksonville, Mississippi, studying at a theological institute. Hearing the news, they knelt and prayed. Yuan reached me by telephone in Buffalo and told me that in his prayers he heard a voice tell him that Fu Li would be

[1]Lin Yutang (1895–1976), Chinese writer and educator, elected president of PEN in 1975. Highly educated and widely traveled, Lin was an early exponent of things Chinese for a Western audience. *My Country and My People* and *Moment in Peking* are among some of his best-known works in English.

saved. At the time, friends from all over the world were sending me messages of condolence, but no one else had given me such a promise. I desperately wanted to believe him, although it was hard to keep up hope, since by that time Fu Li had been lying unconscious for nearly a month. Only those who could reach up to a so-called supernatural power could rise above ordinary human commonsensical considerations and speak as one inspired.

But how do you meet up with one who can reach up to a so-called supernatural power—what in the West would be called a "medium" and in China one with "supersensory functions"? From a mystic point of view, it is still an unknown, out of personal control.

The Qigong Master

One cloudy morning in September of 1993, while Fu Li was still bound to a wheelchair and tapping with her right foot for communication, I left her in Buffalo and headed for Chicago with Su Dan. I was still in a state of shock. I could not understand how such an "unknown" could turn up in our lives so swiftly following our accident.

The fact was, after I had woken from my three-day coma, followed by three days of incoherent ravings, I was told that I had been saved by the Qigong master Yan Xin.

Yan Xin? I had met this grand master of Qigong[2] ten years ago. How could it be possible?

To this day I have not been able to explain away a clear but disjointed dream I had, during the week when I was lying unconscious. I dreamt that one of my legs was broken and a white-haired old man came and put it right. Friends who had been with me day and night confirm that this was what I had been raving about as I lay unconscious. Perhaps it was just a pain induced by hallucination. But my medical record shows that due to trauma in the nerve group of the pelvic area, my right leg was almost paralyzed, and a contusion to my head also caused bloody clots to form in the brain. And yet the moment I regained consciousness, I started walking, with the help of crutches. The doctor could not detect any blockage of functions and had no choice but to sign me out. He remarked that they had never seen a speedier recovery from such a serious auto accident.

Who was the white-haired old man? How come I was saved from paralysis? The minute I saw Fu Li lying unconscious in the emergency room, my mind became

[2]Ancient Chinese practice (*gong*) for cultivating the human body by controlling vital energy (*qi*) through exercise and meditation. Loosely based on Buddhist and Taoist philosophies, Qigong has many schools and some have large followings, both inside and outside mainland China. The Falun Gong, one school of Qigong, was designated a cult by the Chinese government in 1999 and banned, now followed by Zhong Gong, also banned.

blank and I never had a chance to think back to the whys and wherefores of my own recovery. But for me that event, inexplicable in commonsense terms, became the starting point of a new beginning after that life-shattering experience, a new beginning I could not refuse even if I had wanted to. The visitation of a supersensory "medium" is beyond the individual's control.

Stranger still was the fact that after the circumstances that led to our car accident following a night of discussing Chinese civilization at the University of Buffalo, Kang Hua—a Ph.D. candidate in physics—later confided to me that they were all followers of the Qigong master Yan Xin. What he said next sounded incredible; each reader must decide whether or not to believe it. According to Kang Hua, their group faxed Yan Xin straightaway after my accident. Yan Xin on his side was hit by a splitting headache immediately on receipt of the fax and said, "Something has happened, and it's an old acquaintance, too; I must help him."

Now what kind of deity is Yan Xin?

By the end of the Mao era, all the various schools of Qigong, which had been keeping a low profile, now burst on the scene, and from the 1980s onward Qigong masters emerged one after another, rivaling each other in their claims of supersensory powers: moving objects by willpower, seeing through the human body, curing incurable diseases. Within a few years they had convinced the institutions of higher learning, Peking and Qinghua universities, and major media units such as Xinhua News Agency and the Central Television Station, of their efficacy; the Academy of Sciences had even included Qigong among its research projects.

During this period, a young man from Sichuan province who had several miraculous cures to his credit descended on Beijing with great éclat and was listed among the major Qigong masters. He took the capital by storm, dazzling the crowds with his performances. His classes, held all over the country, swelled in size to tens of thousands, everyone collectively doing breathing exercises in the yoga position. China had entered the new and mysterious era of Qigong, wherein official and commoner alike came under the spell.

This young man from Sichuan province was called Yan Xin, and no one knew his exact whereabouts. After June Fourth he showed up in the United States, and rumor has it that President Bush met him in the White House. Mainland Chinese students set up an International Association of Yan Xin Qigong, with branches in all the main U.S. universities. The organization was mainly made up of assistant professors and graduate students in science and engineering.

Two months after our accident in Buffalo, it happened that Yan Xin was holding a Qigong class in Chicago. It seemed to me that he was the only one who could save Fu Li, so I decided to go and beg him for help.

Kang Hua drove Su Dan and me. All through the trip

as I sat dozing in the car, the past rose up in the haze of memory.

It was all because of my mother. During the height of the Qigong craze in 1983, when one school after another took their places on the merry-go-round, literary circles were also caught up in the excitement and had invited a Qigong master from northeast China to perform. Fu Li and I attended briefly. Obviously our "Qi passages" were blocked, because we were not affected by tremblings and contortions as we were supposed to be, and that was that. But just then my mother offered to introduce me to a very particular individual. "Listen to him," she urged. "It might be worth writing about."

My mother's maiden name was Pang, and people referred to her affectionately as "Old Mother Pang." She was a senior editor in charge of health and medical news for the *Guangming Daily* and for years had been advocating the combination of Western and Chinese medicine, though she had no use for quackery. When she heard by chance of a construction worker who was paralyzed from the waist down and set to walking again by a Qigong master named Yan Xin from Sichuan, she investigated quietly and ended up with a positive report. This was viewed by Yan Xin as my mother's contribution to the spread of Qigong in China and, years later, also the reason he decided to come to my help, I was told.

One snowy winter night, I went with my mother to the guesthouse of the Commission for Military Defense

Science and met Yan Xin. He was in his thirties, wearing only a shirt and obviously not feeling the cold, as he greeted us shyly in a strong Sichuan accent. He stressed Qigong as mainly a system of communications, which left me completely in the dark. He evaded all questions about his personal background.

Later, my mother invited him over to our house. He plugged a wire into an outlet while holding the live wire in his hand and asked the members of my family to hold hands in a row and the last one to hold the ground wire. He said that in that way the current would form a circuit every time he touched someone and he could read that person as through an X ray to detect any diseases in the body. I remember he made me close my eyes and he touched my forehead. My forehead where he touched it felt a thrill as if being electrocuted, and I saw stars. "Don't be afraid," I heard him say. "I can lower the voltage." Then he went on to name the locations where I was unwell, some right on the mark, some leading nowhere.

My mother fixed dinner, and he said he was a vegetarian, though he used eggs, like a Muslim. I asked him why and he said, "There are many 'communications' in the biological body, and they are not destroyed when an animal is slaughtered. Whoever eats the meat will take in communications of revenge and consequently will be assailed by disease." It made no sense and left me wondering why eggs didn't carry "communications of revenge" as well.

With him that day at my mother's was his wife, a taciturn young Sichuan woman. I tried to pump her for some background on Yan Xin, but she just smiled at me. Later, I said to my mother, "The fellow's background is a mystery and he keeps himself to himself; what can I write?" Much later, I heard that Yan Xin had been invited by the Commission for Military Defense Science to save the life of Deng Jiaxian, China's "father of the missile," who was suffering from terminal cancer. As far as I know, the cure did not work. Yan Xin often referred to this failure to drive home the fact that Qigong is not a magic cure-all.

The recollection of the meeting with Yan Xin on that winter night ten years ago sent a thrill of fear through me on the way to Chicago—indeed, there was no magic cure-all. Take the case of Deng Jiaxian, for instance, a man who was deservedly cherished as a national treasure. Yan Xin obviously did his best for him, but word went out that there was an obstruction somewhere and the Qi could not get through. Where someone like Yan Xin fails, the blow to one's hopes is most deadly. One should not expect too much, so as not to end up a case over which even the gods have given up. I was seized with fear for Fu Li's fate.

A fter Fu Li's accident, I once wrote to Yuan Zhiming:

I vaguely remember that when the two of us knelt down under the vaulted ceiling of Notre Dame, your shoulders were quivering, and you knelt for a long long time, unwilling to get up. As for me, although I was also moved, I still felt ill at ease. Now I realize that that moment in the cathedral meant vastly different things to you and me; in fact, we are so far apart that I am not in a position to discuss with you questions that belong to the so-called supernatural, or spiritual, realm.

At the time, many people of our group were enjoying themselves in Paris. Yuan, however, was plunged into a frenzy of grief and often acted irrationally. Kneeling in the chancel of the cathedral, he was racked with sobs, while others could not find any tears to shed.

I was told that Notre Dame is the final and supreme example of early Gothic architecture, its stately spires reaching up to the skies, its message beyond our grasp. When I first set foot in this cathedral, my head still spinning from the shock of my escape, the only prayer I could muster under its vast roof was for the heavens to protect my wife and son. But all my piety had been squandered in the years of my youth; all that was left was a desperate personal appeal to the Almighty as I was suddenly plunged into the desperate plight of an exile. It was what we Chinese refer to as "clasping the feet of the Buddha" at the eleventh hour.

Could it be possible that because of my flippancy at that momentous moment, I was struck blind and was totally unaware of the harshness of life as an exile and other disasters to follow? Now I often think back to Notre Dame and deeply regret that I had not knelt there longer and let my soul be touched. I had foolishly wasted my time in Paris.

Later, in the early spring of 1993, I was on a short visit to Paris and my hostess, Tan Xuemei, had purposely chosen a restaurant with a view of the great cathedral. As we drank our wine, I silently admired its imposing profile as it loomed in the dark, content with the view from afar and with no urge to get closer.

Mlle. Tan was very shocked at Fu Li's accident. Wanting to help and feeling helpless, she remembered her teacher of Taiji,[3] Xie Rongkang, a highly regarded master in Shanghai who happened to be in the United States at the time. Across the Atlantic, she appealed to Mr. Xie, asking him to help her friend. This old gentleman was the first of many medics to appear in our lives. On the phone, he said, in a quavering voice, "Over and over again I have pondered your case. Here is something simple. When alone, hold your head straight, face front, eyelids half closed, blank out all thought, and let your spirit concentrate. Imagine that Bodhisattva is in front of you; then imagine yourself as Bodhisattva; repeat, under your breath, *'Namo guangyin buddha.'* Persist for ten minutes or

---

[3]Ancient forms of health-enhancing exercises, tai chi in English, alive and popular both inside and outside mainland China.

longer, imagine that you have transferred this energy to your wife, wish her health. You must have faith, leave no room for doubt. So long as you are sincere, it will work."

I think it was shortly after my own confrontation with the black hole on that morning by the lake that I started to practice according to the instructions of Master Xie, trying to blank out thought and let the spirit concentrate. It was at least a ritual, letting me forget myself and achieve a moment of peace in the midst of my fear.

B e it the Virgin Mary of the West or the Bodhisattva of the East, there is no telling which of them will cross your path first. To use a Buddhist term, it is a matter of "affinity of fate," something that is only met with but can never be pursued. After Fu Li's accident, I suddenly remembered that before she traveled halfway across the world to be with me, I actually had come across the Incarnation of the Bodhisattva but did not realize my good fortune at the time.

It was the summer of 1990, during my second visit to Taiwan. Urged by a friend, Gao Xinjiang, I went on a pilgrimage to have an audience with the renowned woman Master Cheng Yen of Overflowing Benevolence. A certain He Guoqing, a volunteer worker for the Tzu Chi Foundation, flew with me from Taipei to Hualian and mounted the steps of the Abode of Still Thoughts, and finally we had the honor of gazing at the holy countenance of Master Cheng Yen herself. In our conversation, she noticed a

Buddhist talisman that I was wearing and asked to see it. As she turned it in her hand, she asked me, "Where did you get this?"

"I am not sure from which Buddhist school. It seems all of us exiles are wearing one."

"What about your wife?"

"She's still on the mainland."

"All right, I'll give her one."

And she requested that something be brought over and given to me. It was a split half of a peach stone hanging by a string, carved into the shape of a heart and colored a dark crimson. A piece of white jade was studded into the interior of the hollow on the back side.

"The heart sutra is carved on the jade. I wish you a speedy reunion."

She spoke lightly, but her words carried weight. Astonishment was registered on the faces of all the retainers standing around her. I was told later that the Master rarely ever gave gifts; "This goes to prove that there is an 'affinity of fate' reserved for your wife." I had no knowledge of the Buddhist use of the term "affinity of fate." Again, I felt I was in luck when I most needed it and, once back in Taipei, immediately arranged to have the talisman relayed to Fu Li. Fu Li had arrived from China wearing that talisman around her neck, but before she had a chance to have an audience with Master Cheng Yen, she was caught in the accident. When I took out that mini sutra again and hung it around her neck, the flesh already bore the mark of a cut left when they inserted the oxygen tube.

All religions preach faith—if you believe it, it will come true. My lasting regret is that I seemed to have lost all capacity for faith in anything. Even if disaster were hanging over me, I would not know how to resort to faith. It seems that after I grew out of my passionate belief in communism, the capacity for faith itself was eradicated from my very being. And I had prided myself on being a free-thinking intellectual. I had been shocked at Yuan Zhiming's shift from Marxism to Christianity; what was it in the depths of his being that made it possible? I wrote to him:

I am convinced more and more that there is an unsurmountable barrier between the secular world and the supernatural. Neither you nor I realized that something was lying between us—most of the time I did not understand what you were talking about and you could not follow me into my secular world of despair and helplessness and struggle.

Kang Hua drove day and night nonstop; by the time we reached Chicago, several hundred people had already congregated in a Holiday Inn, waiting to greet Yan Xin and acquire his Qi.

Yan Xin met me and Su Dan privately. He was his old self. Perhaps he had put on a little weight; nothing can hide the marks of time, after all. He remarked casually, "Your wife will recover. It takes time. You should both concentrate on practicing the Nine Step Qigong, especially you." He turned to Su Dan and said, "A son's 'communication' is very important for the mother."

This was like stressing an ethical issue. So poor Su Dan sat down on the floor in the lotus position along with hundreds of adults and followed Yan Xin in his nonstop practice of breathing in and out, which lasted three days and three nights. At the end, Yan Xin was pleased with the boy, patted his head, and said, "Why don't you take up the Children's Qigong?"

My back was nearly broken by those three days and nights of practice; I don't know how Su Dan went through it. Every sitting session would last over ten hours without interruption while Yan Xin would talk nonstop through a megaphone, repeating himself over and over again. I myself have some experience of public speaking, but I could never do more than two hours; beyond that my speech would crumble into drivel. I guess Yan Xin's marathon talk did owe something to his "vital energy."

As far as I could make out, Yan Xin was holding forth on a mishmash of popular Buddhist and Taoist theories, seasoned with anecdotes and platitudes that could easily be picked up in any popular handbook of "Buddhist Tales," "Taoist Legends," or "Stories of Outstanding Confucians." As he droned on, my attention wandered and I thought to myself, What a way to advocate traditional culture, obviously more glitzy than Professor Weiming Tu's[4] academic lectures on the subject. But if Professor Tu were here to hear Yan Xin, I doubt if he could sit through it. "Is this the way to promote traditional Chinese culture?" I could imagine him protesting. Besides, those admonitions about kindness, accumulation of virtuous deeds, rejection of greed, respecting the old and cherishing the young, and such like that were scattered through his talk—what do they have to do with sitting in the lotus position and breathing in and out? More to the point, what does it have to do with the imaginary lotus flower lodged in the Dantian acupoint[5] that Yan Xin requests us to concentrate on? I did try to imagine that lotus flower, could almost feel it blossoming in my tummy.

But when all is said and done, would that lotus flower—would it not be the same by any other name: a "rose," for instance?—help Fu Li wake up from where she was in her wheelchair several hundred miles away? With respect to this mysterious theory, my resistance was not

---

[4]Harvard-Yenching Professor of Chinese philosophy, history, and Confucian studies at Harvard University and Director of Harvard-Yenching Institute.

[5]Dantian acupoint, also known as the elixir field, is a point located in the upper two thirds of the line joining the navel to the pubic symphysis, where the Qi, or vital energy, is believed to originate and accumulate.

against the theory itself but its method of communication. As a rule, when Qigong masters effect a cure by instilling vital energy into the patient, they are at least facing the patient. That was how Yan Xin practiced at the beginning of his career when he first burst on the scene, but later he claimed mysterious powers that enabled him to conjure up wind and rain and effect cures over long distances. I had negotiated with the organizer of the class to bring Fu Li over on a stretcher but got a firm refusal. I was told that the grand master Yan Xin had already instilled vital energy into her at a distance, and any doubts I harbored would wipe out its efficacy.

Faith Healing

Fu Li had lost her soul.

According to modern medicine based on physiological science, her condition was diagnosed as brain cells gone dead, causing loss of memory and attendant phenomena; the so-called soul had nothing to do with it. Now, any talk of soul inevitably drags in the question of mysticism, and Western medicine has spent the last hundred years ridding itself of the remnants of mysticism in its development. But with the appearance of Freud, the concept of religious mysticism was freed of the derogatory epithets attached to it, such as "infantile helplessness" and "regression to primary narcissism." The Christian Lin Yutang had said that in the realm of thought, there were only a handful of men who were truly creative—Siddhartha, Kant, Freud, Schopenhauer, and Spinoza—whose thinking soared to unscaled heights while the rest were just repeating what others had already thought through. In medicine as in the sciences in general, there are vast unexplored areas, and the study of the brain is probably one branch that has been left far behind. Freud, on the other hand, must have dug into the darkest recesses of the human subconscious. But is there a "soul" down there? I don't know.

It is now accepted that there are more mysterious cures than those by drugs and the scalpel, one of the most challenging being faith healing. In many areas where modern medicine is helpless, such as cancer, AIDS, or other complaints resulting from pressure or certain lifestyles, such as high blood pressure, stroke, arthritis, or depression, faith healing has indeed reported miraculous cures.

There is a woman named Eetla Soracco in New Mexico who has set up an altar in her home draped in embroidered cloth, laden with candles, and redolent with roses and incense. For a whole hour every day she prays for five victims of AIDS in far-off California. A certain Dr. Targ of the California Pacific Medical Center in San Francisco has enlisted the help of twenty faith healers to help him in the study of the psychology of cancer victims, Eetla being just one of the twenty. This Estonian-born medium claims that, just by looking at a photograph, she can probe the patient's body by the power of her prayers. "I look at all the organs as though they are an anatomy book. I can see where things are distressed. These areas are usually dark and murky. I go in there like a white shower and wash it all out."[6]

When I read this, it sounded like the description of a Qigong master from China. The prayer of the woman from Estonia was neither Christian nor Hindi nor Buddhist (though all have adherents in the United States). Her power to see through the human body is very much like the supersensory powers claimed by the Qigong masters who have been the rage in mainland China.

Although Dr. Targ has not yet revealed the efficacy of his mediums, more and more doctors have overcome their refusal to deal with problems of the soul, while twenty years ago no self-respecting doctor would allow any prayer or "witchery" to invade his practice or his research.

What is the relation between faith healing and the soul? What direct influence does religious faith have on physical well-being? According to the report in *Time,* there are at least two hundred research items having to do directly or indirectly with the role of religion in healing, mostly showing evidence of beneficial influence. For instance, 232 patients undergoing surgery believe they

[6]Quoted from *Time,* June 24, 1996, page 59.

survived through the comfort of religion. Another study shows a five-point lower blood pressure for people who went regularly to church compared to those who didn't. Another study of four thousand middle-aged people who regularly attended religious services shows that they were less subject to depression and healthier than those who did not attend regularly.

In a word, research abundantly shows that when the mind is concentrated on one sound or one image—that is to say, in a state of meditation—the body undergoes changes: heartbeat, respiration, and brain waves slow down, muscles relax, and the secretion of hormones associated with adrenaline and pressure are all decreased. This is a perfect description of Qigong.

As the twenty-first century begins, a new kind of awakening is on the horizon. Annual expenditure on faith healing is around $30 billion, of which more than $1 million is spent on books and tapes regarding mediums (especially those from India) who provide meditation and drugs with Oriental flavors.

I honestly believed in Yan Xin's ability to effect a miracle cure; the problem was whether he was willing to help. There was, as I said, a problem with the method of communication. Nowadays he is surrounded by a coterie, said to have attained the "abstain from grain" level in Qigong practice, who survive on water only. Although practitioners of Qigong number in the tens of thousands, it is only a few of the initiated who have attained this height. They are Yan Xin's spokesmen, and they stood between me and Yan Xin, blocking my access to him. They tell me that, right at the moment of the accident, "the master instilled vital energy for you, else how could you have survived?" Yes, indeed, I did have a dream of the white-haired elder putting back my broken leg, so I have nothing to say to that.

As for Fu Li, they said, "Obviously there was a blockage somewhere." The blockage, they told me, was no one but "Su Xiaokang himself." I asked why and they said, "Think, what have you done about China's tradition?" I suppose they meant my TV series, *River Elegy*. So that was what they were driving at. This documentary, which I had undertaken casually in the 1980s, was first used in the aftermath of Tiananmen as evidence of "sabotage." And now it is the reason for the blockage of vital energies being instilled into Fu Li? This is indeed a major disaster.

Christian Congregations

When the news of Fu Li's accident was first out, many members of Christian communities in our area prayed for her. How dared I refuse such kindness? But there was one thing they kept saying: "If you do not open the gates, God will not enter." I was torn; I felt I could not make a deal with God, like saying, "I believe in You; please come and save my wife." As for Fu Li herself, she had lost touch with the very earth under her feet; what could she know of the heavens above? Many pastors and elders and members of the church came into her hospital room, held hands, and prayed with her, and she would go along. I suspect that to her it was no different from the doctor's daily therapy.

Su Dan was another matter. A Chinese pastor from Los Angeles challenged him: "If you want to save your mother, follow me and believe in God, or else."

On the verge of tears, Su Dan had knelt as he was told, but later he said, "Why don't they leave me alone?" All I could say was, Perhaps it's like Yan Xin's Qigong, the son's efforts are more helpful. Yet this kind of pressure could be counterproductive and stifle any budding leanings he might have had for faith. Who knows?

Fortunately, the pastor was just passing by, introduced to us by Mrs. Xue, a close neighbor. The Xue couple came from Taiwan and were devout Christians, but for some reason they had left the Chinese congregation where they previously worshiped to join a charismatic sect much farther from home but quite close to Fu Li's hospital. "Would you like to try it?" Mrs. Xue asked me tactfully, without any hint of coercion. I couldn't resist the urge to have a look.

It was my first experience in a church of that kind. The huge meeting place was like one of those rented indoor stadiums that can hold thousands. I took a look around and saw that the majority were black and some of the women were already moving their hands and feet. After an interval, two black singers, a man and a woman, got on the stage and picked up their electric guitars. The sound system behind them struck up a thunderous chord, and suddenly the whole assembly broke out in song. They were singing hymns but in a rock-and-roll style and everybody gyrated wildly, totally unlike my assumptions about church service with the choir's ethereal notes resounding from on high to the accompaniment of swelling organ chords. Here, the church service was like a rock concert. Perhaps the members of the flock came on Sunday to shake off the pressures and anxieties of the week by this strenuous singing. Whether it could lower blood pressure and reduce hormones, I was doubtful.

And so, I asked Mrs. Xue, this is a charismatic sect? She explained that they stressed direct communion with God and acquired grace through this means. She also told me that many pastors in this sect had healing powers. One day, sometime after that first visit, she told me one such pastor would be visiting, and we plotted how to get Fu Li over.

It was a night service. I explained the situation and begged the nurse in charge for a favor; luckily she was a Christian herself and allowed me to smuggle Fu Li out for a couple of hours after supper. As before, it was a large gathering of over a thousand people, loud rock-and-roll music roared from the stage, and the whole assembly took part in singing and dancing.

After a stint of singing, a stout broad-faced white minister went onstage and gave a sermon. He pointed out three times in his sermon that there were drug users present, as well as people from broken families and those who were bewitched, all of whom had come to ask help from God. As he spoke, these people streamed onstage and stood in a row before him. The minister mumbled prayers for grace to descend on them as he struck them in the face or on the shoulders with his hands. As he hit them, the seekers of grace would fall back and be carried offstage by several black men.

At the same time, he singled out a young girl among the crowd and said she was bewitched and made her come up onto the stage. She was quite close to where we were, and I could see that she was a sexy-looking girl with a wide mouth and large eyes. The pastor hit her a couple of times; surprisingly, she stood her ground without falling. Finally he seemed to have pushed her forcibly to the ground. Then he asked whether she felt better. She broke into a laugh without saying a word.

And thus with a stint of singing and a stint of curing, a full three hours passed, but the pastor never looked in the direction of the really sick, who were waiting at a corner of the stage on wheelchairs and stretchers.

Finally, we were each given an envelope, and we all

dutifully took out our wallets. Then the pastor talked for another half hour about how this money was going to save the Israelites who do not believe in Jesus. As the meeting was breaking up, many people rushed to the stage and reached out to him beseechingly; he waved his hands as if distributing blessings and then left, smiling.

My heart was chilled. Even Mrs. Xue was angry and began arguing with the pastor's assistants. I said it was not worth it and persuaded her to leave. Around midnight we got Fu Li back to the hospital. All the lights were out. Exhausted, she lay down in bed and muttered, "We're home, aren't we?"

In the spring of 1994, Fu Li was released from the hospital. As soon as she was settled at home, local Christian groups from among the Chinese community came urging her to join an "evangelical camp" to be held in neighboring Pennsylvania. I knew it was a site for collective conversions, and I felt dubious about it. Then something else turned up.

It had been raining for several days. After the sky had cleared, our neighbor picked up a piece of mail that had been lying on the ground; it had been soaked in the rain and the writing on the envelope was blurred. I opened it and saw that it was mailed from a remote little county in the heartland of China. I had been there once. It was nestled in a mountainous region, so remote that the Japanese occupation army had never penetrated, so remote that, a decade after Liberation, the locals did not know that the communists were in power.

The letter writer was a Christian doctor who had left his native soil in the rich southlands and moved voluntarily into this remote region after June Fourth to cure the sick and help the dying. This must be a good man, no doubt. He had heard of my car accident abroad and offered a startling interpretation of my predicament.

Looking objectively at all the co-writers for *River Elegy* from the angle of zodiac animals, it seems you have all offended the dragon and now find yourselves in trouble. Of the five, Wang Luxiang and Xie Xuanjun have been arrested. Yuan Zhiming's father has died. As for you, you have been the hardest hit—in heart and soul.

His letter also mentioned a scholar, Yang Jingrong, whose wife died suddenly after he published a book on *The Dragon and Chinese Culture.*

Why was this? The letter writer proceeded to explain that in the Book of Revelation the dragon is the symbol of the devil, but it is the patron of Buddhism. According to the Pure Land school of Buddhism, when Sakyamuni was born, two dragons spouted water for his ablution.

Only God can harness the dragon [he wrote in his letter]. And you particularly need God's protection.

Xiaokang, you cannot stand up against all the curses hurled at you, openly or covertly. Throw yourself upon the mercy of Jesus Christ, so as to free yourself from these curses.

The arbitrariness of his Christianity was obvious, such as writing off the dragon as the devil, but did he need to take a passing swipe at Buddhism? I did not linger over these side issues. His interpretation of the accident increased my sense of guilt. It is true, I disliked the dragon and had attacked it with my pen, never dreaming at the time that I had committed sacrilege against a symbol of China, provoking such outstanding figures among overseas Chinese such as Chen Ning Yang and Tsung-dau Lee[7] to rise up in indignation, reducing me to fear and trembling, wondering when and where vengeance will strike. And now it is clear where the strike has landed.

Actually, in my despair after the accident it did cross my mind briefly that the dragon might have had something to do with it. Of course it was just a passing speculation. The fact is that our whole family had seen Niagara Falls from the Canadian side in the winter of 1992 with no mishap. On this repeat visit, however, we took the boat and pushed right to the edge of the falls. As we were

[7]U.S. Nobel Prize laureates in physics, 1957, of ethnic Chinese origin.

tossed about in the raging waters, lost to heaven and earth as it seemed, I was suddenly seized by a fear that in the depths of the lake might lurk a mighty dragon that had made its way here from the East. The car accident happened a few hours later, on our way back. Then I remembered that after *River Elegy* was publicly shown on TV in 1989, I had published an article titled "Desolation in the Year of the Dragon." In the article I had mentioned that "my wife's birth animal is the dragon. During every recurring Year of the Dragon, she would wear a red sash around her waist to ward off evil." Although our trip took place in the faraway West, yet Fu Li had stumbled into the dragon's abode, and that may have been taboo. Of course, I don't presume to be seeing things from the viewpoint of zodiac animals.

However, the letter moved me deeply. The very fact that it was lying in the rain, lost and found again, hinted at a message coming to me from somewhere in the world beyond and which I could not understand. Before the accident, I regularly ignored anything that seemed irrational to me, overlooking in my ignorance many warnings that had all been staring me in the face. I am the kind of person who is lacking in certain dimensions, and I had always been oblivious of psychic signals. But this Christian from a remote mountainous area had even devised a prayer for me. That night I repeated the prayer word by word.

· · ·

As for Qigong, I was still single-mindedly looking for answers. Isn't it said that sons are most efficacious when practicing on behalf of their mothers? Su Dan was practicing Qigong a hundred times harder than I was and still had nothing to show. He had never outraged Chinese tradition, had he?

According to Yan Xin's theory for the Nine Steps Qigong, a son meditating on his mother's image will be able to receive powerful spiritual energy from his ancestors. For me, it meant meditating on the image of my mother. Actually, it was originally thanks to my mother that we had this tenuous relationship with Yan Xin. But who knew whether my mother in her eternal resting place was willing to help? This was something I dared not dwell on.

Fu Li never had the good luck to have a mother-in-law who doted on her. My mother had been depressed all her life for being hindered in her career by her bad family background, and it had soured her temper. She did not know how to express affection to her own children, not to mention a daughter-in-law. Ma had always been politely aloof to us all. Both she and Fu Li were strong-minded women, and mother-in-law/daughter-in-law tension is proverbial in China, so I was just grateful that they were polite and no more. Fu Li accepted the situation and kept her distance.

Even after Su Dan's birth, the situation remained as it had always been. Later, Fu Li made the sensible decision to leave Su Dan with my parents so they could enjoy their grandson and Su Dan could qualify for a good primary school in their area. But it was beyond her to see that Su Dan's occasional antics, which she had always tolerated indulgently, were major transgressions in the eyes of his grandparents. This was the first crack in the aloof politeness, a commonplace situation in thousands of families. With me in exile abroad, the mediator was gone; so between a mother worrying for her son and a wife worrying for her husband and a naughty child worrying them both, open conflict broke out.

I do not know the details. But in her delirium, Fu Li had mentioned my mother: "I want my mother-in-law to like me, but it's not working."

She had forgotten that, before leaving for abroad, she had already seen her mother-in-law off on her last journey. She had pushed aside the hospital staff with their clumsy hands and personally dressed my mother in her final burial clothes. Now Fu Li was seriously hurt in an accident, and the person who was instilling vital energy into her was actually doing it for her mother-in-law's sake. Who knows what kind of providence was at work here? As for myself, in my meditations I sometimes actually saw my mother's face hovering above me, and I would pray to her, Please, for the sake of Su Dan, please help Fu Li.

I believe in direct transfers of Qi only when I see it. In 1994, I took Fu Li to each and every one of Yan Xin's

Qigong sessions on the East Coast, wherever they were accessible by car: New York, Washington, Boston. But we were jolted back and forth again and again in our hopes, disappointments, and regrets. Since it was impossible to get Yan Xin to instill Qi into her personally, all I could do was wheel her into the meeting halls, hoping to access the field of Qi formed by the hundreds of believers congregated there.

Once in Washington in a special session of the Nine Steps Qigong, I met Yan Xin by accident and he was quite short with me. "Your wife should walk. If she wishes to walk, let her walk. The force of will is very important."

I ran back into the hall to tell Fu Li, and she immediately started to her feet, but after only a few steps she stumbled. Late into the evening, no miracle happened, and after supper the two of us were too dejected to return to the hall for the evening session. She told me that making her exhibit her handicap in public like that was too humiliating.

But the next morning she was back in the hall again, trying to walk. During the noon intermission, we crept to the end of a corridor and I made her sit on a bench to catch her breath, while I sat in her wheelchair. Suddenly a man shot out from nowhere, his face flushed, with a glass of water in his hands. He thrust the glass at me, shouting, "Drink this!" I was caught by surprise and gulped down the water. Then he shouted at me, "Get up! Run!" I came to my senses and took in the situation. "She is the patient, not I!" I shouted back. For a moment the young man was stunned; then he turned to Fu Li and ordered her to get up and run.

"I can't run," Fu Li muttered timidly as she got up.

"Run! Run!" The young man was jumping up and down as he urged her. I saw Fu Li swaying on her feet, about to fall, and I ran to steady her. Someone beside me stopped me, saying, "Don't interfere with the workings of the Qi!" Fu Li stumbled a few more steps and suddenly slid back. I caught her just in time, and the young man stamped his feet in exasperation and ran back into the hall, where he burst into tears. I was told that these scenes often happen in Yan Xin's Qigong sessions. Some individual would automatically transmit Qi in a frenzy; it is a mysterious means of cure. Well, if it were true of that particular occasion, again it was I who had panicked and wiped out its efficacy.

That night, Fu Li was so tired, she fell asleep the minute we went back to our hotel. I sat by her, in front of the window. Facing me in the distance, the Washington Monument was awash in light shooting up from below, and the capitol of the United States seemed to be quivering in the moonlight. Dry-eyed, I sat unmoving through the night.

Still hoping for a miracle, we went to Boston for one last time. For two days and three nights, Fu Li sat through the Qigong session, and nothing happened. It was the last time we resorted to Qigong. We had been told that Yan Xin had instilled Qi into her and it was up to us to remove the obstruction. But where was it? On our way home I remembered Deng Jiaxian, the man whom Yan Xin had failed to cure, due to an obstruction, and I was suddenly overcome. We were in Manhattan, and I had to stop the car for crying.

"Don't be so sad, Father. I'll work harder at my Qigong and try to remove the obstruction," said Su Dan.

What a good son.

It seems that there were conflicts in the spiritual world as well as in this one. Yuan Zhiming was opposed to our looking up Yan Xin's Qigong from the very beginning. He said it was just a minor form of spirituality and only Jesus Christ was the true Savior. "Turning to a minor god and missing the true Savior, think of the consequences; will you be responsible for the consequences?" His words instilled fear in me. Many Christians had advised me to pray, saying that praying was sure to work. Of course, they meant prayer according to the prescribed form, which includes confession and acknowledging that Jesus is the only Son of God. I prayed accordingly, but nothing happened.

As I was wallowing in confusion and despair, Fu Li went looking for help on her own. She had been to the netherworld to look for Auntie Huang, the nurse who raised her as a baby. Auntie came to her a couple of times in her dreams and then retreated.

Fu Li had been telling me about her dreams day by day, and one day she mentioned God.

"By the sea, there was a boat," she said. "Many people were trying to get on the boat. I couldn't get on; then a voice said loudly, 'Let her get on the boat. Everybody should extend a helping hand.' "

"What voice was that?"

"It was a voice from the Man of God. Many people were telling Him what a good woman I was. Those who could get on the boat will be saved. He orders seats for everybody."

"Shall I go and tell this to the people at the church?"

"No, I don't want preachings. They cannot save me."

As I looked over the details of her dream as I was putting them down in my diary, I was still very stunned. The sea of bitterness, the Ark, the voice from on high— these could only be scenes from the Bible and not something she could make up. Fu Li is totally lacking in any religious feeling or any knowledge of religion. Her mention of "Man of God" was particularly relevant. According to an unmistakable principle of theology, Jesus is God and Man at the same time, is the Trinity, and thus could communicate with men.[8] But had she ever prayed? I don't know.

When Yuan Zhiming heard of the dream, he was sure Fu Li had converted to Christianity and warned me

[8]Translated literally word by word from the original.

sternly over the phone, "Don't try to stop her. You can't, anyway!"

I felt wronged; when had I ever tried to stop her? I was just wondering why I could not hear the voice. Obviously communicating with God is a private matter, strictly between God and the individual, and it is up to outsiders to believe it or not. A miracle is a blessing for the individuals concerned; those not so blessed have to grin and bear it or try to rationalize their lack of good fortune by human logic and stretch their powers of endurance to the limits. There are no reasons, just mystery; any kind of asking for justifications only shows our limitations. There are probably two reasons to turn to religion: misfortunes not explicable by human rationality and good fortune not explicable by human agency. But good fortune acquired through a miracle is not chosen, not transferable, and certainly not to be duplicated. Here, human volition does not have a role.

However, my own atheism had completely disintegrated. I no longer kept myself aloof from the pursuit of the Ultimate. This Ultimate is not seen in the limited terms of personal life and death but could only be reached through the personal. It is futile trying to prove the unprovable. Faith and science are but two sides of Western civilization, science endlessly trying to provide proof to justify faith but always one step behind. God is infinite.

· · ·

In the early spring of 1994, our family went again to Pennsylvania for three days to that evangelical camp. Fu Li listened to the preaching and the witnesses quietly as I sat next her, lost in my own mixed emotions. The so-called search for Ultimate Truth: Is it really asking you to believe in a God who, believers claim, has descended from the supernatural world? He was being described in human dimensions with human expectations pinned onto him, interpreted according to human rationality . . . and in the process Ultimate Truth is lost.

For three whole days, I did not have any religious impulse. Finally I thought it through. Since Fu Li had heard the voice when she lost touch with time and space, and since she believed that the voice was a signal to her, and since God only communicates to each person individually, what more could I ask for? So when the minister asked, "Raise your hands, those who want to receive Christ," I raised Fu Li's hand for her. They have a term for this: seeing the light.

The news spread quickly, but when the minister came to see her, Fu Li said to him honestly, "It was because of the dream that I had. But I still cannot believe. You are so good to me, I cannot lie to you."

Chapter Five

THE EXILES' HOLIDAY RESORT

After settling in Princeton, the exile community from mainland China chose to live in the town of West Windsor in the northeast corner of the area. It used to be rural, settled by farmers, but modernized swiftly under the onslaught of the major companies that moved in. Thus there were many apartments for rent. Yuan Zhiming first discovered a complex called Fox Run; he moved in and the rest of us followed. Thus among peaceful green fields hedged by a placid lake, a Chinese exiles' holiday resort came into being. The area already had a complete education system. With the influx of Asian families who set store by children's education, the quality of the local schools improved and this attracted a new cycle of settlers.

School had opened a few days after Fu Li arrived with Su Dan at the end of August 1991, and she rushed to register him. At the time, neither Fu Li nor I could speak a word of English. A Princeton Ph.D. candidate named

Kent, who majored in Asian studies, could speak Chinese, and he helped us fill in the forms. He asked Su Dan to spell his name in English and remarked casually, "Dan? Then let it be Daniel, Dan for short." It sounded weird to me, but there was nothing I could do. It seems this son of ours had always had his names picked out for him at random.

Like all the mothers among the exile community, Fu Li had been terribly worried that her son could not speak English; these mothers were more worried for their children than for themselves about not speaking the language. It was one of the first culture shocks, and its effects lasted the longest. Actually, what these parents discovered was that their children forgot their native Chinese at a faster rate than they mastered English. At least Fu Li's earnest wish came true; Su Dan loved school and sailed smoothly all the way from primary school to high school without a single academic hitch. That was a great consolation in the middle of our family disaster.

Mlle. Tan sent us a postcard from Italy, where she was vacationing, and I replied:

The postcard with its lakes and mountains was stunning, like a picture of fairyland. I do not take much notice of things around me as a rule, but now it strikes me how hellish our present circumstances are by contrast. I force myself not to think about it, to shut myself away from the outside world, to focus on one thing and one only, so I can concentrate my energies. If I allowed myself to be distracted by other interests, my present situation would be unbearable. The bitterness of this situation cannot be appreciated by anyone who is not experiencing it: the fear, the despair, the daily overexertion, demanding attention to every detail with no end in sight. Even I myself when I look back through my diary of these days feel a chill run through me. To seal myself away from the outside world is the only way to protect my nerves and secure my peace of mind, so as not to lose my own bearings.

You are the only person I can talk to across the Atlantic, as if you were my psychiatrist. My friends are afraid that I might have a breakdown, so I pretend that nothing is the matter. Of course you need not worry for me, now that I have told you. We must face the fact that Fu Li is disabled, although deep in my heart I believe that she ultimately will overcome her condition. But the road to recovery must begin with accepting the fact that she is disabled and start from there.

I will walk dutifully down that road. Nowadays I just make sure that every day goes by without mishap and do not ask too much of life. My attitude is what the Chinese sum up as "strike the bell so long as you are a monk." I feel it is what Americans signal to me too when they say, "Have a nice day." I followed doctor's orders and made a little world for Fu Li in our home. I wrote out little reminders, such as SLOW DOWN and THINK HARD, and directions to her for exercising different parts of her body, and pasted them on the walls, over her bed, and in the bathroom. She has her own table, chair, diary book, medical reading, photo album, and glasses laid out for her. A huge calendar hangs on the wall with my daily schedule: teach her to dress herself, help her take a bath, take her for walks morning and evening. . . . Often she behaves like a child, throwing little tantrums or teasing Su Dan.

My desperate situation is not just emotional. I am so afraid of losing her that I rush about desperately, looking for help right and left, but by doing so I suffer even more. I looked to Qigong, then prayed to God, rather than rely on human remedies. Disappointed, I then placed all my hopes on Western medicine. I learned some commonplace forms of physical therapy, writing down all the instructions in a little notebook. I practiced with Fu Li at home, imitating what I saw. I also learned some tricks of acu-massage. It seems I need to keep busy for my own peace of mind.

Even if life can be lived all over again, who would want to go back and wade through it one more time? But I must keep Fu Li company as she grows up for a second time. Fu Li is an amalgam of wife and daughter, and I cannot not stand on my dignity as husband anymore.

I pushed her to exercise. She would fly into a temper when tired, hit me, shout at me, or throw things around. When she shirked the work or was confused, I could not resist taunting her with harsh words. At these times she would actually calm down, listen quietly, and say, "You must be sick of me."

She is the same old Fu Li. Living together with her for over ten years, I had been totally unaware of where her goodness lay. Only now that her sparkle has been obliterated by the accident and I am faced with what is left of her do I realize for the first time her true value.

She often muttered as if talking in her dreams, "When I'm well I'll work to put you through university."

With only half a life left, her subconscious still struggled to express what was uppermost at the conscious level—to be financially independent, to support her son, and to pursue her career. "Do you think I can still cure people?" she would ask me, already knowing the answer.

That was her lifelong aspiration. It was not eroded by years of overwork or crushed by the destructive accident. Her obsession with her vocation breaks my heart. Once she left the rehab center for head injuries, she began to dream of studying neurology and returning to China to start a rehab center of her own.

Often, as I keep company with her in the dusk, I dream along with her. Yes, perhaps we should return and settle in a mountainous village in central China or a small town in the south. She will open a private clinic and I will help, and thus we will spend the rest of our lives. I should have lived like that if not for the turmoils that came in between. When Fu Li and I first met, she was slim and elegant, coming down the steps of the hospital and taking off her white coat, giving off a whiff of disinfectant as she approached. And now she is half paralyzed, with her memory stuck at the period around our marriage. She was twenty-eight when we married. We were poor, our combined salaries did not add up to a hundred yuan, but she ordered our life so neatly and comfortably it was pure bliss. That tender innocent segment of our lives was cut short by me. And now it seems that only she is still living in that period, with the same well-bred air, the same character of steel, the same deftness and attention to detail. There is not one false spot in her; proudly, she stands contemptuous of all pettiness, a woman to die for.

Oh, to be the companion of a doctor in a small town, living in a little house that doubled as her clinic, a little house with the smell of disinfectant! Wherever it was, I would be content. It gave me a sense of security to dwell on it, as if it were the life I was meant to live and my later fame and fortune and exile to the West were but absurd aberrations. The vainglories of the 1980s in China were illusory and exhausting, so exhausting that many left in search of otherworldly utopias. The poet Gu Cheng, for instance, found a little island in New Zealand and lived by cutting wood and fishing, thinking he could avoid the clamors of Vanity Fair, but he lost his mind, killed his wife with an ax, and hanged himself. I heard the news in Buffalo, and it added to my feelings of despair. I was not personally familiar with Gu Cheng, I just had the impression that he never grew up. It was actually the clue to his marvelous poetry. The later gossip revolving around the murder/suicide was bullshit; nobody really knew him. He had tried to run away and then he hankered after the vanities, he could not put them behind him even when he was on a small island in the middle of the South Pacific. I truly have sympathy for him. This generation is mostly living in lies and self-delusions. Rising to fame is mostly a matter of luck or misunderstanding; there is not much difference between genius and mediocrity; it's a pity that the majority cannot transcend their own self-delusions and return to ordinary aspirations.

If we had not had that accident in Buffalo, would I have retired willingly from the fray? I never even had the courage of Gu Cheng to escape to an island. I began as a writer of reportage but started dabbling in cultural studies and then went on to film, making a lot of sound and fury at home and abroad and deluding myself into thinking I actually was somebody. I could never get off my high horse, while Fu Li, who shared my life, had only ordinary aspirations. At first she thought I was ridiculous; then she felt uneasy and told me to "go easy"—an earthy idiom she acquired after our move to Beijing.

What she was trying to say was, Don't let it go to your head. But by then things were beyond my control.

Only when she was struck down did I realize that what I had lost was the ordinary life. I had squandered it without realizing that I had my treasure in my hand; it is what we refer to in Chinese as "begging for alms with a golden bowl." And now I am reborn as an ordinary man, hoping for miracles, resorting to Qigong, even though it is exactly part of the tradition that I had castigated. In other words, I must bear the effects of this calamity to the full. Friends may offer words of comfort, but the daily disappointment and daily regret I face alone. Without ordinary aspirations, I would have killed myself.

These ordinary aspirations also included a sense of exultation that Fu Li had come out of the accident with her life. I must hold on to the belief that she will be repaired, but that will be another life. The ordinariness of our previous life is irretrievably lost. Lost is Fu Li's soul and her essence as an ordinary person. She is totally innocent, another Xie Ye, the woman who died under the ax of Gu Cheng.

I now avoided the crowd.

It began by avoiding "sympathy." People have a sense of pity, but they only want to help you avoid reality, help you cheat yourself, and always out of the kindness of their hearts. No one around me told me the blunt truth: "Face the fact that Fu Li is disabled." They seemed to outdo each other in bringing me good news: "Fu Li is much better" and "You are with her every day, so you don't see the difference." Actually, in private they were saying, "Fu Li is finished, and poor Su Xiaokang is still in the dark." Truthfully speaking, for a long time I clung to those sweet-sounding lies. It was like opium; you get hooked. But after a spell of self-delusion, I still had to face her, a Fu Li who would never be the same. Only I myself know the pang of that disappointment, and self-delusions only added to the pain. After a string of disappointments, I could not stand the comforting lies anymore. Facing my fate alone was simpler and more in line with reality.

I don't know if some people can deal with two fronts at the same time, accepting sympathy, being soothed like a child, and at the same time facing reality. I couldn't. Ever since childhood I have not known how to put on a mask. Fu Li was always deploring the fact that I had "pliable ears"—I was easily led by a few resounding words—and later, when we settled in the West, she also saw that I could not say no. To this day it is a wonder that I could have gone through what I did in China and come out in one piece.

I don't know how my father and mother brought me up as a child; all they could tell me was to be truthful, don't be mean, don't do to others what you would not have done to you, don't be suspicious of other people's motives, and so on. My father had weathered many storms in the corridors of power, sometimes at the risk of his life. My mother did not have that kind of skill—she had a short temper and she never mixed easily with people—but even so she had muddled through without any great damage. As to Fu Li, she had lost her father when young and had gone through hard times, so since childhood she was always on guard and never gullible. She knew how to preserve distance, had a strong sense of privacy, and could not stand the so-called buddy-buddying of me and my pals. In the early days of our marriage that had been a frequent cause of marital friction. I had been used to an openhanded lifestyle, sharing everything with my gate-crashing pals, while Fu Li had on several occasions given them the cold shoulder. It was only at her insistence that our little family finally built a fence around itself. "If you want to be buddy-buddy with your pals, do it outside" was the law she had laid down.

So I went on buddy-buddying, until I found myself buddied out of the country.

I had gradually been given the kiss of death by my circle of friends, whose praise made me sink deeper into my own recklessness and rendered my ears more "pliable," so totally losing the ability to say no that I put my wife and child in a car and allowed a person who could not drive to take the wheel. The car culture of the "Chinatown" of Princeton finally took its toll on us. Two years after the accident, I came across a diary of Fu Li's that recorded her first feelings after arriving in the United States. There were many references to her fear of cars, including "God protect me from car accidents."

It was I who had brought her to this "Chinatown" to be with me, and neither her wariness nor her standoffishness in personal dealings had saved her.

Fu Li's Diary

A notepad I had used to jot down random thoughts in reading had been taken by Fu Li to write out her own feelings when first arriving in the United States. The front side of the page was her diary, while on the back of the page was a list of daily household expenses, mostly small sums for groceries.

Today is the tenth day following our arrival in the U.S., and Beibei's first day at school. Our lives must get on a new track, entirely different from the past.

Beibei is very tense and did not sleep well the night before. In the morning he hid himself behind me and Xiaokang on our way to school. As we entered the gates, I reminded him again of the sentence that he had made me teach him: "I can't speak English." We saw him in and left uneasily.

In the afternoon, we went to meet him after attending a meeting of our own. He had already left for home. We headed back and, as we entered the yard, we saw Daniel (his new name) happily riding his bike. I felt so relieved. Nothing went wrong, he said, and he liked his school. Let's hope it will keep on like that.

Fu Li never used to keep a diary, but now suddenly she was writing one. Obviously, she had no one to tell of her unease and confusion.

Did some odd jobs, memorized new words, studied traffic regulations in preparation for the road test. Made a pot of chicken legs. Scolded Beibei for an hour in the evening. Another day has gone by. It will be frightful if each day is like this.

Beibei has not behaved well after school today, very frivolous, can't sit still for a minute. Forgot even to take out his work sheet for math. His diary had to be rewritten. Why doesn't this child apply himself?

English classes the whole day. During class, I heard the fire engine and thought I had forgotten to turn off the gas in the kitchen. I asked leave to go home to check. Actually everything was all right. But I was dripping in sweat from anxiety. How can I let myself be like this? Xiaokang says it is depression and everybody goes through it. But am I such a serious case? My memory has never been good, but today I am a wreck and can't remember a thing. This is terrible.

There was a parents' meeting, but I couldn't understand a word they were saying. This is a real problem. Supposing something happened to the child in school? It is so hard to have to rely on interpreters all the time. Our English conversation course has just started, I can't say a word, my listening ability is poor, and my vocabulary is meager. I went to church to practice conversation with a tutor but forgot to carry my electronic dictionary. No way to communicate. The pressure is unbearable.

Fu Li is referring to the English language classes that were set up by the East Asia program specifically for the benefit of the Chinese exiles. There were two groups, beginner and advanced, taught by two professional teachers of English during the summer holidays. Our classes were held in an old building, in which, according to legend, Einstein had given lectures. Zhang Langlang had said, "Hey, we are studying English in the American imperial palace." Later our classes were moved to another classroom.

In such an excellent—I would say hallowed—environment, most of us "elites" made no progress at all in our English. By the time the grant ran out and we could not afford to hire any more teachers, none of us could carry on a discussion with Princeton students on Chinese issues, and even if we did manage to say few words, they were unintelligible. We had to rely on interpreters for interviews with journalists and even to answer a phone call. As for myself, it was only after Fu Li's accident, when I had to deal directly with doctors, nurses, and social workers, that after stammering through two years I woke up one day and discovered that I actually could make out what people were saying.

In 1993, every misunderstanding might have serious consequences. But at the time Fu Li was writing about, I had no clue to the acuteness of her suffering on account of the language barrier. What didn't affect me I chose to ignore. I myself always had volunteer interpreters among friends and students at my beck and call, even for personal affairs. And, after all, it was pleasanter to hold forth on Chinese politics and culture in the Chinese language.

Now this was not only running away from the challenge of English but a fallacy in itself; it was infantile, as well as a typical example of the Chinese mind thinking in the Chinese language. But it was never Fu Li's attitude; she never relied on others for help. Moreover, she did not feel entitled to have her every word spoken for her by others—for her it was a disgrace. (The difference between us was that I did not feel disgrace.)

Fu Li once returned from a parents' meeting at Su Dan's school and spent a sleepless night. After that she threw herself into learning to drive. After passing the driving test, she drove herself everywhere to learn

English—the church, the YWCA, the community college; she went everywhere for English lessons whether
free or not. She seemed to have taken too much to heart
the burden of our son's language barrier, as if his problem
with English meant that he was an idiot. And about all
these internal tortures that she was going through at the
time, I had not the slightest clue.

Sunday morning begins with washing, ironing, and
tidying up, it took me the whole day; my back
ached and I could hardly stand up straight. Looking
back, there was nothing accomplished. Meaningless.

In the afternoon, Beibei found a bread-making
machine in the dump and Xiaokang helped him lug
it back. I was not at all pleased. If a child starts out
in life happy that he got something for nothing,
what aspirations can he have later on? A lot of the
exiles here are like that; I suppose they have no
choice. But would they do the same if they were in
China, considering their previous positions there?
And anyway, we are not really reduced to picking
through the garbage. At least we can afford to get
a cheap one, anything better than scavenging.
Another thing around here is the rushing to church
sales and yard sales, picking up other people's cast-
aways. Do they really need that much? What kind
of consumerism is that? I don't have a clue. I'd

rather dress badly and do with less. Perhaps I am too stubborn, or perhaps it is what they call the cultural difference. But anyway I cannot accept this kind of scrounging.

The exiles taken in by Princeton, being "elitist" and yet strangers to the English language, had no choice but to keep to themselves, and thus a Chinatown with parties every weekend gradually emerged. No party could end without singing songs of the Cultural Revolution or other revolutionary songs such as "Signed in Their Blood" and so on. No one had any academic training, but there were frequent "scholarly panels," and no one could resist holding forth at length, mapping out the future for China. Furthermore, we could all dabble a little in the discourse on "culture"; else how were we to distinguish ourselves as "visiting scholars"?

Another focus of interest was the car craze; old and young alike played with cars like children with new toys. We haunted car lots, attended car auctions, and even flitted to the junkyards.

Flea markets were another unending source of delight, but the greatest satisfaction came from picking a piece of furniture from the dump. As I relive these scenes it seems that apart from possessing a used car and dispossessed of admiring fans, there was no way to tell that we so-called Chinese celebrities were living in the United States. After June Fourth, there was a saying in mainland China: The "elites" are either inside (prison) or outside (abroad)—but what a world of difference between the two!

During the first few months after her arrival, Fu Li was bursting with unvoiced fury. Now I realize it was the shock of coming from the desolation of post–June-Fourth China to this "exiles' holiday resort." The contrast between "inside" and "outside" was just too stark. More than once she said to me in sorrow, "How can you ever face them?" and I had thought lightly to myself, How come Fu Li is turned to moralizing? After she scolded Su Dan roundly over that breadmaking machine, she had broken down and cried. At the time I felt vaguely that something was wrong, but she wouldn't say anything, just kept begging me to leave this place and go some-where to study; she was most insistent. But I lingered over the life I had, as if in leaving this place I myself would wither away.

Visitors in and out all day. Exhausting work, this entertaining. A splitting headache, I suspect it's a migraine. Have been taking these pills for two days and they make me sick. Everybody is busy and enjoying themselves. Nobody has time for anybody else. Why am I so out of sorts? No one to talk to, and I dare not send letters to China, really want to have a good cry.

Weekend. Set out in the morning to look for used bookcases for Xiaokang. Ran around for a whole morning. Also picked up a few odds and ends, all used stuff. So long as they are cheap and still serviceable. No sense of security at all, no jobs available, this is life in exile; after what I have gone through, I am resigned.

Afternoon, shopped for shoes and stockings, spent twenty-five dollars. On my return, Xiaokang joked, "Spent so much of my money?" I know he didn't mean anything, but I still felt hurt. I don't know how long I can bear to be without an income of my own. Having to ask my husband for the tiniest expense. You don't enjoy spending it, it's not money you earned on your own. Can I rely on my husband for the rest of my life?

Again some U.S. holiday or other, no school; all the children are here at our place and absorbed over their games. I shopped for groceries and cooked. Xiaokang is giving an interview. Again. Yesterday he gave an interview, and today it's another interview. At noon I heard that someone had a car accident. The news sent a chill down my spine. Heaven knows what will be my luck with cars.

The exile wife shopped, cooked, entertained guests, and minded the child, while the husband did one thing—gave interviews. The description in the diary is a perfect capsule of our life in Princeton, true for every family here. Journalists flew in from all over the world, with their cameras and recorders and flashlights, flashing their way right up to Fox Run, following their subjects even to their English lessons and their driving tests. This kind of exile must be unprecedented in world history. Life was good indeed, except for one thing; we were all risking our lives in cars.

We were mostly over thirty-five and drove used cars—two factors that contribute most to the frequency rate of traffic accidents in the United States. Thus the chance of accidents among our community was frightfully high. The accident that Fu Li mentioned in her diary happened to a woman exile. She went to meet someone at the train station, saw a deer in the middle of the road, and panicked; the car overturned and landed in a grove by the wayside. Her wounds were not serious, but there was a big cut on her forehead. During the last couple of years, there were a string of car accidents in our community, mostly minor ones.

Before I finally settled in Princeton, I had visited briefly in early 1990 and stayed the night. I remember that the next morning there had been an accident; an exile had driven his car right into someone's home the very morning that he got his driver's license. Later, the same gentleman had another accident after his wife arrived. It was on a rainy night.

By then I was settled in the area, and I drove with Su Wei to the hospital to fetch him and his wife. It turned out that he had run into an electric pole on his way back from the train station and his wife, sitting in the back, was actually propelled to the front of the car! The pole, which had snapped, was lying on the roadside for a long time; I passed it every time I drove by but never gave it a thought. Who would have imagined that our driver on July 19, 1993, would be none other than that gentleman's wife?

All the men in the exile community were taking it easy. Once outside donations stopped, it was obvious we would have to rely on our wives' working to support us. This particular gentleman had a famous saying, "Wives support the Party." What happened in fact was that his wife drove my wife into a disabled state, perhaps for the rest of her life.

Awake most of the night, had to take Beibei to school in the morning, head swimming. What I want above all is a copy of the test for a registered nurse and see whether it's workable for me.

I suppose one's lifelong state of mind has something to do with childhood. But somehow the more I seek something, the more it eludes me, and finally it settles into a permanent psychological burden. The trail ahead must be blazed alone. Lost the way? I suppose losing one's way is nothing more than not achieving what one has set out to do. Each person's ability is limited, so why worry? The present is probably the most confused period in my life. No goals. Unattainable even if I had them. Perhaps I haven't tried hard enough? I am confused.

Fu Li's lifelong ambition had been to be a competent doctor. I do not know what this has to do with her childhood. I know she had a hard childhood; she lost her father at seven, and that frightful experience must overshadow her whole life. But she never said anything to me about it.

She was settled in Beijing as a doctor, but when she decided to share my life in exile, she had to give it up. As a typical professional woman, she must have been in the depths of despair. Losing her profession must have been just as painful as losing love. But as Fu Li used to say, you blaze your own trail, and this of course included her choice in marriage. She did not put the responsibility on anybody else. She would walk down the road she had chosen right to the end.

Two months after arrival, she calmed down a little and went around looking for work. In Food Town, a neighboring supermarket, she saw a baker who looked Asian, so she went up and spoke to him. He was Chinese, it turned out, and helped Fu Li get a job at the seafood counter. She was the first wife in the "exiles' holiday resort" to go out and look for a job. Her diary ends here. She never wrote another word.

Scenes of Long Ago

Fall is here, and, as we say in Chinese, the firmament is high and the air bracing, and the yearly season for crabs has come around again. In the days at Fox Run, Fu Li would come home from work at the supermarket with a box of crabs; it was easy, as she was at the seafood counter. Before she worked, when all the household expenses came from her husband, she would only buy vegetables and chicken, although she herself does not eat chicken. She would never buy seafood. Now that she is spending her own money, we have fish every day; she can afford crabs by the boxful.

Fu Li dislikes fatty food but loves shrimp and crabs. Although I was born in the south, I always fumble helplessly with crabs, often ending with bits of shell caught between my teeth while the tender white meat lies tantalizingly beyond my grasp. Crabs for me always meant more frustration than enjoyment. It was Fu Li who taught me how to handle them. Back when we had just begun dating, she could barely cook, yet her expertise with crabs was amazing. First she sliced ginger into a bowl of vinegar. When the crabs were steamed and brought out brick red, she pulled off the big claw for use as a pick. Then she lifted off the top, which would be filled with yellow eggs, turned it over, and used it as a plate. Then she used the claw to strip off the white meat, put it over the yellow eggs, and poured the mixed vinegar and ginger over the whole. Every mouthful was pure delight. She was perfectly cool and collected in her operations. Eating crab like that, before the first season is over, one starts looking forward to next year's crab feasts.

Where did she learn to do this? It was during a trip to Shanghai that I had an inkling of the Shanghainese craze for crabs. For them, a crab during the fall, especially a big crab from the reservoir at Yangcheng Lake, was the culmination of the year's culinary delights. Fu Li's father studied journalism at Shanghai's Fudan University, so he might have acquired the knack of eating crabs and passed it on to her.

I remember a writers' gathering on the banks of Yangcheng Lake when we were treated to a special banquet of crabs from the lake's reservoir. It was a big deal; the crabs were counted the minute they were out of the water and recounted when going into the steamer, yet somehow, when they appeared on the table, several were missing. The uproar couldn't have been worse if there had been a major robbery. I thought it much ado about nothing.

A Shanghainese corrected me. You don't know what you are talking about, he said. Do you think that reservoir crabs are to be had every day? Every single one of them in the lake is targeted, some for the capital in Beijing, some for the provincial capital in Nanjing; we Shanghainese can barely lay hands on any.

At the table every guest had two. We all fell to in earnest, not even giving up a leg. What was funny about the feast was that, at the end, there was one left over and those "celebrities" at the table actually fought for it.

Later, during the fall—the first I spent in exile—I actually was treated to exactly the same kind of big crabs in Paris. My host, a friend from Taiwan, said that they were airlifted to preserve the freshness. By then I had acquired the knowhow to eat crab, but the crab party only highlighted the absence of the person who had taught me the art of eating them. She was still on the mainland, and to me the crabs were tasteless.

When I finally settled in New Jersey in the fall of 1990, friends called me up to join them for a trip to the shore where we could fish for crabs. We started out at the crack of dawn for a little bay where there were motorboats and fishing tackle for rent. We sailed into the bay, threw the lines, and waited for the crabs to bite. You couldn't call that fishing; we could grab a couple of crabs just by dipping our hands into the water. In a twinkling we had several barrels. But the flesh of the saltwater crabs was coarse, no comparison at all to river crabs.

At that time Fu Li was not yet with me. Soon after she arrived, she threw herself into working while I was busy trying to keep up my reputation as an elitist by gallivanting about making speeches. I had totally forgotten about crabs. One day I accidentally mentioned our fishing trip and Fu Li wanted to go immediately. We started off the next day at dawn with Su Dan. I kept driving east along the former route until we reached the water. Waves were lapping idly at the coastline. The Atlantic was deserted except for a breeze. The season was over. We had forgotten that it was already November.

By the year 1994, our moods had shifted dramatically. That summer a friend gave us the use of his summer house for two days. It was on the East Coast, and all the restaurants were flush with crabs. Su Dan and I wheeled Fu Li everywhere for crab dishes. Western restaurants served crab meat either broiled or baked; though lacking the playful expertise required by the Chinese way of eating crab, it was still very tasty. But Fu Li seemed totally uninspired and ate as if chewing sawdust.[1] River crabs were also available in Chinatown but we were not tempted. Somehow we had lost interest.

I still remember the time when Fu Li was working at the supermarket and would sometimes bring home crabs and serve them with vinegar and sliced ginger as in the old days. But I would rush through the meal getting bits of shell between my teeth and couldn't enjoy it. As for Fu Li, she first had to tempt Su Dan with snacks to make him settle down, then she patiently picked the meat from a crab and pushed it over to him when she had a plateful. Then she would strip a plateful for herself. She tried to teach her son how to eat crab, but he preferred hamburg-

[1]In the Chinese original, *weitong juela:* "tastes like chewing wax."

ers and pizza and she finally gave up. During those time-consuming crab dinners, Su Dan and I would be in front of the TV while Fu Li patiently sat at the table, picking crabs.

And now fall is here again. I saw crabs in the store and could not resist bringing back a dozen. Nowadays Su Dan can take care of his own crabs; following my few instructions he actually managed to put away two or three. Fu Li meanwhile waited for me patiently, watching me expectantly as I stripped the crab the way she had taught me and put it over the yellow eggs in the upturned shell. Then I poured vinegar with sliced ginger over the whole and pushed it toward her. As she savored every mouthful, I saw the shadow of the old Fu Li enjoying her crab—the only difference being that now it was I who would fix one for her and then one for myself. After eating two crabs in this fashion, she sighed and said, "That's enough. It's wonderful. But the sight of you stripping crabmeat, I can't bear to watch."

The main road in front of Princeton runs straight through many little towns like a kebab,[2] with the little towns like cubes of meat on a skewer. The two ends of the skewer were two stretches of highway running north and south. To the

---

[2]*Tanghulu* in the Chinese original: candied fruits skewered on a bamboo strip with two ends of bamboo protruding.

south, U.S. 206 was shielded by ancient trees on both sides, providing shade through the summer months. When I first arrived in Princeton, I stumbled here one day in my aimless driving, was delighted with the tall trees and their generous shade, and by association fell in love with the little town beneath them.

Three years later, as I drove along this shady path, Fu Li was sitting beside me, unable to move.

I asked her as I drove along, "Do you still remember this path? Think. Think hard."

"What is this place? Who lives here?" She looked abstractedly at the passing trees.

As we drove farther down, she became restless, trying to remember something. "There used to be a family here. What was the name . . . ?"

Her memory seemed to be galvanized. After another half mile, I pulled the car up to a house. Before we drew to a stop, Fu Li shouted urgently, as if calling to a child, "Trenner, Trenner!"

Mr. Trenner, an old gentleman close to ninety, was at that moment in a wheelchair in the sitting room. I wheeled Fu Li toward him. Fu Li grasped the old man's hand, saying in English, "How are you? Do you still know me? I am Fu Li."

The old gentleman smiled innocently like a child as he nodded and stroked her head as if she were his little girl.

The scene reduced the old man's daughter to tears.

I was completely stunned.

Trenner was an old man whom Fu Li had taken care of. He had been a senior investigator in drug research.

In the past, when Fu Li studied English at the YWCA evening classes, the teacher had been a young Jewish girl who was friends with the Trenners and had mentioned Fu Li to them, a woman doctor arrived from China. The Trenners' children then had the idea of asking Fu Li to come and take care of their old father, offering to pay her by the hour as a nurse. At the time Fu Li had quit her job at the supermarket and was studying to take the test for a registered nurse. She thought the income would come in handy and she could practice English with the old gentleman, so she said yes. She sometimes brought over homemade dumplings for the old man's lunch and sometimes drove him to McDonald's, his favorite. After lunch she would draw a hot bath and lay out his bathrobe and towels. She would leave after she had tucked him in for his nap. Fu Li was a doctor, after all, so whenever she detected the least sign of irregularity in his blood pressure, heartbeat, or body temperature, she would alert the family to take him in for a checkup. The old gentleman was her only patient. She was extremely concerned about him and could not stop thinking about him even when she was at home. It was always "Old Trenner" this and "Old Trenner" that.

After Fu Li became a wreck physically and mentally, the old man's second daughter, Kathryn, a lawyer, showed up one day with a bouquet. She said it was for Fu Li's birthday. I was surprised that she remembered. The old man's children had kept track of Fu Li's condition but did not want to intrude. Now they felt they could come. Shortly after that visit, the old man's eldest daughter, Idamae, invited us to their house. I was worried whether Fu Li could recognize him.

The fact that Fu Li was reunited with her old patient and still recognized him was a great stroke of luck. Strangely enough, a few days later, Chen ShuPing phoned. She saw in the papers that the old gentleman had passed away and told us the location of the funeral home. I took Fu Li over the same night. The family was surprised to see us there. Fu Li could not bring herself to view the body, so I went and paid my respects to the remains on her behalf. He was lying there peacefully, in a happy release. I thought to myself, Isn't it strange, it is barely a week since our visit. As if the old gentleman had wanted to say goodbye to her before he left for good.

After Mr. Trenner's death, his sons and daughters were always ready to help us. They were the only American friends we had in the Princeton area.

The Woman Doctor

"Has Fu Li gone and taken the exams? This is Li Wen-pei calling."

It was another phone call from someone who did not know of her accident. I dreaded them all, unsure of where to begin my explanations, but I dreaded a call from Li Wenpei most of all. She was asking whether Fu Li had taken the exams for registered nurse. Fu Li had sought her advice on the subject, though I don't know how Fu Li had gotten hold of Doctor Li, a woman her own age, also from the mainland, who lived in a basement in Queens.

In 1992, Fu Li quit her job at the supermarket and immersed herself in study, preparing to take the test. It was the first step in our plans to make a living. It was futile to survive through clinging to the Democracy movement; we would only become more and more lazy and sink into the habit of waiting for handouts. I had by then totally given up hope of returning to China and had to think of how to strike roots in the United States. Fu Li was certain that she must get a stable job so I wouldn't have to run around selling myself as a "visiting scholar." And the starting point for her was no more or less than to pass the test for registered nurse; she felt it was closest to her own profession and not beyond her reach. This, then, was our American dream. I looked over my own diary and saw this passage:

How should I sum up my year of 1992? I look over my notes and realize that I basically have not participated in any political movements over the span of a year. But I have given the most number of talks. . . . Mostly organized by students from the mainland, a lot of hot air, argument for the sake of argument, very tiresome. . . . I have also written quite a number of articles through the year, but nothing of substance. . . . I suddenly feel sick at heart.

"Hey, I found someone called Li Wenpei, let's go and see her."

For several days running, Fu Li had been in animated conversation with this person over the phone. When we arrived at her street in Queens, Li Wenpei, a slightly built woman of few words, was already on the sidewalk waiting for us. She led us to the back of the house and entered the basement through an iron-plated side door. The interior was like a warehouse, stocked full of odds and ends. The woman had cleared out a cubicle for herself and pasted it up in brown paper, a space big enough to hold a nice clean bed and not much else. It was the first time I came across anything so sparse; it was miles away from the aggressive world of *A Chinese Woman in Manhattan*[3] or the rough-and-tumble world of *Beijinger in New York*.[4] The two mainland woman doctors were deep in conversa-

[3]Autobiographical rags-to-riches story by a woman from mainland China. A best-seller in Chinese translation in 1991.
[4]A Chinese TV series based on the novel *Beijinger in New York* (New York: Cypress Book Company, 1993) by Glen Cao, starring the Chinese actor Jiang Wen.

tion about the U.S. nurse's exam as they leafed through the study material.

After we left, Fu Li told me that Li Wenpei inspired her with the deepest respect.

"She is so unfortunate. She came as a spouse when her husband was a student. When she was sick and nearly died in the hospital, her husband deserted her. She survived and started taking odd jobs but was determined to qualify as a nurse."

"Why doesn't she just go back?"

"She wants to get her daughter out through her own efforts. She wants to show the stuff she's made of."

Li Wenpei had already passed the test and at the time was working in a major hospital in New York. She told Fu Li her plan was to save some money, move to the Middle West for a better job, and then bring her daughter over. That was her American dream.

I never exchanged a word with Li Wenpei; her life experience never touched me. Actually, it should have been of consuming interest. During the 1980s when literary reportage was all the rage, I had roamed the length and breadth of China looking for people and their stories, dogging them for interviews, making them open up (something I used to be good at). Only after I had in my hands dozens of extraordinary stories did I dare pick up my pen to write an article. It was nothing like the figure I cut later when I passed myself off as a "culture specialist" and wove reams of words with nothing solid to back them up, buoyed by nothing but fanciful assumptions. In 1993 when Fu Li went down in the crash, I suddenly thought of Li Wenpei and realized I had lost the knack for reportage through the kind of life in exile that I had been leading.

Li Wenpei and other spouses like her often suffered breakups in their marriages, but most of them managed to land on their feet and struggle on alone to realize the American dream. Their husbands also belonged to the type who achieve success but share it with a new family. As to girl students from the mainland, generally regarded as the smartest and toughest, their stories are even more arresting. All these stories are known as the chronicles of the "sent-out" youth.[5] Regrettably, no one had written them down. I had been urged by students here to write on the subject myself, but I was then dallying with "culture studies" and lost interest in live human beings.

The murderous rampage of Lu Gan[6] in Iowa was actually the first time a Chinese mainland student had his story converted to fiction, all of three hundred thousand

---

[5] A playful variation on the Chinese term "sent-down youth," referring to the millions of young people, mostly high school kids and ex–Red Guards, who had been sent down by Mao to the countryside during the Cultural Revolution. Some of them later settled in the United States and thus became "sent-out youth."

[6] Lu Gan, Chinese student at the University of Iowa, shot several people to death and hurt others in a murderous rage over a perceived grievance.

words, written by another student. The writer had dumped the pile of manuscripts on me, honoring me by asking for my opinion. I flipped through a few pages and put it down. I had no stomach to read about psychopathic behavior as part of the ordeal of being "sent out." But later on, when I saw the flood of nationalism engulfing the students abroad, I thought I could see some of the same psychological patterns that went into the making of a person like Lu Gan. The novel about him was put on the Web and greatly enjoyed by Chinese students here.

Anyway, mine is a good example of the exiles' obtuseness about events with human interest. One would think that living in another culture among people of another nationality would enable a person of genius to flower even more spectacularly, especially in arts and literature. Milan Kundera is a good example. But looking at the Chinese exiles from the mainland, the situation is the exact opposite. There were many writers among the exiles after June Fourth, but no works of merit have appeared from their pens. "Exile" has become a political label, a justification for rejecting normalcy, a state of hollowed-out numbness. Life in exile is so comfortable. Many complain of the language barrier, especially poets. Anyway we all claim that our talents and inspirations have withered outside our own language, and there is nothing anybody can say to that.

But at least this I know: The Chinese in other professions do not dwell on this disadvantage. The first thing they do on arrival is to learn the language. They either learn English or they give up pursuing their professions. Take Fu Li, for instance. Even though she was willing to be a nurse, the language barrier seemed almost insurmountable. She pored over the dictionary and completed thousands of quizzes for the nurses' exam. She armed herself with flash cards of English terms, pinning them over her bed and stuffing them in her purse. But on the eve of the exam, she was still sweating with anxiety: "What is the term for the muscle on the buttocks where you push the needle in?"

In spring she went to New York to take the exams. I drove her over. We had taken the trip a few days earlier to make sure of the location and to have an idea of how long the drive would take. The exam was held in a huge waiting room of the Hudson River ferry, right next to a retired aircraft carrier that was now on exhibit. Examinees poured in from all sides; they were of all races and colors, but mostly women. The room was stifling with heat as if about to explode. And there was Fu Li, nearly forty years old, still having to go through this. I was sad at the thought and after seeing her inside I wandered over to the retired carrier, feeling quite glum.

After the exam was over, I met her as she came out. She was dripping from the heat but as excited as a high school girl who has taken her college entrance exams, and chattered all the way back. She said she didn't expect to pass at the first try: How can you have everything your way so easily? she had said. I knew she would go on taking the exam until she passed. That was Fu Li all over. I felt sorry that she had to work so hard, so after she had taken the exams for the second time, I dragged her off on our outing. Barely two weeks later, when her mind was still stuffed with terms about skeletons and nerves and drugs, she was flung into chaos and lost touch with her memory. In her dream she may still have been harping on one idea: I don't mind toiling away so long as Xiaokang gives up his restlessness and settles down to write something worthwhile.

I had no heart to say much to Li Wenpei, who had made the call. Fu Li's situation was much worse than hers.

June Fourth, who cares for this date anymore? But every year as the date approaches, we feel involved and take refuge in words of frustration. As for the situation in China—a China that according to many will never reverse itself—the exiles saw it defined in terms of the demand for democracy formulated in the Tiananmen movement, the liberalization achieved in the so-called ten years of reform, and the burning hatred in reaction to the bloodshed in Tiananmen. Yet all the above were replaced by the magic word "nationalism." I can never forget that after Tiananmen had been wiped clean, many mainland elitist intellectuals announced to the media that the Chinese Communist Party would fall shortly, and the basis for their prediction had been the famous saying of Mao Zedong: "Whoever crushes students will come to a bad end." Thinking back on it now, my feelings are not only of frustration but actually of absurdity.

During the first anniversary of June Fourth, when I was in Taiwan, I borrowed a term from Kundera and said that the anniversary would be like a "solid mass permanently protuberant."[7] But I later discovered that I had misunderstood Kundera because I did not understand frustration. That "solid mass" is a sense of frustration, frustration over history, frustration over the self.

Three years later I understood in a flash. The day I awoke, I heard through the hospital broadcast that Wei Jingsheng had been released. I should have been in prison, but I had escaped. But can you really escape? If prison is to be replaced by a car accident, I would choose prison.

There is not much choice for the individual, whether it is fate or accident. Take that sudden outburst of 1989, for instance. Scholars can make all kinds of conjectures about inevitability, but in essence it was an accident, especially to the young lives who died on the Tiananmen Square. Most of them could not have realized that it was to be their last resting place. No one among the living will

[7]Milan Kundera, *The Unbearable Lightness of Being,* translated by Michael Henry Heim (New York: Harper & Row, 1984).

take responsibility for these deaths. The Communists and the democracy activists point at each other—which is to say, the whole thing was like a major car accident.

The deepest sense of frustration usually hits in the aftermath, when you realize that all is beyond repair. People always say, "The blood of June Fourth was not shed in vain," as if the price paid in young blood can extract something in return. The concept of blood being a mandatory price must have started with the famous words "If blood must be shed, begin with mine" by the martyred Tan Sitong.[8] But from his time to ours, isn't it true that the more Chinese blood is shed, the murkier politics have become? Take the period from June Fourth on. After eight years had gone by—the war against Japanese aggression took but eight years, after all—what had changed?

PBS showed Carmalita Hinton's *The Gate of Heavenly Peace,* the best film on the subject. The material and the editing are excellent, but, conforming with Western attitudes, there was an overdose of the subjective and not enough distance. The maker of the film was too involved, too biased toward the political angle, too occupied in highlighting the distinction between mass movements and democracy by due process. It is well meant, but in a

[8]Participant of the Hundred Days' Reforms of 1898. Tan was one of six men executed when the plan to introduce constitutional monarchy was overthrown by Empress Dowager Cixi.

documentary film a lot of the human interest can be lost. There were too many shots of minor details regarding the process of the movement, while more arresting issues may have been submerged. For instance, the interpretation of the students' naive idealism, I felt, was a bit simplistic and biased in favor of the good intentions of the so-called reformers. It is an ideological position that overstresses the role of so-called mass consciousness. This documentary actually has a merciless subtext, which implies that the confusion and fanaticism of the masses was justification for the shooting. This is a marked neoauthoritarian stand. What it lacks in depth is the unasked question, Why did the students behave the way they did? Out of frustration. And therein lies the real tragedy.

Thus the "solid mass" goes on "protruding" itself, turning cancerous, and neither China nor the world can do anything about it. The yearly memorial is only meaningful for the dead and gone, gone forever. We the living owe that much, not to China, not to "democracy," just to each and every one of them as individuals.

I myself finally realized that I do not owe anybody anything for Tiananmen. I only owe a debt to Fu Li, a debt that cannot be repaid in this lifetime. As we are more and more removed in time from June Fourth, only the victims are savoring their pain; it is a down-to-earth daily reality for them, not something that calls for a few words of glib retrospection every year when the time comes around.

This conclusion finally made me realize the meaning of politics in China. Fu Li had always disliked politics and disapproved of my dabbling in them in the name of "anxiety on behalf of the nation." She had never liked my literary reportage, which she thought was playing with fire. She was right. I played with fire and she paid the price. I am in her debt. I can't deny it and no one can help me pay what I owe her. She poured out the sweetness of life into all our years of marriage, to which she devoted her heart and mind on a daily basis. If she lost sight of it for one single day, she would be ill at ease. And all this was unaccountably destroyed. So what if the government's verdict on June Fourth is reversed?

Generation X

Su Dan noticed that I like to put on music while driving on the highway, so he taped some rock-and-roll for me, mostly Michael Jackson, Whitney Houston, and so on. I listened a couple of times and put the tape aside. Too much hype for highway driving, I thought. I still preferred the melancholy tune in *Godfather,* while Su Dan said it is old hat. Popular music is the clearest dividing line between generations. Actually, Su Dan himself was not a fan of Whitney Houston and company. When I said I rather liked Whitney Houston's "Nothing," he scoffed and said she spat out the word "nothing" too hard and sent saliva flying around. I was upset. "How do you know?"

"I read it in a mag."

It's often these little things that make you realize you don't know your own son anymore.

One Sunday he sat watching a live performance of an MTV concert. He often sat in front of the TV alone with an earphone. He knew it was an interest his parents did not share. I was in the kitchen and happened to glance at the screen and over the thousands of bobbing heads, I saw some writing in English about Tibet. I wondered what a rock-and-roll performance in San Francisco could have to do with Tibet, the plateau of the world.

"The concert is a fund-raiser for Tibet."

"How can they help?" I didn't get the point.

"They are making an appeal not to buy goods made in China."

I was shocked. "Who will listen?"

"Who?" Su Dan broke out angrily. "Well, let me tell you. My generation. And the generation older than me by ten years and all the coming generations. We are the MTV generation."

One year later I saw this term in *Time* magazine and remembered what Su Dan had said. Of the MTV generation, it seems that the common assumptions were that

Beavis and Butt-head were their icons; Beck's "Loser" was their song ("Savin' all your food stamps and burnin' down the trailer park"); Richard Linklater's *Slacker,* with its Austin, Texas, deadbeats, was their movie. This was the MTV generation: net-surfing, nihilistic nipple piercers whining about McJobs; latch-key legacies, fearful of commitment. Passive and powerless, they were content, it seemed, to party on in a Wayne's netherworld, one with more antiheroes—Kurt Cobain, Dennis Rodman, the Menendez brothers—than role models. The label that stuck was from Douglas Coupland's 1991 novel, *Generation X,* a tale of languid youths musing over "mental ground zero—the location where one visualizes oneself during the dropping of the atomic bomb, frequently a shopping mall."[9]

These cultural signifiers are as far removed from me— a father, a marginalized person who only reads Chinese, and an exile on top of that—as the Stone Age or the dinosaurs. My only consolation is that so far Su Dan has not yet turned into that much of a monster. As I turned back to the TV screen there were indeed demonstrations of how to identify China-made goods inserted in intervals during the concert. To me they were much more appeal-

[9]Quoted from *Time,* June 9, 1997, page 58.

ing than the political wrangling about Most Favored Nation status on the channels of CBS, ABC, and CNN. Might as well let the MTV generation take over the world.

"Isn't this the same as boycotting Japanese goods?[10] Can you find it in your Chinese heart to go along?" I kidded Su Dan.

My son may have been influenced by the many discussions on the identity crisis of Asian youth; anyway, he usually stood up for China and had contempt for the Asian boys who dyed their hair blond or red. But to my question his answer was ready: "The Chinese government is not China."

"But boycotting Chinese goods will hurt the people of China."

"And so? That's not what's hurting them most."

My my, I must take a good look at Su Dan. He has more sense than the Chinese graduate students here who abuse Taiwan and damn Harry Wu[11] as a traitor. When I say *sense,* I don't mean "postcolonialism," "nation-state," or other Western jargon. What I mean is, Here is this Chinese boy living in an atmosphere where he may feel

[10]Boycott of Japanese goods during the war of resistance against Japanese aggression.
[11]Author of *Bitter Winds: A Memoir of My Years in China's Gulag* (New York: Wiley, 1994), and *Troublemaker: One Man's Crusade Against China's Cruelty* (New York: Times Books, 1996).

discrimination, but he can still go beyond that crass talk of nationalism, a trap I myself could easily fall into.

And so it occurred to me that the MTV channel was not such a threat after all. From 1993 on, I had been running to the hospital every day and leaving a teenager to the teachings of American television. It had been a burden on my mind; I knew it was dangerous even without warnings from the American middle class or the Christian church. Yet I left Fu Li's dearly beloved son to sink or swim on his own in what I had been warned is a mire of "sex and violence."

I don't blame MTV, but I really hated the local computer store.

Su Dan had begun to resist going to the hospital with me to see his mother when Fu Li was moved from Buffalo to Princeton. It had been the minimum that I required of him—to visit his mother on weekends. I felt that seeing her son once each weekend was the least Fu Li deserved. First she had met the other dead twin in her dreams; then she had thought the elderly black woman on the bed opposite was Su Dan. It would dispel her fears to see him once a week. It never occurred to me that it was a torment to Su Dan. In that frightful winter of 1993, he had submitted quietly, but he talked to her less and less.

Every weekend, I had to persuade him to go with

me—holding out rewards like buying comics on the way or CD card games, something I detested. But it was the one treat he most looked forward to throughout the week. A thirteen-year-old looking forward every week to shopping at the computer store. What is the world coming to? This thought always struck me when we had to stop by the store first on our way to the hospital. Here we were in our own private hell as we heralded the coming of the computer age. In the year 1994, not even many American families had a CD-ROM.

Su Dan's love affair with the computer began with the installation of our CD-ROM. This was not the same thing as the Nintendo I had bought for him in Beijing when he was four or five years old. It had cost me twice my monthly salary to buy him that imported Japanese toy. At the time Fu Li had said, "You're ruining him." In 1991, after they arrived in the States, I again bought him a Nintendo, one that could be manipulated on the TV screen. The two of us had great fun playing it, driving Fu Li into bursts of fury. It was then that the idea of card games caught on in his mind and will probably stay with him forever. In this country, adults also play card games. Thus, at the time when Fu Li's soul drifted back from the netherworld, her son's soul had drifted away from two-dimensional games to surfing in a three-dimensional world.

It was in that particular computer store that I had hesitated over the purchase of the CD-ROM, daunted by the price. Su Dan was seething with anger, and after reaching the hospital he started quarreling with me right in front of Fu Li. Then he turned and ran off. I left Fu Li in her wheelchair and pursued Su Dan, bringing him back in the car. What I did not understand was that he was already gone for good, a leavetaking that began the night he boarded the Greyhound in Buffalo. I was trying to drag him back into our world. According to the rules of filial piety, he had no right to leave his parents in hell and go off on his own. The fact that he needed to do this never crossed my mind. It was beyond my imagination to register the psychological damage that a boy like Su Dan—who had always relied on his mother—might be suffering to see her in this state. This was the beginning of his resistance. He had nowhere to hide except in the world of games.

But with the computer he entered another world, especially after the Internet. That world seemed to jump to life only for his generation. They were perfectly at home there. Su Dan started by tinkering with my old 286 until he reduced it to a pile of garbage, went on to dismantle two other used computers, and then demanded that I buy him a new one. All his generation cares for is speed; they reckon everything in terms of megahertz and are crazy about the movie *Speed.* Speaking of this generation, *Time* magazine had warned that they might be a bunch of loafers, equivocators, and vagabonds, but we should not to be fooled by their laid-back posturings.

Su Dan was not really a slacker. With a comforting degree of self-knowledge, he told me he was not sure whether he belonged to Generation X or Generation Y, or perhaps he was one of the New New Men. Obviously he was not too damaged by the accident and not affected by my own spiritual breakdown. He just got up and started off on his own, drawing the meaning of human endeavor from martial arts novels, American movies, computer games, and Japanese cartoons. I often made sarcastic remarks about the way he lost himself in these idle amusements, but then, remembering the harshness of the world, I felt he had not done so badly for himself. Without the mediation of Fu Li, he and I were facing each other across a wilderness. When he first arrived, he was just a kid; when he got mad at me, the worst thing he could say was, "I won't miss you anymore." Now that he was older, he would flare up at the smallest provocation and rush out of the house in the snow. Often when I went out to search for him, I would find him sitting moodily on the swing.

It is Halloween. In the morning Beibei was at a party in school and went trick-or-treating in the evening. But tonight we caught him in a lie and I am in a very bad mood. What hurt me most was Xiaokang saying that I am taking it out on the child. That night we had our first big fight since I came to the U.S. He said I was not fair; he was always giving way, he said, and I still fly into tempers at the drop of a hat. Now that it has come to this, what can I say? You forge your own way through life. Now if I return to China I wonder what I will be stepping into, the political environment being what it is. But I will not be happy here if life drags on like this. He said, You are already forty and still so restless. I thought to myself, Precisely because I am forty already, I can't bear to live my life for other people only and not do justice to myself.

For me, this was the most shocking paragraph in Fu Li's diary. The date was 30 October 1991, which is to say that after barely two months she had already thought of returning to China. How unhappy and despondent she must have been! As for me, I had completely forgotten about that quarrel. But reading her account, I realized that the quarrel was just part of a pattern.

The fact is, I had treated Su Dan as a friend ever since he was a child and had never tried to discipline him. After June Fourth, I felt guilty for deserting them, so when we were finally reunited I tried to compensate. But Fu Li was different. She showered him with love and care, but there were two things she could not tolerate, lying and not doing well at school, especially the first. If he was caught in a lie, Fu Li would hit him and then hug him as she broke into tears. I used to tease her by saying, Hit him and be done with it, but if you break into tears it won't stop him from lying again. Anyway, in the days when we were living in Fox Run, I was content to be reunited with my son. But Fu Li was plagued by a hundred anxieties. She had not adapted to life as an "exile's holiday." Seeing no future, she felt it was a gamble in which she might lose her son.

How could she have foreseen that in a few years, when she was suffering from brain trauma, she would lose her son even more thoroughly to the computer age? *Time* magazine described the X Generation as much more ambitious than their parents and grandparents; they were self-confident, quick-witted, and materialistic, and "high-tech wunderkinder, such as Yahoo! Web-search founders Jerry Yang, 28, and David Filo, 31, [were] role models because of their affinity for risk and their entrepreneurial spirit." They are a generation on the make, the article had said.

Well, there we were, saddled with such a one at home. Su Dan treated homework like a game, he looked up everything on the Net; that was his idea of being good at studies. He chatted on the Net as he did his homework, not caring with whom he was chatting, it could have been a typewriter for all he cared. He had the knack. There was a period when he was hooked on "magical cards"[12]; they were very much like the costumed figures I

[12]English term supplied by author.

had shown on slides when I was a child. Of course, Su Dan was playing with popular mythical figures of the West. The figures could be matched, just as the "One Hundred and Eight Heroes of the Marshes" or the "Twelve Beauties of Jinling" could be matched in my games. The kid actually succeeded in matching up many sets of characters and sold the sets to his schoolmates and neighbors for a good price. I was shocked when I found out what he was doing, but he said it was his own business. Fortunately Fu Li was unaware of what was going on, or she would have had a fit.

Su Dan was hooked on *The X-Files* and news of UFOs and was genuinely concerned about visitors from outer space. He totally believed in extrasensory powers, worshiped bioengineering and life science, and was sure that gene therapy combined with advanced computers would bring about the perfect human being. And thus was Fu Li's baby gone.

Before leaving China, Fu Li had taken Su Dan to Henan to see her mother, and her mother had said, "If you take him to the United States, he will be lost to you forever." The old lady had gone straight to the point. As for me, I sometimes wondered whether Fu Li, if there had been no accident, would still be able to lay down the rules for Su Dan. Or, if I had not been exiled and the three of us were still in China, would Su Dan have become one of Generation X? Or if I had come to my senses and left the circle of exiles in Princeton earlier, would there still be such a big generation gap between me and my son?

But right after we were driven out of China in fear of our lives, the Cold War was over; doomsday cults and fundamentalism flourished, with Europe and the United States softening and the Asia-Pacific area rearing up—all these unexpected happenings were totally beyond our imagination. To be hit by the computer age and Generation X may have been as inevitable as the car accident.

Chapter Six
FU LI'S "NOBLE DAMES"

I am just a passerby in Manhattan. Many people are enamored of New York, but I cannot understand this city, just as I cannot understand America. To me, New York is not American, it is a world in itself—a global village, to use a trendy term. I go there through a dark tunnel, as if entering another world. From the west bank of the Hudson River as I am driving along the superhighway, the island standing in the morning light does indeed look like a separate world. Packed among the cement forests and deep gullies are desire, money, art, excitement, you name it . . . but, in the end, merely signifiers.

In 1994, on the off chance, I took Fu Li to Manhattan to look for help from Chinese acupuncture. The failure of the spiritualists and the Qigong was a great blow to me, and now I had been told that the insurance company was cutting off Fu Li's medication. "Why?" I asked. Only then did I hear the whole truth: "She suffered cerebral hemorrhage in five spots. There is a limit to recovery."

But I wouldn't believe in this limit. Who knows where it is anyway? Our only choice was to expand the limit, to press as far as we could. I became attracted to another of China's mysterious cures, acupuncture. It is related to a system of acupuncture points, or acupoints, which have never been located in the human anatomy. Since the mysticism of the spiritualists and the Qigong were closed to us, acupuncture was our last resort.

Nowadays acupuncture is neither as mysterious as Qigong nor as popular. As far as Oriental mysticism is concerned, it seems that the more shrouded in mist, the greater its appeal. But one thing is common to all of them: You must find someone who has been handed the mantle by a true master. I took Fu Li first to Philadelphia, then to New York. There were many licensed practitioners of acupuncture, but none seemed to have the golden touch. They stuck needles into Fu Li from head to toe, with nothing to show by way of results. We did meet one great specialist of scalp acupuncture within a year of the accident, when Fu Li was still in the hospital. He had a reputation of working instant cures and was passing through New Jersey, traveling from California to the East Coast. A friend from the Chinese Christian group begged him as a special favor to see Fu Li. We had to keep it from the hospital nurse, so we smuggled Fu Li to the cafeteria, where the doctor gave her acupuncture. Afterward, he shook his head helplessly and said she was too badly wounded.

Dr. Bao

By 1994, I had had so many disappointments that the later ones drove out the earlier ones and new hope was rekindled. Hope really has magic powers, a magic nurtured in despair. Buoyed by hope, I persisted in going to Manhattan for a full ten months. Ten months of racing on the highway, of creeping through the tunnel in fear and trembling, all for the sake of seeing a woman doctor from Hangzhou. America is really full of surprises; we actually found her in the summer of 1994 in lower Manhattan. It was said that she was the last disciple to be initiated, right after the Cultural Revolution, by a leading master in Shanghai, and that with her the line ended.

Her last name was Bao. She said, "How can there be instant cures? I feel she can recover, although I'm not sure how far. Let me try. She has been badly hurt; it is like a stroke."

Hearing the old familiar tones of Hangzhou speech made my heart leap. She was indeed exceptional. She pushed one long needle into Fu Li's left arm under the armpit, rotating the needle from left to right, and Fu Li immediately felt stimulated from her shoulder right to her fingertips. The doctor then pushed two needles into her tongue while she was chatting with me, and lo, the needles immediately reached the yamen acupuncture point[1] and Fu Li's speech became clearer.

We ended up going for treatment every other day. With time I became used to the sights of lower Manhattan, the dirt and the people who insisted on washing your car during red lights. I even got to enjoy the crowded street scenes as we moved along in a sea of cars. Before that, we never ventured into the city unless we had to, just as a Chinese peasant would not venture into Beijing. I had an inexplicable fear of New York, probably dating from the winter night when I got off the Greyhound at Forty-second Street and was immediately surrounded by drunken panhandlers. I had just arrived from Paris, and the harsh welcome was a contrast to the safety, warmth, and varied night life of Europe. Actually, Broadway and SoHo were just as rich and vibrant; the problem was that we had never been part of the life there. My fear of big cities in America is ridiculous, seeing that I was considered Western-oriented. I had inserted many snippets of picture-perfect American life (cut from TV ads) into *River Elegy:* lyrical scenes of beaches, lawns, and swings in front of little houses. That

---

[1] An acupuncture point located in the center position at the back of the neck.

kind of gap-mouthed naïveté regarding America now seems even more out of sync than the May Fourth era of 1919.

Standing on the curb one day, it suddenly occurred to me that the Big Apple, as New Yorkers call their city, was like the apple of the Bible, full of temptation. Once God has left (inane to quote Nietzsche's "God is dead"), mankind must fend for itself. Hope and disappointment are mixed, and you must swallow them all like the mixture of New York's wealth and poverty, luxury and crime. It is a veritable Eden, neither Paradise nor Hell.[2]

For the last three years, you have been my companion, silent and faithful, while I never gave you a second thought. But the day before yesterday, you were damaged, and only then did I realize that you have been hurting silently but cannot cry out in pain. That day, I left the mall and was hit by a woman who was close by your wheels. I got out and looked at your wound, a big dent in the right-hand taillight. This was my second car accident. I was unhurt but you were damaged. While waiting for the police, I was very calm, thinking only of the ties between the two of us. You have been a companion in vicissitude, working uncomplainingly, never giving trouble: a real buddy.

As time went by, you have aged, with a hundred and

[2]A literal word-by-word translation.

fifty thousand miles to your credit. Yet in the coldest winter mornings, you would hum the minute I started your engine, and thus my day would begin on a note of confidence. To get on the superhighway and crawl through the tunnel in order to reach New York—I cannot do without that confidence. I also suffered brain trauma during the 1993 accident; nowadays whenever I get on a highway I always feel I am heading for disaster, as if that calamity that struck like lightning could repeat itself and I would again be flung into another existence, Fu Li, sitting beside me, unconscious of everything. I must go to New York every other day. Without your reliable support, I don't know how many times I would have died there.

Over a period of ten months, everything was smooth sailing, you were sometimes out of breath, but you were still light and nimble on your feet. When I am in an ugly mood, I sometimes give chase or am chased by others. And you were always with me every step of the way, breathlessly making eighty miles an hour, as light and nimble as a filly. Remember that time in the jammed highway south of New York, a fellow cut me off without signaling? I stepped on the gas and tried to overtake him, and you also showed your mettle, leaving the fellow, a youngish man, behind in the traffic jam. He didn't catch up with us until we were approaching Manhattan. He blocked our way and stuck out his head, challenging us. We remained locked in silent defiance for a while and then each went our way. But you were usually so civilized, sticking to the slow lane, taking your time, trying to reassure me that I was in good hands.

Once inside Manhattan you really have a hard time. I usually leave you on the street outside the clinic. You worked hard to get Fu Li and me there, but I could never spare the money to park you properly. It's over ten dollars and, over time, would add up to a considerable sum. Once you were caught and just about to be towed away when I arrived in the nick of time and had to pay several hundred dollars to rescue you. Traffic violations are a main source of revenue for New York City; the police do not go out in police cars, they come out in plain clothes and take you by stealth. I can't begin to tell how much they made me pay in violations. I cracked the whip and made you pull the cart until finally, one day, you collapsed from exhaustion right in the middle of the Holland Tunnel. The tunnel was immediately closed and you were dragged away by a tow truck. The moment we were out of the tunnel, I dropped you at a garage and took Fu Li off in a rented car.

After you were cured, you resumed life as my slave, as devoted and hardworking as before. I never gave a thought to our relationship. You were just a thing to be used to the fullest extent. I was not always like that. I had acquired you on a chance, but once you were mine, I cherished you and never let anyone else borrow you; I would change the oil every two thousand miles and wash you regularly every Sunday. Adults are fond of silent companions. I suppose that is why Westerners keep pets like dogs and cats, for the sake of the communication. But Fu Li and I had been afraid of animals since we were children. Fu Li especially feared cats. After the accident, Su Dan in his loneliness had wanted a puppy but I absolutely forbade it, and Su Dan had been very hurt. I felt sorry about it later. Why is it that I myself am so lacking in certain dimensions of feeling and have so little capacity to open myself to others? I dared only approach insensate creatures—like you, for instance. In my subconscious, I suppose I felt secure that with you I would not be hurt. It must be a compensation for my inability to communicate with humans, the most sensate of creatures.

After the accident, I lost all sense of pleasure and never bothered about you, just kept on using you. I used you mercilessly, never washing you once. Yet you kept up your slim good looks. In those three years, although you never said anything, you seemed to know my feelings and never bothered me. You are very sensible of human feelings. And now I have hurt you, it suddenly occurred to me that for the last three years, you have never murmured in complaint. I was seized with uncertainty, wondering how much longer you can be with me.

The acupuncture specialist tried her skills on Fu Li, wielding her needles in the Shanghai style, the Tianjin style, and the Beijing style. A few days after her treatment one evening, Fu Li suddenly threw away her cane and started walking, saying, "I can walk, I can walk!" and just as suddenly fell flat on her back. After falling down like that three times, she would cry whenever she saw Dr. Bao in Manhattan. "Will I ever walk?" she asked, and Dr. Bao too started crying. She said she had treated the paralyzed in Hangzhou for twenty years and had seen all kinds of human wrecks but could not bear to see Fu Li. The two clicked at first sight and became like sisters, as if their friendship were more important than the cure.

Dr. Bao ran through the gamut of all her skills, sometimes calling long distance to China to consult other specialists. She tried scalp acupuncture, spine acupuncture, and even "wisdom" acupuncture, which is supposed to restore the memory. Once she inserted the needle into Fu Li and went to look at another patient whom she suspected of a growth in the vagina. She suggested that the woman have an X ray. But Fu Li chimed in: "That's not necessary; a gynecologist can diagnose it by an internal check." Dr. Bao was very happy, telling Fu Li that her profession had returned to her.

One morning Fu Li said that everything that had seemed so remote was now approaching—"Both you and Su Dan seemed so far away, and now I can see you though I still can't reach you." She was emerging from chaos like the gradual focusing of a film camera. Su Dan was running a fever one day, and Fu Li asked him to open his mouth; she wanted to check his tonsils, and she muttered a prescription, reminding me to make sure of the dosage.

Dr. Bao's silver needle seemed to have the trick of gradually adjusting Fu Li's inner and outer film screens so that Fu Li could distinguish between her view of herself and that of the outer world. Some changes were very subtle, such as Fu Li's fine sense of appropriateness, a most endearing quality. When friends dropped in, she had the perfect touch in greeting them and answering questions, and I would feel that the old Fu Li was back again. If we were eating out or dining at friends' houses, she would first ask, Are there any taboos to observe? I was perplexed and she smiled and said, "Didn't you complain of my table manners? Give me a kick under the table to remind me." When eating out, she would always sit quietly on the side, not speaking much herself but listening carefully. She would wait for a lull in the conversation to whisper shyly that she needed to go to the bathroom.

Fu Li told Dr. Bao she felt the world was clearing up for her. Dr. Bao inserted needles on the lids and pouches of her eyes. As the doctor extracted the needles, she was greatly surprised to hear Fu Li say, "Dr. Bao, this is the first time I see your face clearly. You are so beautiful." And then I also noticed for the first time that Dr. Bao was indeed beautiful, the delicate southern type of beauty typical of women in Hangzhou, with sparkling eyes and pearly teeth.

When she had a relaxed moment, Dr. Bao would talk about her husband in Australia and how she missed her son, who was still in Hangzhou, but she never mentioned why she was in New York.

The tension of driving into Manhattan was so draining for me that not even sleep could restore me, as it usually did in the past. Dr. Bao said she had many patients among Americans suffering from this kind of fatigue and stress. She said it was one of the common complaints in America, as hard to cure as AIDS or cancer. She had been trying to cure this kind of chronic stress by acupuncture.

Being unable to sleep I would sit up and watch Hollywood movies, including R-rated films on cable television, too tired even to care that Su Dan, still in the category of those who need "parental guidance," was often watching beside me. After watching, the two of us would end up in a row. We had no common language nowadays.

There was one film, *The Professional,* that we both enjoyed. It was about an assassin in New York called Leon, who was a silent witness to his neighbor's whole family being killed in a D.E.A. raid. Leon was moved to shelter a young girl, the only survivor. This was breaking the rules of his profession, and he was on the run. Ultimately the girl's thirst for revenge brought on an attack by the armed police, Leon fended off the attackers, drew their fire to himself, and succeeded in saving the girl before dying in the final debacle. Both Su Dan and I roared our approval of this Hollywood movie by a French director.

Su Dan was familiar with Hollywood movies and said that this was much more fun than *The Specialist,* a similar action movie with Sylvester Stallone and Sharon Stone. I didn't understand what he meant by fun. Both movies depended on the tension between the reckless naïveté of an avenger and the impassive professionalism of her rescuer. But the Stallone movie was just a hackneyed love story while in the first movie, the contrast between the teenager secretly learning to smoke and the illiterate hit man who lives on milk only and sleeps in a sitting position raises the tension to a climax. The innocent child's cruelty and the reawakened conscience of the cold-blooded killer come to a deadly clash and send the sparks of humanity flying. But I could not appreciate the hints of simmering love between the young girl and the muscular killer, which seemed to be at the core of the story. I said to Su Dan in a casual warning, "Watching too many of these action films is not good for your psychological health." To my surprise, he said that violence and terror in entertainment are just sensations; no point in looking for meaning. I was shocked. So this is the essence of the postmodern entertainment industry? It seems that the entertainment industry of the West is designed to relieve fatigue and stress; to lose yourself in a Hollywood movie and be stimulated by the music is a relaxation. So the true function of entertainment lies in providing relaxation—who cares about meaning?

Wang Jingjuan

During the ten months that we had been going to Manhattan, an old lady had kept us company for a full four months.

I refer to Fu Li's mother, who, at seventy-odd years of age, flew over the ocean alone. Arriving at Kennedy Airport, she spotted Su Dan before we saw her. As she walked toward us among the crowd, I was afraid to look her in the eye. Her decision to come was quite sudden. She had a heart problem, thanks to the Cultural Revolution, so Fu Li's sisters and brother had kept the news of the accident from her. But they knew they could not keep it from her through the Spring Festival. She was wondering why she had not heard from her daughter for so long and was expecting some message. Fu Li's siblings had urged me to help Fu Li write a card for her mother. Fu Li tried several times, but the cards were just not presentable. The truth finally had to come out. The old lady merely said, "Get me a plane ticket."

Her heart was broken. Late at night, when Fu Li and Su Dan were safely tucked away, she would let go of her grief with me.

"Why am I cursed with such a fate? Losing my husband when I was barely thirty, and left with five children. And now at the end of my life, to have this daughter in such a disaster!"

I had never seen her so downcast. Her fortitude was proverbial among the people who knew her. Her family name was Wang, and they were members of the local gentry of Zhengzhou. There were four siblings. She and her younger sister had left home to join the revolution, and her sister had died on the battlefield. But after 1949, the revolutionary government executed her brother, imprisoned her father, driving him to his death, and left the widowed mother to her care, an old woman who was in the strange position of being associated at the same time with a revolutionary martyr and two antirevolutionary elements. Thus fate had been cruel to Fu Li's mother, even before her husband died suddenly of brain cancer while still in middle age. For the sake of the five children, she never remarried but worked and brought them up on her own. During the Cultural Revolution, she was targeted and struggled against, made to parade the streets in a dunce cap, and did labor reform. The household help, Auntie Huang, was driven away, and the five children were all sent down to the countryside, four of them girls in their teens, and for a long time she never heard from them—how could she face her dead husband? The years of anxiety left her with a heart condition. When the political storm was over, she had to maneuver to get the children back one by one, give them an education, even sometimes to arrange their marriages, as in the case of Fu Li.

I was the one she chose for Fu Li; she entrusted her daughter to me, including the trust of the father. Finally she could give an accounting to her dead husband. She always treated me courteously as her son-in-law, saying that her daughter had a hot temper and I had to put up with a lot. She gave me the purest of her four daughters. She allowed me to take her to Beijing, and then to America, and in the end all I had to show her was a Fu Li with her body disabled and her mind in chaos. I cannot begin to imagine the mother's unspoken regret; she could not render an accounting to her husband. But to me she never breathed a word of reproach.

She was not fit to travel overseas but she would have no peace of mind until she saw her daughter. Fu Li was not her favorite among the four daughters, but Fu Li resembled her the most, from looks to temperament, as if she were her own mother as a young woman. Over seventy years old, Fu Li's mother accompanied us to Manhattan, sitting alone in the car at the curb, helping me shop in Chinatown for cheap groceries, carefully preparing every meal. When I was away, she would take the place of nurse, but she was not strong enough to move Fu Li, and mother and daughter sometimes tumbled to the floor in a heap. To her, this experience was like another Cultural Revolution, but her force of character still upheld her.

Her mother had arrived, the mother who was first on her lips when she woke up from her coma. But Fu Li was anxious and repeatedly asked me to book her mother's return flight. She was concerned about the heart condition. Suppose something were to happen, how could she account for it to her siblings at home? Seeing that I could not bring myself to raise the question, Fu Li finally brought it up herself when I was away. Her mother cried her eyes out. The evening we saw her off, Kennedy Airport was unusually deserted. Fu Li was afraid of breaking down at the last moment and stayed in the car. I went with the old lady, but before we arrived at the terminal, she said in a low voice, "Don't come any farther. Li is alone in the car."

With that she turned and walked away. For the first time in my life, I was seized with the kind of forlornness described in "The Back View."[3]

---

[3]Famous piece of prose by the modern Chinese writer Zhu Ziqing, describing the narrator's view of his father's back as the old man walked away after seeing him off at a train station—a thoughtless young man's first glimmering awareness and sense of loss of a father's caring.

On the eve of her departure, Chen ShuPing invited Fu Li's mother to dinner and gave her a diary book as a souvenir. The old lady leafed through the blank pages until she saw her hostess's address and telephone number at the end. "Now my heart is easy," she said.

Chen ShuPing

Chen called from that phone number and chatted with Fu Li for the last four years, a call a day. Sometimes, when the call didn't come, Fu Li would start fretting. On the average of a call a day, it comes to fourteen hundred calls.

Fu Li and Chen ShuPing had gotten to know each other quite late. From the beginning, Chen had kept her distance from the exiles from mainland China, except for Chai Ling[4] who had been widely reproached after going through the terror of June Fourth. When Professor Yu invited some of the exiles over to their home for chats, Chen would be the hostess, and on these occasions she had been disheartened by the exiles' accounts of their internal strife.

Internal strife was also what Fu Li herself detested, and

[4]Chai Ling, one of the student leaders in Tiananmen on June Fourth.

perhaps it was on this account that the two women clicked the moment they finally met. Anyway, by a piece of good fortune, Chen liked Fu Li, saying she was clearheaded and many cuts above the rest. But they had known each other barely a month before the accident happened.

Chen had immediately rushed to Buffalo. Leaving her husband in the Hilton, she came and stayed with Fu Li for two days running. And then later, in the rehab center hours away from their home, Chen was again with Fu Li as she did her exercises in bed, or she kept me company as I sat in the hospital shedding tears.

Chen ShuPing never drove to Buffalo. She took the train; getting off the train she would take a taxi. As I saw her standing alone on the platform in the dusk, I would feel that only she could empathize with my despair. When I went to Qigong for help, dragging Fu Li to several cities on the East Coast, she never tried to stop me. On the contrary, she said, "When a man is crying to heaven and earth in desperation, nothing will stop him." But she did drop mild hints: "Listen to the doctor, but seek a second opinion." Later, when I taught myself acupuncture and started putting needles into Fu Li, she didn't mince words. "Take care. If you miss by so much as a fraction of an inch, you'll end up miles away from your target!"

As I look over the years that I stumbled through, I realize that, were it not for Chen ShuPing and her hus-

band, holding my hand in quiet support, I would probably not have survived. That Chen liked Fu Li was one
thing, but for her and her husband to involve themselves
in our disaster was an entirely different matter.

In fact, they had been most saddened. As far as they
were concerned, there was this bunch of exiles in Princeton, waiting for handouts and torn by internal strife. At
the time, Professor Yu was already asking himself, "Why
did I let myself get into this?" Chen ShuPing had urged
him to go the extra mile in helping out, and that was
when the accident happened. Chen knew that if I
couldn't hold out, Fu Li's recovery would be affected, as
would the teenage Su Dan. It would be the destruction of
a family. While I was totally disoriented, Chen ShuPing
was the epitome of tact. She never intruded into my private domain or ordered me around but tried to exert an
influence over crucial decisions. That was her consistent
behavior in dealing with all daily affairs, big and small.

Chen ShuPing was having a hard time herself over the
same period. In the fall of 1995 she and her husband flew
back from Taipei, arriving at midnight to hear a message
on their home phone that Chen's brother was seriously ill.
She flew to Los Angeles the very next morning. Within a
month her husband, Professor Yu, was diagnosed with
kidney stones. Chen ShuPing brought some reading and
was with him in the hospital, while on the West Coast
her brother was dying of cancer. I couldn't imagine how
she survived that period in her life. Later she called on the

phone and said, "The other day, I tripped on the street and cut my hand. It's all due to anxiety. Yu was discharged from the hospital right after the operation, but my brother died the same day so I must be in California for the funeral. I put Yu in a hotel with his drip dangling over him. . . . This is the unpredictability of life. You never know when it will strike."

Sandy

Here we were, vacillating between East and West. Medically speaking, the East and the West are more apart than they are in any other field. We went back to Fu Li's attending physiatrist, Dr. Elovic, and he was stunned by what he saw. He said to me, "Dr. Fu's recovery to this degree"—he always insisted on acknowledging her status as a colleague—"is definitely not owing to Western medicine. It's probably due to acupuncture—and to your persistence in helping her exercise."

We ran into Sandy quite by chance that same day. Sandy was a rehab specialist in the hospital, and she offered on the spot to give Fu Li physical therapy at home. She was the person who had first helped Fu Li find her feet. Luckily she was taller than Fu Li and could manage to hold her as she took her first steps since the accident. Even in her then semiconscious state, Fu Li had somehow felt that this native English girl was out of the ordinary. On leaving the hospital, she had said to me, "Let me find that necklace, I want to give it to her." It was her favorite white jade necklace.

Thus a new cycle of treatment started. From fall into winter and persisting into the following spring, this treatment spanned the cold months of 1995. But this time it was Sandy who came over. She would take the train after work and I would meet her at the train station. The first day as I took her back to the station, I asked about the woman who had been kicked by a horse. She said the woman was still the same and her husband still came to see her every day.

"Perhaps I shouldn't say this," said Sandy sadly, "but if that woman goes, the man could start a new life." Her words did not make me shudder in fear for myself; on the contrary, I realized my own good fortune. That poor Argentinian husband. I am in seventh heaven compared to him.

Professor Lin Yu-sheng of the University of Wisconsin was in Princeton for a meeting and asked Fu Li and me to have dinner with him. He was not really keen on attending the meeting, he wanted to see us. The fact is, during our fateful trip of July 1993, we were heading eventually for Madison. Professor Lin had asked me to bring Fu Li and Su Dan to visit him and his family. On the eve of our setting out, he realized that a group of us were going to travel together and called the same night.

"What is this about traveling with other people? Are you going to drive your old car? You'd better rent a new car. Make sure to have full insurance coverage, even if it is expensive. Who's driving? Don't stretch yourself; you should stop to rest even for a short while when you feel tired."

I said I would rent a new car with full coverage and I would do the driving with great care.

A few minutes later he called again. "Promise me you absolutely will not let anybody else drive! Or else I'd rather you not come at all."

I promised, thinking to myself, This is so like Lin Yu-sheng. But I cheated him. And I was punished for cheating such a man, so earnest and serious. The idea had flashed across my mind soon after I regained consciousness.

For a period of nearly two years, he was in the habit of calling every day. He was very sad and felt he had something to do with the accident. He is also a Chinese like no other for his firm stand on the Weberian "ethics of responsibility" that he has long been advocating to the Chinese audience. He does not know how to offer words of false cheer. In my panic-stricken days of darkest despair, only he could bring himself to speak to me with complete frankness, warning me never ever to meddle with the doctors' treatment. He couldn't stand people who scurry around mindlessly looking for magic cures. After all, his professional expertise lay in critiquing the intellectuals of modern China who had been looking for magic cures for China's problems. Professor Lin was one of the first people abroad to criticize *River Elegy,* pointing out that it was full of exaggerations, simplistically seeing things in a black-and-white dichotomy, totally in line with the wholistic rejection of Chinese tradition of the May Fourth iconoclasts. Seeing him after the accident, I suddenly realized that I was still scurrying around looking for magic cures, but by then it was not the wishful thinking of saving China with "blue"[5] but dreaming of instantaneous cures for Fu Li.

I was reminded of his saying that "for China's modernization, the problem is not competing for speed, but competing to hold back speed." This famous saying of his had struck me with the force of an epiphany when I first heard of it in China in 1988, and it had inspired me with the idea of making a sequel to *River Elegy.* Back home

---

[5]Referring to the West's "blue" civilization of commerce and enterprise as contrasted with China's conservative, landlocked "yellow" civilization—a central theme in *River Elegy.*

from having dinner with him that day, I took out his article "On the Reconstruction of the Humanities in China," and reread one passage:

> For the last few years, I have been harping on the theme of competing to hold back speed, and one of the reasons is that I feel deeply our cultural crisis is not to be fixed by solipsistic rhetoric. Our problem lies precisely in the fact that there are too many self-anointed geniuses old and young, and now their ranks are swelled by cultural stars. The speeches and writings of this stellar constellation, apart from reflecting the very cultural crisis they are claiming to fix, are just a pack of self-delusions. These people must be conscionable in matters of knowledge and culture if they do not want to be dismissed as hopeless and their activities written off as totally worthless. Hence, they must go through a re-education.

I felt these words applied to people like myself, hitting the nail on the head. Another passage preceded the one just quoted:

> Competing to hold back speed is the result of a dialectic fusion of a sense of achievement with a sense of true humility which nurtures a certain state of mind. For people who have never experienced that kind of fusion and never acquired that state of

mind, competing to hold back speed is just empty jargon. On the other hand, once you have acquired that state of mind, you will naturally transcend the quirks that Chinese intellectuals are prone to: emotional instability, excessive modesty to the point of self-abasement, or frivolous and vain to the point of boastfulness.[6]

It seemed I had never really understood "competing to hold back speed," though its true meaning is much simpler than the highfalutin theories that had attracted me. But now I see that Fu Li's disability, like China's problems, is a chronic disease, for which there is no prescription for a "fundamental solution"[7]; it must rely on gradual cures and long-term effects. Perhaps acupuncture, Qigong, or even praying to God are all forms of gradual cures and long-term effects. I have been caught by the media that promote everything as miracles. It seems that advertising "miracles" is the only way to catch the public's attention, so much so that the practitioners of these "slow cures" themselves are afraid to mention the word "slow."

[6]The foregoing paragraphs have been amended by Lin Yu-sheng at the request of the author.
[7]A famous quote from an essay by Li Dazhao, librarian of Peking University, editor of *New Youth* magazine, one of the leading lights of the May Fourth movement of 1919. Later cofounder of the Chinese Communist Party in 1921.

Sandy undertook a new rehab project—to reconstruct the brain's control of the left side of the body, so as to help Fu Li make the shift from right-handed to left-handed; that is, to change the habits of a lifetime. This is still in the experimental stage in brain science. According to Sandy, tests on monkeys show that once function is suppressed on one side, it will automatically turn to the other side. But the human instinct is so geared to what has become second nature that it is resistant to manipulation, with the additional problem that acquiring left-handedness is particularly dependent on natural reaction or it will not work.

Sandy put Fu Li into a specially designed program. She first checked her condition with a computer for her ability to maintain equilibrium; then she brought all kinds of knickknacks and made Fu Li perform movements such as squeezing toothpaste, pouring water, lifting a glass of water to drink, throwing a ball, lifting an object to the top of a chest of drawers, and so on, and everything was placed on her left side so Fu Li would have to use her left hand. After every movement Sandy would note down the distance and the time involved. She taped everything. Sandy also asked us to note the frequency with which Fu Li used her left hand on her own initiative in the space of half an hour. Everything depended on figures, changes in figures denoting changes in Fu Li's condition. I guess it is the basis of scientific experimentation. Scientists may believe in a supernatural religion but in real life they reject all illusions, miracles, and the like and only accept precise figures and facts. This was my first understanding of the spirit of the West. Sandy strictly forbade us to remind Fu Li or urge her to do anything. Scientists do not believe in results that are not naturally acquired. They are not in the habit of cheating themselves.

I had never been so frequently at a train station to wait for arrivals, waiting for that familiar face to appear among the tired-looking faces of people after a day's work. Chen ShuPing once said, "It is another of Fu Li's 'noble dames'[8] coming to her help." When I think back to all the people who had shown up on their own initiative, I know it was a blessing that is not to be had for the asking. I have no complaints.

The snow was thawing in the warmth of spring. The train station had quieted down in the evening dusk.

"I can't do anything for you anymore. You have learned to do everything yourself."

Finally one day Sandy had said it. This was the last time she was coming. I took her to the platform where I had been meeting her for the last several months and

[8]Thomas Hardy: *A Group of Noble Dames.* Here, "noble" conveys both "high birth" and "superior person" of the Chinese original, *guiren.*

wanted to cry. I had not had the impulse for tears over the last two years. It now felt strange, and I controlled myself until I was back in my car.

It is like being in a trance. Things you had tried to suppress or silently swallow are now dredged up to the fore of your being. You truly feel you are about to collapse; you feel you are jolted out of time and space and swooning in the most tender core of your vulnerability. I instinctively resisted. Sandy's farewell left me feeling deserted. From now on Fu Li and I were on our own.

Tan Xuemei

Among the first batch of letters Tan Xuemei wrote after Fu Li's accident was this one, written in the winter of 1993.

Right now I am writing to you from the Café Flore in the Latin Quarter. This is the spot where Sartre and his group of existential philosophers, writers, and artists used to meet. Last time when you were in Paris I had wanted to take you to a few such places, but we were rushed for time. When Fu Li is recovered, bring her to Paris and we'll go together.

I received your letter and Fu Li's photograph.

Thank you! She is not changed, only deeply wounded. We are so far apart, I can only kiss her picture and can't help saying "poor girl." The mark of the inserted tube is still noticeable on her neck. I'll keep the photograph in front of me, but I won't show it to anyone. Don't worry, I absolutely respect her privacy.

In the last couple of years, Tan Xuemei had sent innumerable letters, innumerable cards. To greet Fu Li's first awakening from her coma, she sent a postcard of the famous painting of the Italian Renaissance, "The Birth of Venus," inscribed with the words *Fu Li, my sleeping beauty, you are awake at last!* After that she sent a series of Impressionist paintings. "The colors suit you; luminously bright, they draw you out of yourself," she had said. She never missed any of the Parisian art exhibitions, and she kept sending over to our Chinese community the latest information about Parisian literature and art. She was the perfect go-between. She also communicated with Fu Li after her own fashion—through postcards. In the spring of 1994, Fu Li had been released from the rehab center just as her birthday was coming around, so all the way from Paris, Mlle. Tan ordered a huge bouquet to be sent to us in the United States. And the postcards kept coming; she never asked whether Fu Li read them, just kept on sending them.

Some years ago I had been at the Pompidou Center

with a bunch of other "elite" figures, standing on a platform making speeches, and that's when I met her. By
then I had lost the appetite for that kind of role and had
sneaked out of the meeting. I was standing idly in the
lounge smoking when she walked up to me, a lady with
black hair and blue eyes. "I teach Chinese in Paris. I really
can't stand this kind of speechifying. Though you were
more modest."

She told me that in 1988 a delegation of Chinese writers had also been here making speeches and she suggested
from the audience that everyone stand up to pay tribute
to the imprisoned Wei Jingsheng.[9] She said that of the
writers seated on the platform, only the youngest, Zhang
Xinxin, stood up; all the others sat unmoving where they
were—writers with resounding reputations in China. She
told me this story the first time we met, and it left a lasting impression on me.[10]

That was Mlle. Tan Xuemei. I had assumed she was

[9]Democracy activist, author of "The Fifth Modernization," arrested
in March 1979, sentenced to fifteen years in prison, released in September 1993 on parole, rearrested in 1994, released in 1997, and
now in the United States. See *The Courage to Stand Alone: Letters from
Prison and Other Writings* by Wei Jingsheng (New York: Viking,
1997).

[10]"In the summer of 1988 a large delegation of Chinese writers, during a visit to Paris, was stunned when a Frenchwoman in the audience assembled before them proposed that everyone stand for a
moment out of respect for Wei Jingsheng. The writers—including

French; after we became friends, I learned she was actually of mixed Chinese and German parentage and born in China. She was an exceptionally beautiful woman; approaching sixty when we met, she still had style and flair. Later, when she heard that Fu Li had arrived in the United States, she flew over the Atlantic to spend a summer holiday with us. We sailed on the Hudson. She and Fu Li stood together at the railing, their long hair fluttering in the wind.

> You mentioned that Fu Li saw the other twin in a hallucination. Actually it might not be a hallucination, she might really have seen that dead child. Poised between life and death (or a deathlike trance) people are often able to see their departed beloved. There is a monthly TV program here called *Mysteries* where many people (mostly victims of traffic accidents) testify to such experiences, and psychologists travel all over the world to gather and document such experiences and write books about them. As for Fu Li's nightmare, I think that your being on the wanted list and your two-year separation was too

some of China's brightest minds—were transfixed for several embarassing seconds. (Finally one, who had already lived a few years in the United States, gathered her wits sufficiently to propose a salute to 'all people in every country who have struggled for ideals.' Then the writers could stand up.)"—Liu Binyan, *"Living in Truth,"* translated by Perry Link, *New York Review of Books,* July 17, 1997.

much for her to bear. Dreaming of Su Dan's emergency rescue was actually a reflection of her life in that kind of emergency state, and her subconscious wish for Su Dan's twin brother to be rescued. As you have said, this is the deepest wound she ever sustained in her life, and the dream also reflects her anxiety and guilt toward Su Dan.

These hallucinations will recede, but how will Fu Li recover her self-confidence? You have new obligations now. Fu Li is a strong-willed woman, but she needs even more of your tender love. Women are not the same as men; their need for love tends to be more spiritual. You should make her feel that she has the same place in your life as she always did. The two of you have been through such a trial, you nearly lost her; I am sure you love her more than ever. But on Fu Li's side, I am not sure how she will respond. She cannot cope, she is easily angered. . . . She had always been so self-confident, self-assured. I remember we once chatted about makeup and she stated that a woman cannot attract her husband by making up her appearance. But now you should often tell her how well she is looking, encourage her, say things like "This dress is just right for you" or "You look so young today" or "Your hair looks nice this way." . . . Fu Li is very good-looking, but she was never aware of it. Right now you must make her feel that she is still attractive to you.

All Fu Li's guardian angels are women: her mother, Chen ShuPing, Mlle. Tan Xuemei. . . . What a world of good deeds she must have stored up in a previous life to have such good karma!

I have gone over the photographs again and again. At first I was surprised to see the changes in Fu Li from two years before. But after comparing the photographs closely, I also saw obvious improvements, especially the two last ones, which showed traces of her old spirit of fortitude. I think we should avoid making comparisons with her former self. The Fu Li of today and tomorrow may not be the Fu Li of old, but you should discover new delights in her, that is where hope lies.

Victims of brain trauma have been known to change personalities after recovery, sometimes becoming even smarter than before; this has happened repeatedly in many clinical cases. What kind of new person would Fu Li change into? I waited in hope and trembling. I did not want her to be smarter, I just wanted my own Fu Li back, the old self with all her ways. But Tan Xuemei was talking about something else when she made the reference.

In a later letter, she told me two stories.

Last month I saw a French film called *Blue,* one of a series in which the director planned to include *Red* and *White.* In the film, a couple was driving with their five-year-old daughter when they met with an accident; the man and the little girl died on the spot. After the wife woke from her coma in the hospital, she returned to the castlelike house where they had lived and decided to make a clean break with the past. She burned the unfinished symphony that her composer husband had left behind. Taking only her clothes and a blue pendant of her daughter's, she stifled her sorrow and lived in a Paris slum. Quite by accident, she discovered that her husband had had an affair with someone who was a judge. The woman lurked outside the cafés near the court and finally met with the judge, who, she discovered, was pregnant by her husband. She took the judge to the castlelike house and said, "Your unborn child is his, naturally this house belongs to you and your child."

Of the second story, Mlle. Tan wrote:

A few days earlier I saw on TV a piece of news that moved me to tears. I mused over it for a long time and thought of Fu Li and you. An American couple was vacationing with their eight-year-old son in Italy when they were robbed on the highway. The child was shot and died. In their grief the parents decided to donate their son's organs, and as a result five Italian children were saved. A few weeks later, the suspect was arrested, but the American couple appealed to the Italian court to commute his sentence and give the man a second chance.

Don't you think that this couple are perfect saints? Apart from a humane spirit of religious tolerance, I am afraid there are deeper reasons for this generous gesture. Perhaps in so doing they have found a means to release their suffering. Fu Li and you, instead of struggling in this bottomless pit, perhaps you should also find a means of release?

I don't want to linger over these two stories; I could not bring myself to write to her about my reaction—especially to the second story, which really happened. To endure pain, to chew on it, to swallow it, this I have achieved, but release is out of the question. This last requires the strength of faith, and I am lacking in faith. I have read the Bible, but I cannot grasp the meaning of "redemption." I just feel that human suffering is absolute, and man must bear it alone; no one can help him. Jesus died on the cross to redeem man's sins, but this is part of a Western concept of "storing up," implying a "free choice" of "storage" and "withdrawal." Although one is free to store up and use for redemption, I discovered that I had never stored up any good and could not bring myself to believe in that "heavenly bank." I know very well that I am not eligible for an entrance ticket. Fu Li's case is even stranger. In her semiconscious state between living and dying, she said that she had heard the voice of God, "a voice coming from a great height." But with the gradual restoration of consciousness, she drifted farther and farther away from that "voice from on high." I cannot tell if she would be happier in a semiconscious state caressed by that voice, or if she should regain "consciousness" and return to the earthly state of existence. If that "voice" had really been there, why didn't it keep her from coming back?

If returning to the earthly life in full consciousness meant the loss of "release," then do we have a choice?

On the day of Fu Li's forty-fourth birthday, I asked a Cantonese restaurant to order a big turtle from New York. I had half of it stewed for soup and the other half braised. There were also "long-life" noodles and peach-shaped "long-life" buns. I invited Chen ShuPing, Sandy with her fiancé, and Wu Meng, a Chinese computer student and our neighbor, and we all enjoyed the meal.

I was caught in the rain one night, it was the first rain of spring. Chen noted that Fu Li is increasingly calm and collected; "The old Fu Li is coming back," she said. She also reminded me that Fu Li has been deeply wounded inside, and Fu Li is the kind of woman who realizes how badly she has been wounded, not like others who are not so aware and are easily persuaded that they have gotten over it. Not Fu Li. She needs time to heal her wounds, external and internal, and she must consciously go through the process. No use trying to persuade her that she has gotten over it. Chen ShuPing really understands Fu Li.

Spring has come. I can feel it in my bones.

People tend to bemoan their own fate as the harshest in the world and envy other people's good fortune. After the accident, I myself was plagued by the enigma of misfortune, savoring it to the full, torturing myself day and night. Beethoven's Ninth with its thunderous knocking of Fate sent me into shocks of fear and trembling. I tried to treat misfortune as a philosophic encounter, but I was out of my depth. Religion could have provided an answer, but I just couldn't bring myself to believe. My mind was in a turmoil. One day I went to see a film, and suddenly I saw the light.

The title *Forrest Gump* was translated very aptly as *"Ah Gan Zheng Zhuan,"* perfectly catching the movie's spirit. It has enjoyed a long show time and the highest box office returns of 1994. I went to see this modern American dream on an impulse. Success for Americans is not achieved through natural-born ability but by acquired vitality. The capacity to take the slings and arrows of fortune comes in the shape of denseness and a mad adaptability. And this was Forrest Gump's good fortune. The case of the girl Jenny was the opposite: She paid the price for her bad luck with her own life, dying after giving a son to Gump. The film seems to hint that she is happy, but I can't see it that way. Does it mean she has found self-fulfillment, or that she has filled an obligation? I cried for her as I was watching the film. I felt that man's dream of happiness cannot atone for her sad fate—it is something beyond the human capacity for endurance, beyond the reach of happiness. I felt that therein lay the heart of the story.

Fu Li was tired and didn't care to talk. On my part, however, I felt that to have what we were having at the moment was already a piece of great good fortune. All the other alternatives—death, turning into a vegetable, dementia, loss of limb, loss of speech, serious psychological scarring—were all 99 percent probabilities, yet we ended up with the 1 percent odd chance. It cannot be explained by just good fortune. She is now basically a normal person, and all the other sadder possibilities have gradually departed like silk threads being slowly pulled away. This is an issue beyond the question of fate.

Three months later, I went to see *Forrest Gump* again, determined to find out what it was that attracted the American audience to the film, and I think I got an inkling. It is probably the average American's secular view of life that a Chinese would consider "dumb," that is to say, dumb but lucky, lucky and yet unfortunate, slow-witted but strong, as if man living without consciousness of fate is always living in good luck, as if luck is God's domain, while men are all unlucky and the only thing

that man can do is to not give in to fate, to be unconcerned with good luck, and not even bother to enjoy good
luck. This is very American, lucky yet unfortunate. Of
course it is a screen illusion, the public gets a kick out of
seeing bits of real history edited into the story, the American audience likes it, an American version of "dumbness."

The Chinese are too "clever" by far; they are all out for
luck and can't bear misfortune. Take me, for instance.
Ever since the accident I had been groaning under a burden of misfortune, yearning for a miracle to descend, as if
God owed me one. In my shallowness, I was only asking
for things to be fair, not knowing that unfairness is a pro-
founder question. Fate sentenced me to one misfortune,
and I used it to deny all my former good luck. It is the
opposite of Gump. Born disabled, he was showered with
good luck all his life. Yet he remained dumb, never aware
of the meaning of "luck."

During the Christmas sales of 1995, I bought an electric treadmill. In three years' time I would be fifty. Rather
than buying it for Fu Li, it's truer to say that I bought it
to satisfy my own state of mind. On the morning of New
Year's Day, as I was installing it, I sensed a rustling
behind me. I turned and saw Fu Li totter toward me and
then collapse on the floor. She saw me installing the gim-
mick and couldn't resisting coming over for a look. I
helped her up and saw that her nose was cut. I was wild
with rage. If the location of her cut had been ever so

slightly off to the side, it would have caused internal damage to the brain, or a cut across the face.

What kind of ending am I compelled to face? I see it approaching inexorably, reducing all my efforts to ashes. Is my dream bound to be shattered? How easy it is for a man to fool himself in his despair, self-delusion being one way to dispel pain! Today, I am aware of a new kind of despair, an icy low point in my mood. How much longer do I have to bear it all? How much longer can I hold on? What can I do with the rest of my life? Those were my thoughts and feelings to start the new year.

I have crept out of the abyss of existence, the years of torture seem to be coming to an end, and new hopes for life are kindled in my breast. These hopes range from things to people but are mainly focused on Fu Li, hoping that my old Fu Li, calm and down-to-earth, will still return to me. To snatch back all that I have lost is my only motivation and my goal. But this in turn gives rise to new frustrations, as if a new round of failures is waiting for me and new disappointments are brewing. Can it be true that life on earth is a series of traps, so that the minute you are out of one you fall into another? Moreover, can these traps work in a vicious circle, so that the bad karma resulting from the former life will set off the next trap in an endless cycle? I know I am descending into the Buddhist concept of karma, and this concept runs counter to my hopes for starting a new life with

Fu Li. I cannot understand the extreme tension between living and dying.

Su Dan asked me, "Do you remember that feather in *Forrest Gump?*"

In the film, a feather appeared under Gump's feet. It grew and grew in size as it floated lightly in the air until it finally disappeared into the sky. "The theme of the film is that feather," said Su Dan. In my surprise, I almost missed the words that followed, obviously said to impress me: "Are you aware that the feather is a digitally manufactured illusion and cost one million American dollars?"

Is it possible that Su Dan realizes that life is uncertain? Life is as light as a feather, I thought to myself, totally different from the Chinese saying that life is "weighty as the Tai Mountain." The Chinese ancients were always bemoaning the transience of life, how it is weightless, like a feather. They were always striving for monumental achievements resounding down the ages. Could it be that asking for the meaning of life is an invalid question? Take Jenny in the film, for instance; she never could believe that Gump loved her; later she accepted that love but then left, feeling that she did not deserve it. In his grief Gump began to run, and Jenny kept up with his movements but would not contact him to relieve his mind— that was something that Gump had to cope with on his own. Her responsibility was to raise their child, send it to him, and die herself.

At the end of the year, Su Dan scored A for all his courses. I wanted to give him something for a reward. He considered the question for several days and came up with what I always hated: computer games. I bought them for him, of course. Later on, Fu Li let on when she was half awake that Su Dan for the first time in his life was planning to buy me a gift. "I have ten dollars only," he told his mother. He bought me a Christmas card. On New Year's Eve, I sat with him in front of the TV until the moment when the ball dropped. He got up and walked out the door, took a few turns, and sighed as he returned. "The air outside is so fresh." Suddenly I had the feeling that everything starts afresh. He has grown up.

Chapter Seven
TULIPS

Out of the wastelands of desolation, the craving for life awakened and I felt the tingling of hope. I can pinpoint its appearance to one sunset during the summer of 1995.

We were going to leave Fox Run, with its ponds and green lawns, where we had rented for the last four years. Ever since the day in the fall of 1991, when Fu Li arrived with Su Dan, I had been living in bliss, spending life in exile as if it were a holiday, without a clue to what the future had in store. Then, while packing, I came across Fu Li's diary of those days, tension and repression and fear splashed across the pages. The same question on each page: How can a woman live without having to rely on her husband, without having to ask him for money? For her, America was nothing but despair. And now all the spirit was knocked out of her.

In the rush of moving, I had actually forgotten that it was July 19, the anniversary of that day of darkness.

It was Su Dan who muttered, "Dad, it's been two years. . . ."

By sunset, I decided that our family should celebrate this anniversary. I hastily made two dishes, steamed spare ribs in cured black beans and three-flavored chicken, and got out two bottles of wine. A year ago, Fu Li's mother had brought with her a bottle of Confucius Family Wine and a bottle of Western wine. I lighted candles, and the three of us started drinking. I raised my cup and apologized to Su Dan for the neglect and bad temper he had suffered at my hands for the last two years. But the words were barely out of my mouth before I broke down. Su Dan hid his head behind his drink. I could not make out exactly what he was saying, but I could sense that it was full of genuine feeling. Fu Li sat apart, moving her eyes in scrutiny from father to son and back again from son to father. Finally the three of us all got drunk, and thus we took leave of the hell that was the last two years.

The next morning, Su Dan helped me move everything to our new address, carload by carload, like ants moving from one hole to another. We were looking forward to a new life, though not sure what it would be like. How I wished to have a house by a quiet wood, to wake up after an afternoon nap for coffee and pastry together with Fu Li. It is life, but in the past I had despised things like that. It is only when I am myself managing the house that I appreciate such pleasures. Formerly, when Fu Li ran things, I was not really living my life with her; my life was spent dragging pen over paper, filling up blank squares,[1] or running around basking in praise. I had never taken up the role of husband and father in our twelve years of marriage. Now, however, Fu Li had become a "daughter" and I started from scratch to be a "father," while Su Dan had lost his right to be a "son."

Su Dan told me to "transport" his mother to the new house, get her settled there, and stay with her while he took care of the odds and ends at this end. He vacuumed the carpet, leaving the place in perfect condition so the fault-finding management would have to return our eight-hundred-dollar deposit in full.

The new place was quite close, housing for low-income families that we were subletting. It was nothing compared to our place in Fox Run, but it was close to the railway station and the rent was low. I wanted a change of scene, and leaving on the day of the anniversary somehow meant a clean break with the past.

Behind the house, a piece of farmland lay across the road from us. There was plenty of breathing space, with something of a pastoral air. After we were settled, I drove around, taking in the lay of the land. I discovered I had been here before, in 1991, when I had first arrived at Princeton. The supermarkets and Chinese restaurants and

---

[1]Literally, "crawling over blank squares," a homely expression for writing Chinese characters on paper printed with squares, usually referring to practicing the writer's craft.

video stores all looked familiar. How arrogant I had been as one of the survivors of Tiananmen! The atmosphere of terror that pervaded the Chinese mainland after June Fourth had only heightened my sense of good fortune, of being a smart aleck. Six years later, I discovered that I had been running on the spot, the most unfortunate of the whole lot. Such a life in exile is preposterous. As I made my way home very late, Fu Li and Su Dan were already sound asleep. Had they acquired a sense of security? It was dark in the room and I couldn't see their faces, but it warmed my heart to think that they had.

H ome is a nest, a haven of safety. Fu Li used to say with a tinge of sadness that we had built our nest and broken it up several times over. In the summer of 1991, when she was allowed to leave the country, she broke up our last home in Beijing. All our things were scattered, some given away, some sold. She was sad. She said she was destroying a home that she had built bit by bit with her own hands.

When Fu Li married me, her bridal chamber was a single small room in the dormitory of a newspaper office in Henan province. The lavatory was right next door. The room could hardly hold anything else once a double bed was installed. It was in this small room that she conceived Su Dan and his twin brother. Shortly before her confinement I changed jobs to work as a reporter for a radio station, the reason being that they offered me a three-bedroom apartment. Fu Li, already far advanced in pregnancy, busied herself in ordering furniture, and we soon had our first comfortable home. But I started gallivanting across the length and breadth of the country, never staying with her long enough to enjoy our home together.

Then I moved to Beijing, taking Su Dan with me, leaving Fu Li alone in our nest. In the end she had to give up everything and follow me to Beijing, where we lived in my parents' house. Fu Li missed the first home that she had ever built; she said she had lost the heart to ever do it again, but she did.

The home she had to destroy before leaving the country was a two-room apartment in a towerlike building in the Haidian district of Beijing. It was an ugly edifice typical of dormitory buildings at the time, but we had been ecstatic when we were first assigned to it. At the time I had some author's fees, so once again Fu Li started nest-building. We visited several furniture exhibits before deciding on a model complete with bedroom and living room and had to go to a plant out of town to order the set, making sure also to get a single Simmons sofa bed for Su Dan. After the furniture, our next concern was electric home appliances, carpets, and so on, which also took a lot of energy to acquire. Fu Li was dead sure that this was our final home and did not spare expenses to get what she wanted. At the time, washing machines were a novelty in mainland China, but Fu Li did not hesitate when a friend offered to get us a washer with dryer for an exorbitant price. As far as I can remember, the hot water was not yet installed before she had to leave again, bag in hand. So again it had been an empty dream.

Am I a nomad by temperament? I had no feelings one way or another over the building and breaking up of these nests. Even when Fu Li joined me in the United States and had to resort to picking up discarded furniture, I was still totally unaffected. I only thought of nest-building when my life of roaming came to a halt with the accident and Fu Li herself was nearly destroyed. Suddenly I had to bustle about for three meals a day, two shopping trips a week, and a pile of bills to pay every month.

We were the last to leave Fox Run. With us gone, the place ceased to be "the holiday resort for exiles" anymore. In 1994, when I was still being buffeted by the winds of fortune, the exiles in Fox Run were all buying their own houses and leaving one by one. When we were settled in our little sublet by the train station and Fu Li had lost all consciousness of nest-building, I too started to dream of a house of my own.

It was literally just a dream. There were many detached houses in the environs of West Windsor, many of them with swimming pools, but the prices and property taxes were way beyond our means. In the past I had often wondered why Americans wanted to saddle themselves with a house where they must remove their shoes on entrance, cannot smoke indoors, rarely cook for fear of smoke, and on Sundays mow lawns under a hot sun. But now, looking at the beautiful houses in West Windsor, I realized why a house is a top priority of the American dream. I suddenly regretted the loss of our apartments, in Henan and in Beijing; they had been furnished bit by bit by Fu Li's own hands, more endearing to me than the beautiful houses and lawns right before me.

I have read somewhere that, according to Indian tradition, life is divided into four periods: youth (learning how to live a life), caretaker (supporting a home in adulthood, taking up social responsibilities, and participating in secular life), philosopher, and finally hermit (overcoming worries and devoting time to philosophic speculation). In this view, life is obviously a passage, a transition between life and death, something to do with transmigration of the soul. I thought I have entered the stage of caretaker. Sure enough, one day as I was in the supermarket, I picked up a copy of the popular magazine *Home Plans* and became totally engrossed in their descriptions of different designs. I actually went and looked at builders' models without telling Fu Li.

But I knew in my heart it was a dream, an enticing trap that would swallow my energies for nothing. I suddenly had an inkling of the Buddhist concept of rejecting worldly desires. But then it ran counter to my wish to start life again with Fu Li. I really didn't know which way to turn.

The Limits of Freedom

In the small hours of dawn as you are catching your last sleep, someone is waiting for you. If you don't get up, she is fettered, unable to move. At some point in time in the innumerable hours that have passed by over her head, her biological clock adjusted itself. Now every day she wakes at dawn when the whole world is still asleep. She gazes at you in your sleep as if trying to make out a stranger, how many wrinkles on your forehead, how many lines on either side of your nose. She tries little tricks to rouse you. By four or five o'clock, she has to get up. But without you she cannot get off her bed. For the sake of your freedom, she chose to share your exile and lost her own. Only by relying on mechanical appliances such as braces, canes, a wheelchair can she be free.

Stubborn beyond reason, for a long period of time Fu Li refused. "Relying on these appliances means disability, and I cannot bear the thought," she said. All preachings and persuasions were useless. No one does anything without reaching the decision on their own. There are no such things as quick fixes or miracles.

Loss of freedom takes away one's dignity. Having to ask help for everything, even from her own husband or son, was an effort for her. She expected unquestioning service, but the kind of life I lived for the last two years deprived me of awareness. One day I was so sleepy I disregarded her calls and lolled in bed till nearly nine. Fu Li dressed herself and tried to get off the bed. Seeing me wake up with a start, she said in a low voice, "I'll never speak to you again."

I moped for a whole day, and slept away the whole morning. In the afternoon when I tried to speak to her, she smiled like a child. "Oh, so we are still on speaking terms?"

I suppose the subtle balance between one's sense of disability and the power of endurance differs from person to person. Suddenly one day Fu Li decided to accept the walker, a kind of four-legged aluminum support. After trying it out for a few days, she got used to it. From then on she woke up in the morning, got out of bed, used the bathroom, made tea, and moved about . . . all on her own. To go to the bathroom without help from either her husband or her son—it was amazing that this bit of freedom could make her so deliriously happy. For several days running, she reveled in her newfound freedom, finding excuses to move about the room, her heart bursting with happiness. It is heartbreaking to see her this way, but I finally understood that freedom cannot be forced. It is a matter of personal choice.

But freedom has limits. In 1994, she would shed tears on seeing her son. A year later, she took every opportu-

nity to tease him, and the two of them would tumble
about on the sofa like kids. Her son tickled her, and when
she was losing the game, she cried to me for help, laughing aloud.

One day, however, they had a falling out. Fu Li
snatched the pills and the cups on the table and threw
them at Su Dan. I rushed out and shouted at the boy to
stop it; he turned without looking at me and locked himself in his room. Fu Li was unable to handle her bit of
freedom and joyfulness. I waited until dusk to say a few
words of remonstrance, telling her that the boy was looking for the love he had missed for two years. She broke
down and cried. While I was cooking, she went into her
son's room and they were huddled there for the longest
time, talking about I don't know what.

Can I provide motherly love to our son? He has already
reached puberty. In terms of psychological development,
it is a period of rebellion, of confrontation with parents.
However, I cannot remember such a period for myself.
Perhaps it is because my own period of puberty coincided
with the Cultural Revolution and I was a Red Guard,
bringing down this, that, and the other, and that distracted me from the confrontation with my parents.
Nowadays in the United States, however, it is commonplace for kids to rebel against their parents, to walk
out, to cut off ties. It is really scary. How will this boy
turn out? Without a mother, isn't it natural for a boy

to be confrontational with his father? What can I do about it?

"What do you want me to do?"

"Don't tell me you are against it!"

"Nobody can understand who you are!"

Fortunately the kid can still speak Chinese with a perfect accent, though he slips into English grammatical forms, which makes it sound weird. He's not going to walk out. After all, his mother is there. He surfs on the Internet, has his own website and home page, and calls himself Zen in that world. I asked him why Zen. He said no reason, he just liked the word. I wanted to ask him the meaning of Zen; then I thought to myself, Why bother? Possibly it has something to do with the Qigong and karate he started practicing after the accident. An unconscious reaching out for the East, I guess.

O nce we had left Fox Run, I had to drive him to his karate lessons after school. Six times a week, and he was not going to miss a single lesson. I thought it was asking too much, and for the first time I refused. He flew into a rage, also for the first time. He dashed his glasses to the floor and ground them under his heel, looking at me fiercely all the while. I was stunned; I turned and walked away. Back home, I discovered that he had fiddled with the two computers. I could not access the windows on them. To him, monkey tricks like that were mere child's play.

I realized that an adolescent rebellion was on the way.

I have no authority at all over him. What's more, in this electronic age, all the authority is on his side. There is no arguing with him. For instance, when I had not connected his new computer to a printer, he seethed with anger and threatened to cut computer lessons. I hastened to install the printer. A few days later, he asked me to order software for him and his buddies. I wasn't sure it was a good idea. He mocked me for not knowing how to save on costs. I said, You should have asked me first. He snorted and said, "What do scribblers like you know?" I could only smile, wondering whether he was saying this to put me down or had always regarded me with contempt.

I have no authority to tell him what to do. Probably all parents of Generation X or the New New Man are in the same fix. They have contempt for their parents, thinking themselves superior. At least that's better than loss of confidence. But if children are not equipped with the minimum rules for behavior and are only boosted by this bit of self-confidence, how will they go through life in this harsh world?

Is it because we have not given him enough love? How do you offer love to a boy? It seems somehow that boys are only oriented to accept maternal love. How is a father to pour out love to his Generation X son? The traditional wisdom about love solving everything somehow doesn't work with the postmoderns. I had made innumerable attempts at communication—heart-to-heart talks, shows of concern—but nothing seemed to move him. Only when he got what he wanted out of me did he show any affection, but then he would immediately come up with more demands, and no matter how many previous favors I had showered on him, he would turn on me the minute a new demand was not met. These kids react swiftly to technological communication but have lost the capacity for human affection. Is this the defining characteristic of Generation X?

The alienation of his son can bring on a father's sense of futility, of being beyond caring. But then, Su Dan is his mother's very life. Fu Li cannot live a single day without him. Feeling the futility of my endeavor, I had only a sense of duty to hold me up and give me patience to go on.

For our family of three, having escaped death and overcome many vicissitudes, the psychological space has tightened. Formerly that space was upheld by the heart of a mother, but now that she has become a "daughter," beginning to grow up all over again right in front of her husband and son, what can that mean for the son who is reaching puberty? How will it affect him psychologically to see an authoritative mother turning into little sister?

A Return to Writing

Wen Tingyu has these famous lines describing a vigil: "Upon the wu-t'ung trees/ Falls a midnight rain,"[2] though as far as I am concerned, "In my chamber a dream fades at the fifth-watch bell."[3] Fu Li makes rustling noises at the crack of dawn, sometimes talking to herself in bed or blowing up my nose.

One morning after helping her settle down, I was at a loss for what to do and picked up Yale professor Kang-i Sun Chang's short articles on poetry that she had just mailed to me. One article, "On Melancholy," discourses on the poems of the Tang poet Li Yu. One paragraph read:

The hardest thing to bear in life is to be overtaken by misfortune at middle age, when the heart is inextricably sunk in "sorrow and resentment." Halfway through life's journey, one is suddenly hit by fate and cannot replace emotion with rationality. One is tortured day and night by pain and has to swallow it

[2]Translated by William R. Schultz, see *Sunflower Splendor,* ed. Liu Wu Chi and Irving Yucheng Lo (New York: Anchor Books, 1975), page 251.
[3]Poem by Yan Shu, translated by An-yan Tang. See *Sunflower Splendor,* page 310.

alone. This is what is meant by "Past events may only be mourned/Facing the scenery, I find it hard to dissipate my grief"[4] and the lines "How much grief can one bear?/About as much as a river full of the waters of spring flowing east."[5]

I had always loved the last two quotes, but mainly for the beauty of the sound and the rhythm. I had never deciphered their meaning. You must be in the situation to appreciate it. The only problem is that my middle age was passed in flight from my country, life in exile, and trying to live out the aftermath of the accident. I am at loose ends, suddenly faced with the coming of old age. I now finally realize the meaning of "*kalpa*." According to the current definition of generations on the mainland, my generation has been capped as the "last three classes"[6] in polite terms, or crudely referred to as the Red Guard generation. Right now this generation is highly regarded. Whether in government or trade, literature or the arts, this generation behaves as if they are the only people that count, as if China is in their hands. The exceptions, like Wei Jingsheng,[7] who is my age, chose to go to jail when barely thirty. He lost his

[4]Translated by Kang-i Sun Chang in *The Evolution of Chinese Tz'u Poetry* (Princeton, N.J.: Princeton University Press, 1980), page 83.
[5]Ibid., page 80.
[6]Referring to the high-school graduating classes of 1966, 1967, and 1968, before the schools were closed down.
[7]See chapter 6, note 9.

teeth in the first fourteen years in jail, something I dare not contemplate for myself. And now he has chosen to go back to jail for another fourteen years. With incomparable strength of mind, he is willing to pay this price for his ideals. This is genuine moral strength. My situation abroad is like sitting in jail, but without the moral strength, just the "sorrow and resentment."

My only way out is to return to the world of writing. Yet even on my native soil, I was not the sort of writer to weave words out of pure imagination. I always had to have material to work on. And now I am not only uprooted but also "modernized" into weaving words on the computer—with the result that my imagination has dwindled even further. When I have nothing better to do, I play games on the computer, like my son. The modern man's traditional forms of communication have withered away, resulting in spiritual hollowness. Sitting in front of a computer feels like being sealed in the house. I feel as if I am shriveling up. TV and the Internet seem the only things that the mind can accept; emotional human ties are all compressed into an exchange of information. On the Net, people are "back to back." Man is turned into a terminal.

Surfing the Net in the United States, I felt it was virgin soil like the pioneering West, a mass of unexplored wilderness with no laws to go by. The fact that legislation against cyberporn was vetoed on the basis of freedom of speech is a good example. Ever since the industrial revolution, all technological advances have been mixed blessings for mankind. Just when people were beginning to sing the praises of the "revolution in communication"—the reorganization of space for human activity, the rise of a minimedia, the possibility for groups with special hobbies to communicate with each other without personally meeting—in a word, praising the Web for reversing the trend in the popular media to reduce everything to homogeneity, scholars sounded the alarm over the destruction of social coherence. The multitudinous rise of marginal discourse and the voices of minority groups on the Net that cannot be drowned out by the popular media is certainly not a bad thing. But in today's world, when Europe and America are the dominant cultures, the future of the marginalized Chinese language on the ever-growing Net is full of uncertainties.

Chinese on the Net is a fascinating world emerging from nothing. The first pioneer use of Chinese on the Web might have been by a group of "media have-nots"— students from the mainland—a voiceless group rejected equally by the English language and the Chinese language media. The free website was their only means of communication. So, in moments snatched from the toils of their lonesome studies, they began to play with "Little Sister E" (e-mail),[8] searching on the Web for partners to

---

[8]The word "mail" is roughly homonymous with "little sister" in Chinese and carries vague sexual overtones in a certain context.

share their interests, whether it was car repair, chess, gardening, or stir-fry dishes. During the bloodthirsty spring of Beijing 1989, several students in the California area who had never personally met managed to launch a Chinese news website. The next year someone posted Bei Dao's short poem commemorating June Fourth in Chinese. These were probably the first Chinese words to appear on the Web.

Looking at the Chinese on the Web, it seems that the highly regarded news magazine *China News Digest* has satisfied the craving for news, and therein lies its attraction. But it is not the only one of its kind. The Web holds an attraction for marginalized groups because it satisfies their craving for publication, for two-way dialogue, for relief from the anxiety of belonging to a minority group overlooked by the media. Newgroup, a website closely associated with Chinese affairs, is the best indication of the fierce desire for publication that has been repressed so long. Every kind of writing is posted there: political commentary, cultural chitchat, religious debate, first attempts at verse. No one is embarrassed because everything appears under pseudonyms. There are many such news groups. They come in different shades and colors, here today, gone tomorrow. However, they have one thing in common: They are totally uninhibited. Though the quality of the writing varies, they should be appreciated for being such a fresh departure from the jingoistic moralizing of official Chinese newspapers.

Only now that people have found a voice do we begin to know the pain of silence; only now do we know that a hitherto silent group is actually filled with resentment. These kinds of news groups are subdivided through the Chinese Code into Traditional Chinese and Simplified Chinese. It is a vast uncharted expanse, totally unknown to the publishing and film industries. Here, words are free to roam like wild horses; here, anything goes: personal opinions, comments, attacks, abuse. Students from the mainland and Taiwan cross swords over the unification/independence issue. At one point mainland students cut their teeth on what was called the ten inexhaustible topics. One such topic was stir-fry dishes; another was abusing Joan Chen, the mainland actress who had made it in Hollywood; still another was the mockery of people from Shanghai. The comparative merits of the major universities of China was also a hot debate, some claiming their alma mater to be first under heaven while damning other institutions as so much trash, others resorting to self-depreciatory mockery, calling Qinghua a "toad," Fudan "hatching eggs," and the University of Science and Technology "baggy pants."[9] At some point Harry Wu[10] and Chai Ling became targets, some abusing them, others speaking up for them. Anyway, it was a melange that was

[9]Wordplay on the names of three Chinese universities when pronounced in Chinese speech.
[10]See chapter 5, note 11.

very revealing of the quality and tone of Chinese writing on the Web.

This is obviously not purely a problem of communication. The Web provides a kind of absolute freedom: free of charge, and also "free" of authorship and therefore free of responsibility. Under such circumstances, people do not respect their words; nor do they respect themselves, scattering filth wherever they go. It is one of the reasons for the proliferation of porn on the Web. We think that pornography is a Western obsession, that at least we Chinese do not go for pornography; all we want is to have our say. This is probably because there is no freedom of speech on mainland China, and it probably also has to do with the marginalization of the Chinese language. Thus the desire to communicate is overwhelming, and the Web is their medium for release. But judging from the recklessness of what they spill out on the Web, the elegance, understatement, and subtlety so characteristic of Chinese culture are all gone without a trace, and that is a greater disaster than obsession with pornography. This only goes to prove that modern science and technology can do nothing for a civilization that has lost its vitality. I wrote a piece called "A Free Spirit, Naked I Come and Naked I Go," just for the fun of it. It was published in a newspaper in Taiwan or Hong Kong, I don't remember which. Someone posted it on the Web, and it drew a burst of abuse. I felt vaguely that there was an active Web population out there in China, but I didn't know them.

"What generation do people like me belong to?" Wu Meng, our Fox Run neighbor, asked me one day.

Good question. His generation followed my Red Guard generation but they were older than the June Fourth generation. They seem to be left out in China's drawing up of generational divisions and of course are left out in the mainstream discourse in literature, film, and history. Many Chinese students in the United States belong to this generation. They caught the tail end of the Cultural Revolution, left for abroad during the "reform and open up" period, and thus missed Tiananmen.

"I suppose you'd be categorized as the sixth and a half generation," I said to Wu Meng, and asked him to go and interview others of his age.

He sent me a very good piece titled "Our Childhood Was a Black-and-White Film." He added, "We are not the wounded generation,[11] nor is our blood boiling with indignation." I conducted an open discussion on the subject on the Web in *China Monthly*.[12] Wu Meng asked some of the most articulate among his buddies to talk about themselves. It turned out that their hero was Wang Shuo.[13]

---

[11]Named after a 1978 short story, "The Wound," by Lu Xinhua. The story describes the psychological scars of the Cultural Revolution for the teenage generation, later referred to as "the wounded generation."
[12]Journal on the Web edited by Su Xiaokang.
[13]Dubbed a representative of "hooliganism" in contemporary writing, Wang Shuo uses an earthy Beijing dialect to celebrate a group of

In the years following, Wu Meng was almost the only one with whom I kept in touch. He helped me run the magazine and helped me in my negotiations with the doctor, the accident lawyer, and the insurance company. He was very Westernized in his behavior, always calling for an appointment before he showed up. He consulted me in everything but always kept a distance. He had great sympathy for Fu Li and me, but he knew the greatest favor he could do us was to respect our privacy.

The computer is the most inflexible of autocrats: One bad strike and you're out. I am the living image of those people you see in the comics. They get stuck on the computer and rush to school to get their sons. One late night I was stuck again in the middle of writing and shouted for Su Dan, but he was not around. Outside it was raining hard and totally deserted. My heart contracted in fear as I reached into the car for an umbrella. I looked around and there, under the pavilion by the tennis court, a dark shadow sat, unmoving, like a ghost.

"Su Dan!" I shouted, and the shadow jumped up and ran toward me, saying, "The rain is so beautiful!" Before the accident the kid would never venture out by himself in the dark. I wonder what he was looking for, alone in the rainy night.

amoral and reckless young people in such works as *Playing for Thrills* (New York: William Morrow, 1997) and *Please Don't Call Me Human* (U.K.: No Exit Press, 2000).

I gradually felt myself being flung away and lost to the world. I had long ceased to miss friends and didn't care for consolation and concern from others, totally focused as I was on Fu Li's recovery. That was my own *Waiting for Godot.* In the intermissions, I looked over discarded drafts and went over my notes and letters of the first period of my life in exile, when I had lost my sense of orientation and had been afraid of solitude. My fear of prison was so obsessive it had taken over all my faculties, and I had survived on cheers from the public. That was a blank period in my life.

One entry in my diary was from a day in late spring of 1990. I had left Paris dejectedly for San Francisco and jotted a few worthless thoughts on the problem of solitude on the flight. I wrote that solitude is unbearable because the emotional props enabling one to confront the world are taken away. The price for maintaining solitude is psychotic eccentricity. In the years after the accident, although the outside world had lost its attractions for me, solitude still extracted an emotional price. I did not want to meet new people, and I brooded about walking away from it all.

In 1994 I had wanted to be forgotten by the world, and two years later I had my wish. I was confused. The loss of self-esteem gives rise to a sense of unreality, but the greater problem is the loss of goals altogether: "I think of heaven and earth, without limit, without end/ And I am all alone and my tears fall down."[14] Solitariness does not mean freedom from the worry of fame and gain, the relief from responsibilities, the sense of security in being away from the crowd. No, solitariness is the impoverishment and emasculation of the self, an internal withering and further loss of the sense of security. The individual is submerged in—and at the same time protected by—the collective. The choice of not being submerged entails a simultaneous loss of protection. I often asked myself, Need I throw myself into another community, say, a religious community? In a community of moral love, there is less hurt and less affectation, but the individual would be submerged even more deeply.

What does life in this world mean for an individual? What meaning is there in maintaining a reputation for oneself in the world of the Chinese people, or, in other words, in the world of the Chinese language? Should one rely exclusively on family affection, without reference to any outside support, and deny the possibility of communicating with a higher being? Formerly I had turned excessively to society, immersing myself in it. Now I was extricating myself, with neither faith nor family to replace it as a resting place. The individual was suspended in midair.

[14]Poem by Chen Zi'ang, translation contributed by Kang-i Sun Chang.

I suddenly felt drawn to a little island, and Hawaii often popped up in my dreams.

L
ater, I did go to Hawaii. It was an attempt to go outside myself and check out my feelings, also to see how Fu Li and Su Dan would adjust to my leaving them temporarily. But I first made a short trip to New York and recorded my feelings in my diary.

A friend arrived from the mainland, and I took a night train to New York to meet him. The pitch darkness outside brushed silently against the windows. I felt my heart being enclosed in a hard core, away from the unknown terrors of the outside world. It was a long-lost feeling left behind in Paris, when every night I had to return from the city to the suburbs.

For the first time, I am traveling on my own. It is a refreshing feeling, reminiscent of the time when I was led out of that darkened room where I had been cooped up for nearly fifty days; I suddenly experienced a blast of coldness and a sweet satisfaction. That feeling reminded me that the past is dead, sealed in a cave, closed to the world. Only when you are aware of being consigned to a place do you have the urge to get out. The outside seems like a new point of reference. Now I have rejected the outside world for a whole two years and have let myself sink into a hole. I feared the outside world; there was safety in being sunken. But I am not sure whether I really want to get out. There is nothing outside that I need.

That summer I made a trip of four days and recorded the first day on my flight on United Airlines.

This morning as I left for the train, I felt as if I had been lost somewhere in the Western world. I had an indescribable feeling of fear and strangeness.

I was driving at night through a street in Trenton once with Zhang Langlang. There were few people about; a couple of blacks eyed us coldly. Langlang had said "What a postmodern scene," which fitted in perfectly with my own feeling of being lost. Even in the busy streets of Paris I would be seized with that feeling, especially at dusk on weekends, when emerging from the subway. It had been a long time since that feeling had crept over me. Now suddenly it hit me again. I realized that I often feel like that when I approach an unknown world.

But on the other hand, I had known that kind of feeling since childhood. I dreaded the dusk during the rainy season in the south. Standing under the dripping eaves with my back to the dim light within, my heart would contract, and for a few moments I would be filled with melancholy and distaste for the world.

My Hawaii diary:

Sitting in a restaurant in Wakiki, listening to people speak English about the Chinese trying to smuggle themselves into the West. It makes me sad. They seem willing to listen to my talk. I was only saying, I am here to talk about the Chinese, but I do not expect to be believed. Sitting on an island in the middle of the Pacific, speaking of unanswerable questions, it seemed I was not Chinese myself.

Everything is okay with Fu Li and Su Dan. I called in the morning. Su Dan sounded very responsible, I must reward him for giving me this chance to get away. But having come here, I do not have any sense of freedom; all my thoughts are with my wife and son at home, as if they were floating on a sea and might capsize at any moment. I am incapable of leaving them. To force myself to leave is not a solution.

Hawaii is a beautiful place: the sun, the sea, the relaxed crowds. But for me they are remote. I am not touched. What are people busying themselves about? What goals are they pursuing? Myself, nothing rouses my concern except my wife at home. All I can do is to look at the world detachedly; it is the only position possible for me. I like this position.

Back home, Fu Li told me that the night I left, Su

Dan stayed with her until she went to bed. The minute he left the room, "I cried," she told me. I asked why. "Because I am a loser."

This is Fu Li all over. People's temperaments are unchangeable. I was only gone for four days, but she had thought deeply about it.

Just then the news broke of novelist Eileen Chang's death.[15] The Chinese media buzzed with the news and with such comments as "the beauty of solitude," "standing alone rejecting the world," or "epitome of the critical moment where madness and genius meet." Others said that the last years of her life were "narrow, dark, but profound." Actually no one really knew the real state of her mind during her last years. It is the darkest mystery of this unmatched genius.

There is a young Chinese woman called Nancy who is an Eileen Chang fan. She grew up in the United States but decided to live in Paris. She likes to dabble a little in writing and tried to imitate Chang's style. She faxed me an article she had written commemorating Eileen Chang, which I thought a cut above the rest. Of the writer's eccentricities, Nancy wrote: "Chang's hermit-like life during her last years must have been a source of mortification for her. A hedonist, she loved beautiful clothes and

[15]See chapter 1, note 3.

dainty food. [Her first husband] Hu Langcheng had once said that she pampered herself like a red-beaked green parrot, that she loved strong tea and the smell of paint and gas. A full-blooded woman of the world, she loved physical stimuli, understood human nature, and was full of compassion. But somehow, somewhere, at some point in time, all earthly delights melted into dust and ashes. . . . She died, totally rejecting the pleasures of the senses."

To me, Eileen Chang's aloofness to all mundane concerns is absolutely fascinating. Yet, with no faith in immortality, no prop of religion or any outside force, what supported her in maintaining her solitariness in old age? Is it something unique that she discovered for herself? Nancy had written: "I concede she had her independence to hold on to, but I will never believe that she was happy." According to Nancy, Eileen Chang was "far, far superior in her being as a woman," and all the men in her life were "way, way below the mark." But I still can't imagine how this seventy-four-year-old woman managed to drag out her last days, since her aloofness from life was not misanthropic despair; neither was her coldness born of hatred and contempt. It must have been hard. Had there been no stirrings in her heart? Finally, what was she waiting for as she still clung to life? Did she imagine herself still in old Shanghai?

In her article, Nancy ended by writing: "There

was at least one man in her life who was her equal in superiority, a soul mate—Hu Shih.[16] Our generation does not sufficiently appreciate Hu Shih the pioneer. In the tradition of Chinese scholarship, Hu Shih is the last of his kind. He had predecessors but no followers. The last time the two of them met was in New York. They stood in the freezing cold and stared at the Hudson River. 'It was as if a cold blast from the cavernous depths of the ages had blown over from across a hundred thousand miles,' Chang had written of this encounter. Time was not on the side of these two remnants of China's literati. Every time I read over the above quote of Eileen Chang, I feel that that moment on the bank of the Hudson was for her the beginning of the end."

Chen ShuPing was also on the phone with me, talking about the death of Eileen Chang. She lent me a book by Sima Xin titled *Eileen Chang and Ferdinand Reyher*.[17] The account of the last lonely years of her life makes me shudder. For a period of over three years, she had actually moved about from one

---

[16]See chapter 3, note 1.

[17]Ferdinand Reyher (1891–1967), American leftist writer. Harvard M.A., 1914, taught at MIT. Reyher traveled widely in Europe, was friends with Ezra Pound, James Joyce, Joseph Conrad, Bertolt Brecht, Sinclair Lewis, and others. Associated with Hollywood through director John Huston, Reyher gave up creative writing to write film scripts for Hollywood. Married Eileen Chang in 1956.

motel to another in L.A. just for the sake of avoiding lice. At the end, of all the furniture that she had collected throughout her life, one piece only was left— a brass desk lamp. Eileen Chang's best work was done in her twenties and thirties; later on the ways of the world did not feed her with material for writing. She tried, but it did not work. Genius is not everything. Emotional state and mood must adjust to the outside world. As a woman, her lot was also tragic; she loved two men who were unworthy of her and had to pay a devastating price in the bargain. But she never touched on the subject in her writing. I finally understood her rejection of the world. The world was not worthy of people's optimism, or hope, or illusion, or ideals. Optimism is but self-consolation. As for ideals, they are infantile, ignorant, even cruel. If one is unable to protect oneself against the world, the only way out is rejection. Chang's fiction resonates with the sights and sounds of worldly pursuits; rejection of the world deprived her of subject matter. What is more important, her despair in human relationships took away the magic of her pen. Her English was excellent, but command of English does not make a writer. Her incompatibility with the modern world was another factor that held back her writing. All of which goes to prove that writing is the expression of life itself. If life is damaged at the source, it may produce sentimental outpourings, or it may kill off writing altogether.

As for myself, I have resumed writing. All Eileen Chang's fans are imitating her, but none of them have met with her kind of fate, so none can write like her. She had reached a spiritual state that was beyond imitation.

I never tire of wielding the pen, though I do not want to write the kind of tragi-heroic cultural critique that I used to do, nor enigmatic political comments either. Mr. Yang Ze wrote, asking me to write something for his paper. After the accident, when I was still in Buffalo, he had called from Taipei, asking me for contributions. He could not offer words of comfort; all he said was, "Write; writing may give your heart relief." I said I didn't want to write that kind of nonsense ever again. He said, "Then write about yourself." After that he asked me to write a special piece once a week for the daily column on the "Human Affairs" page of his paper, *China Times*,[18] and I started scribbling before I knew what I was about. As I went on writing, I looked up my diaries of those years, which were scattered in notebooks and on diskettes.

---

[18]The name of the column, "*sanshao sizhuang*," could be translated loosely as "a few good fellows" or "fellas." By the author's request, it is just referred to as a daily column, to which he contributed a piece every week.

Reading over some of the passages, I sometimes broke down in tears and the screen would blur while my hands shook so much that I couldn't type. When I took off my glasses, there would be droplets of tears on the lenses. My tears did not fall silently, they actually burst out. The ancient Chinese saying about tears being "splattered" is no idle hyperbole. After I'd had my cry, I'd run to wipe my face with a hot towel so Fu Li would not notice anything.

The jumble of writing retrieved from the notes and diskettes painted a living image of a man in despair. In the first shock of losing the best part of my life, I was weak and vulnerable. The sharpest pain lay in the fact that my loss was irreparable—I realized that from the very moment of its happening. This is because I am a person who believes in certain values in life, such as continuity, tenderness, love, commitment, and so on. Before the accident all these were taken for granted and submerged and displaced by other things in life, such as personal achievement, fame, and gain—until disaster struck. It highlighted what was basic and it pierced my heart. The world has too many vain distractions to take us away from the essentials of life, and man is lost in meaninglessness, unaware. The so-called pitfalls of existence sometimes catch us up in their sweep and hold up life's true aspect. This moment is too cruel, but without cruelty you cannot see yourself in the mirror.

Furthermore, when man is stripped clean, what is he

like? I never had such an experience before. There may be several different kinds of reactions. One would be to try to regain what is lost, not in a repaired state but restored in its entirety. This had been a great source of frustration for me and the reason I had been attracted to religion and Qigong, which cater to these kinds of wild expectations. But ultimately I realized the illusory nature of their promises. I could not be satisfied because I had been expecting a bona fide miracle. My expectations did not drive me into fanaticism. On the contrary I was rational, and it is precisely the rational expectations that are bound to end in disappointment. There are no miracles in the world, only people's craving for miracles. I also discovered that sometimes people who have been cruelly hurt become realistic. They only want back the part that they have lost and do not accept illusionary systems: The latter only provide the tools of self-consolation, a kind of spiritual drug. I had at one time craved that drug, but it could not dispel my deep sense of catastrophe and reconfirmation of the value of what I had lost. That is seared into my being on a daily basis.

Another problem is cause-and-effect. One of the worst parts of all your troubles is that you can't find a pattern of cause and effect. All your self-reproach is meaningless when you can't find a point of departure. You haven't got an inch of ground to stand on. To attribute your troubles to abstract reasons such as guilt or karma or fate or the will of God is one solution, but it is no consolation to me because the impact of my pain is concrete and objectified and has to be borne. To transfer the burden of the pain to something abstract by pure force of faith would render the concrete pain unbearable, because that kind of pain only concerns itself with your role in it and what you can do to relieve it. Anyway, transmitting the pain to some-thing abstract does not help me. Perhaps it is because my burden of pain is not heavy enough. Who knows?

I also began to realize that my pain of the last few years could be traced to human nature itself. The life force that is stripped bare is greedy and given to illusions. Its redef-inition of happiness is limited to the basic and the primi-tive but, on the other hand, given to inflated desires. Such desires are drugs, to sustain the individual in his terror of being exposed.

What I wrote offhand at the urging of Yang Ze was probably the first thing I had written with my hands unfettered. Now if I continue writing, will I be putting on fetters again? There is this question of distance. With distance will I be more clear-sighted, or will I lose my sense of reality? I do not know. Anyway, one thing I don't have to do is make a draft. All the details are right before my eyes. Writing about myself, I feel that the subject is way beyond the horizon and at the same time right in the marrow of my bones. That column expects me to turn out a little something every week. This is the first time I am writing without a public in mind.

I seemed to be writing for myself, but after a few

months of writing the column, one reader, Miss Li Zhende, wrote, "I've been following you step by step, in and out of Fu Li's hospital room." A friend, Ke Yuanxin, told me he was praying for me during his long journey across the ocean. There were other letters from readers: Qiu Liandao, Lin Jikai, Yang Shizhi, Xiang Yun. . . . Thus I was aware that there were people who were indulgent enough to read what I had been scribbling.

One night, Professor YingShih Yu phoned. "It's very moving, what you are writing,"

"Which piece do you mean?"

" 'Ordinary Aspirations.' I just read it. They are your true feelings. You couldn't write like that if you were writing for an audience."

"By now I am incapable of cooking up something just to please the readers."

"That's right. That's what we call 'ridding oneself of the vanity of the word.' Man must have dignity. It is not something acquired from outside of the self, it comes from within the self."

Professor Yu went on to tell me that he had been talking to the visiting Japanese writer Kenzaburo Oe about the question of human dignity. Oe said that when he was young he had asked his father about human dignity, and his father had uttered one word: "Benevolence." So Oe asked Professor Yu for instructions regarding Confucianism. Professor Yu said that Confucianism has it that "benevolence is the self." He said that the ancients also held that benevolence is man, meaning that human dignity comes from the inner man. This is the source of human freedom in the Chinese culture; it is not something that can be instilled from the outside.

As I kept writing for the column on a weekly basis, I suddenly realized that I should thank Mr. Yang Ze and also the editor of the supplementary page, Mr. Liu Kexiang. I was not just writing a special column. I was healing myself. They let me go on scribbling my "pitiful wretchedness"[19] for a whole year, giving me a chance to pick up the language again.

Two Dressing Gowns

It was late fall. I opened Fu Li's suitcase to look for warmer clothes. It was easy to dress Fu Li. All she wore are loose-fitting tops and pants, the kind of casual wear popular in Taiwan, in two styles, one for summer and one for winter. She had several sets of each. But as I opened the suitcase that day, what met my eyes were her clothes from the old days—shirts, skirts, sweaters—as if a woman's whole life were on display.

[19]Borrowing the term from a well-worn line of Chinese poetry by Li Qingzhao.

She came in, sat down, and started asking me one by one which pieces had been brought over from China. She did not recognize the clothes she had chosen so carefully to take with her before leaving for good. Fu Li's family had been poor. Since childhood she had never had any good clothes. But she had very good taste and knew exactly what was right for herself. In 1981, when we were married, I had wanted to buy her an overcoat. We scoured all the stores in Qianmen Street in Beijing before we finally found one that was perfect in price, quality, and cut. That was the only thing I ever bought for her that she wore. Even so, she only put it on for special occasions. Exiled abroad, I went on mad shopping sprees from Paris to Taipei. The first letter she smuggled abroad said, "Stop buying me clothes. For whom am I dressing up, here alone?" But when she left for abroad, she did buy a whole set of clothing for herself, saying that women's clothes were too expensive abroad.

As I turned over the clothes in the suitcase, I picked up a brilliant red silk dressing gown. We looked at each other in amazement. "Did I bring that?" she asked me.

She must have bought it when preparing to leave China. Suddenly I had a glimpse of her feelings at the time. She'd had enough, she didn't want to look back, ever. Buying the silk dressing gown meant breaking away; it was a souvenir. But she had never worn it. She had also bought me a white one, which she never even showed me.

The two silk dressing gowns had been lying at the bottom of the suitcase ever since like the fragments of a dream, a woman's lifelong yearning for home and family. The home had been destroyed by the nation-state. No, only half destroyed as far as she was concerned—there was something else waiting for her in a foreign land, although she didn't know what. Her dream had come true when she married me; what was needed was to keep nourishing it daily with her life's blood. The two dressing gowns seemed like the dried remnants of that life blood, which had been buried away under humdrum daily affairs. Looking at them after our time in hell, I felt for the first time the heart-searing impact of what they stood for.

After Fu Li left the room, I sat unmoving for the longest time, overcome by sorrow. A man's relation with a woman had never before seemed to have taken on such enormous proportions. It was as if a wife lost years ago had suddenly returned. I left the clothes aside and dug up her letters of 1990, written during the worst period of terror. Page after page of yellowed printing paper, stored away longer than the clothes in her suitcase. As if in response to the groans of pain registered on the pages, I sorted them out in chronological order, sat down, and started to type them into the computer. I didn't know why I was doing this. All I knew was that I must get it done.

Going over those letters was like seeing her in a previous life, every word brimful of the old Fu Li. She never bothered with punctuation in letter writing, and as I typed them out, a feeling of consolation stole over me as I added the punctuation for her. Some of the letters were so moving. In one she said, "Sometimes I feel that in the few years since marriage, I had so few peaceful days." She ended with "I always feel like crying." She would never have said that to my face. Another read:

> Thrown apart, I really want to say something else, but to whom can I talk of my sadness except to you? Don't take my words too seriously. All you need to know is that your wife has the truest heart under heaven. Your letters and phone calls have dwindled. I suppose you are busy. In the past you were always busy, and I put up with it. I don't know if I can stand it for a lifetime.

I did not have the words to describe such pain. Actually it was only after the lapse of years that I was able to feel its full weight.

As I typed her words into the computer, I let myself go through her pain. From the outside our marriage was perfect; only she knew what it was really like, but she still went on giving. She never reproached me with one word, never cried, only submitted to me quietly in everything.

"Let's go see the doctor."

"All right."

"Tomorrow is acupuncture day."

"All right."

"I need to go out, don't try to get up on your own."

"All right."

She seemed more unquestionably submissive than ever, saying "all right" countless times through the day, in a small thin voice.

In 1996, her sister wrote, saying that the family had found a rehab place in the seaside resort of Beidaihe and wanted me to send her back. I had been taking care of Fu Li for three years and, our life abroad being fraught with difficulties, they felt that things couldn't go on anymore and thought up this plan. But I pictured Fu Li alone on the deserted beach in winter and couldn't bear the thought. Besides, I knew what it would mean for her to be deprived of Su Dan. I did not tell Fu Li of her sister's suggestion. I only thought to myself, Is there really no way I can make it up to her?

August 25, 1996. Today is my birthday. I am not going to make a fuss about it. Fu Li didn't even remember. In the past, she would have prepared a banquet. I am forty-seven years old. My hair has not yet gone white. I remember exactly thirty years ago when the Cultural Revolution broke out. My father was forty-three years old, having been born in 1923, but his hair had turned completely white by then.

Thus I am luckier than he, although I am swamped with housework all day and feeling more and more tired. The plus side is I have learned to be handy around the house. And yet I am smoking more and more.

In the three years between ages forty-four and forty-seven, the meaning of life for me has changed completely. I have only come to realize what it means to be born when I am already in robust middle age. Before that I had muddled along unconscionably, lost in a mire of ignorance, shallowness, vanity, smugness, pseudo-scholarship, and craving for creature comforts, what Lin Yutang[20] had called "heathen pleasures," though I was obviously fated never to be a follower of any faith. The absurdity of existence is a tragic blunder of forty-odd years. I was deprived of a proper education, as a child, but was steeped instead in atheism and cheap idealism and barbarous politics, making me a very inferior sample of the human species. If not for the automobile accident, which descended like a bolt of thunder, I would have gone through life without looking back in regret. I and many of my peers have thrown ourselves into some major issues and actually succeeded in making a lot of noise, while barely equipped with the tools of knowledge and totally uninspired. We

[20]See chapter 4, note 1.

strutted on that filthy stage where there were no rules to speak of and played pranks on forces that we did not understand—whether they were the cold-bloodedly astute "clique of marginal persons"[21] or the ignorant, smug populace. We felt that we had prevailed, while actually we were just playing childish games. In my self-satisfaction I was further estranged from the essence of my humanity, removed from man's soulfulness. It was harder to return to an ordinary mundane existence because I had never been able to accept religion. But I feel lucky to be restored to my everyday self. I am going to rethink my life from this solid position. It is not too late. That is what I congratulate myself on.

The rhythms of my existence are clear. The first thirty years, I was involved with idealism; the middle ten years I was contending with worldly evil (tyranny, nation state, and other cultural monsters), and the last seven years I was struggling with fate— that is to say, struggling with an intangible force— and I am exhausted. The initial feelings of having fallen into an abyss have subsided over the last three years, but I realize it has only eased me into an unending torture. Everything just goes to show the limits of human capacity and the denial of supernatural miracles, which probably do not exist anyway.

[21]Term supplied by Professor YingShih Yu of Princeton University.

The damage was irreparable. Did God condemn me to this despair before He let go of me?

I can only take a step backward and retreat to a quiet life. Nowadays the farther I am removed from the crowd, the better I feel; I begin to appreciate the blessings of retreat. Distance is such a privilege. To draw a space for the self—how come I had never thought of that before? Why do people fear solitude and never sing its praises? In solitude the heart is at peace and rarely disturbed by vexations, which usually come from brushes with the outside world. I have now settled into a mood in which I do not want outside invasions; my heart is like a pool without a ripple, the best possible state to be in. Of course this condition is very fragile; any ripple will set off alarms. But I have no urge to pour out my grievances, only hoping to forget them quickly and return to tranquillity. Life does not need a big stage. First and foremost are rice, salt, oil, and firewood; second is to experience the magic of existence. As to nation state, progress, and development, what are they to me? On the stage of life, a wife and a son bring enough complications, quite beyond the scope of what my energy and wisdom can manage.

In the morning drizzle, Fu Li takes one walk around the building with no support. She does this every day; she may walk perfectly one day and fall down the next.

Muscle contractions on her left side cause extreme tension, a common effect of paralysis. When helping her to exercise, I concentrate on her heels and knees. I make her sit up and stretch her heels, and I massage her thighs and the soles of her feet after a hot foot bath. I taught myself acupuncture; it has always concentrated on a few known acupoints for paralysis. There might be other mysterious acupoints, I suppose, the knowledge of which is passed on in a single line of descent that is closed to me, of course. Well, that can't be helped. Fu Li told me that when she was studying to be a doctor she had looked down her nose at Chinese medicine and never put her heart into learning about it. "And now," she said, "I am your guinea pig!"

I pored over a copy of a book on physical therapy, translated the paragraphs on the treatment of the heels and the knees, and tried bit by bit to put their instructions into practice. The human body is really a marvel of construction; any little disarray anywhere will dislocate the whole structure. For instance, if you cannot raise your feet by ninety degrees, your feet will make circles instead of going forward when you walk. The knees are especially important, but Fu Li could not control them and her knees were always bending backward. I told her, Your knees are like the knees of British troops in the imagination of Lin Zexu.[22] For some reason Lin had thought that

[22]Lin Zexu (1785–1850), official of the Qing court. As governor of Guangdong province during the 1840s, he stood up to British powers and took strong measures to try to stop the opium trade.

the British soldiers could not bend their knees, so he presented a memorial to the emperor Daoguang, saying that all he needed was to hack at the knees of the Western barbarians in order to expel them from China. Fu Li laughed so much she nearly toppled over. "That is 'biological bending,'" she told me.

Because her left side does not work properly, Fu Li is instinctively afraid of putting her foot forward in walking. I encourage her to make a big step with her right foot. Every time she puts out her right foot, her left leg shakes and I help steady her from behind. Her left leg could never stop shaking as we walked along. I was so discouraged. After taking a break, I would make her resume walking in the afternoon and keep it up until she started shaking again.

That was how we passed through the year of 1996.

She was walking back into the world. It was a long way to go.

As she sweated profusely in walking, one day she said in a low voice, "Now I realize how serious my accident was."

When I returned from Hawaii, I didn't feel like traveling anymore. Soon after that, Fu Li refused to leave the house and refused other people's visits. I knew she did not want former friends to see her in her weakened state. She thought it was "loss of face." She had always played to win; one can imagine how painful it must have been for her to still want to be a winner. But nothing I said could change her attitude. In the old days, she could never sit silently doing nothing. She would always look for something to do. If there was nothing, she would turn on the TV or read the papers as a kind of passive distraction.

Now Fu Li was asking why. All her pain—disability, acupuncture, physical therapy, the guilt of neglecting her son, her son's growth under conditions beyond her control with consequences beyond her powers of conjecture—she cannot accept that there is no explanation for this. She will not be satisfied by brushing everything off as accidental. That would be too remote, too disconnected from her sufferings.

Soon afterward, Fu Li lost confidence in any further recovery. Obviously, her emotional defenses were breaking down. If this went on, what would happen to her?

One day at around three o'clock in the morning, I got up for a drink and couldn't go back to sleep.

In the silence of the night, I began to muse on this woman. This woman never took any nonsense from anybody, but there were two things she dreaded: failure in marriage and failure in the proper upbringing of her son. This might have something to do with losing her father at an early age. But if the two things she dreaded came to pass, how would she react? I could not imagine.

Fu Li had always been the kind of person who did not let her thoughts fly off on a tangent; she just dealt with things at the practical level as best she could. No one can remain untouched by the shock of such disasters; despair and depression are a natural reaction. Under such circumstances, religion (including Qigong) does have a healing effect, offering faith and dispelling anxiety, which is conducive to healing; best of all, the individual is not in pain in the process, though no one can tell what supernatural agents are at work. But all this did not help Fu Li. She did not operate in that dimension. My own explanation for her being afflicted like this was that, contrary to accepted opinion, the times are evil.

One winter night, I ran a high fever and could not get up in the morning.

In three years, it was the first time I had been brought down. I felt burnt out, as if my last hour had come. To give up, to die, is not such a dreadful thing. But I could not leave Fu Li; she couldn't walk properly. Trying to take care of herself, she had fallen into the bathtub one morning when washing her face at the sink.

She sat by my sickbed chatting with me.

As I lay in a raging fever, my thoughts wandered. Is there no place for the soul? At least two hundred years ago, men in the West sincerely believed they were under the protection of God. There was a source for the meaning and value of life, and there was a place for the soul when men died. But for the last two hundred years, men have been "disenchanted."[23] So now as we live in this world, we are facing a wasteland. We must look for the meaning of life on our own and face death on our own. But can man return to the times before the "disenchant-ment"? For the last two hundred years, it has been proved futile. For the last three years, I had the feeling of being stranded in a wasteland and for a time had wanted to return to the world before the "disenchantment," hoping for miracles to appear. But now I knew it was hopeless.

In the afternoon, Su Dan returned from school and immediately volunteered to go and get pills for my fever and buy dinner. It was snowing. When he came back his down coat had a second coat—a sheet of ice. Who can complain with a son like that? That evening I took the pills and had a hot bath, and the next morning the fever was gone.

The New House

In 1996, during the third winter after Fu Li's accident, we moved again.

[23]Term supplied by author, borrowed from Max Weber's *Essays in Sociology,* tr. by Hans H. Gerth and C. Wright Mills (New York: Oxford University Press, 1946), page 319—Trans.

I had my eye on buying a condo in a secluded corner of an area near Su Dan's high school. I had gone over to look at it in the summer. A patch of greenery embraced a deck just off the sitting room, and beyond that was a little pond that seemed to highlight the surrounding stillness. But it took three months' wrangling before we closed the deal, and by then winter had arrived. I rushed to have a look at my little pond but it was gone. All I saw was a dried-up patch connected to the Princeton Canal nearby. So be it.

Now I knew what Liu Zongyuan's feeling had been when he bought, jointly with two friends, a piece of land including a stream and a knoll west of Gu Mu Pond for four hundred pieces of silver—"that joy of possession, was it meant to be?"[24] Although I am not, like he was, in the wilds of Hunan, I feel exactly as he did when he wrote in his "Prelude to Poem on Foolish Stream," "As to stupid creatures, none can compare to me, therefore none under heaven could challenge me for possession of this stream; I have the right to name it."

In spite of my excitement, however, the deal almost fell through. When I applied for a mortgage, it turned out that my credit was bad. Add to that the fact that I did not have a stable income, and there was no way I could get a mortgage. Chen ShuPing was all worked up. She took me to the bank, made me put all my papers in order,

[24]From prose by Liu Zongyuan (813–852), "On the Little Knoll West of Gu Mu Pond."

and even paid my debts. The two of us worked our heads off. I discovered that in the United States to clear your credit history is just as arduous as it is to remove a counterrevolutionary stigma in mainland China. I was pissed off by the structuralization of this consumer society and, in a huff, declared that the deal was off. Chen ShuPing tried to persuade me to the contrary, saying that it was not a moral issue, only a problem of lifestyle and attitudes, and asked me not to cut off my nose to spite my face. One day she got me and the agent over to her house to talk it over. She even offered the house she and her husband owned as collateral. The agent finally agreed to give me the mortgage, probably on Chen's account.

Chen was even more excited that I was. The day before we exchanged papers, she called me on the phone: "Your dream has come true!" The afternoon after everything was all signed and sealed, I wheeled Fu Li over for a look at the place. Chen ShuPing came along with her husband. He brought out two bottles of white wine, saying, "This calls for a celebration!" "Look," Chen said to her husband. "There are three willow trees, a real 'Retreat of the Three Willows.'"

The wine made us slightly tipsy that same night over dinner.

S u Dan didn't spare himself during the move. It actually put him in a good mood. Fu Li said the child was like herself and took no nonsense from anybody; what we call in Chinese the donkey that only works with stroking. As I was busy with the moving, I thought to myself that I had been treating Su Dan like an adult since his mother's disability. I had robbed him of his childhood, and he was standing up for the rights due to his age group, and resisted sharing my burdens as an adult. He may have been right. He had lost so much. He wanted to keep what he could get so long as it didn't interfere with his studies or caring for his mother. You can't argue with that, I suppose. There was a party at his school on Christmas Eve. I asked him whether he was going.

He said, "Consider yourself lucky. There's a party every weekend. I never go."

"You can go."

"I don't want to."

"Why? I can drive you over."

"I'm only interested in sports. It's also a kind of party."

Fu Li heard every word of our conversation. At night she asked me softly, "Don't you think the child is a bit lonely? Can't get on with people? Or perhaps, because we don't give parties, he doesn't want to go to other people's houses." She added forlornly, "Let's give him a birthday party."

"Good."

"I'll practice harder at walking. I'll make a few dishes."

"Let me fix a few dishes."

"No, I want to do it." And she started crying.

She was in low spirits for several days.

Su Dan rarely gave us a chance to talk. But each conversation we did have opened up a world of information. For instance, one day he blurted out, "Asians like me who don't dye their hair are getting rarer and rarer in school."

I was shocked. "Why dye your hair?"

"See? You haven't got a clue! Asian kids all feel different. The first year they're just dumb. The second year they start to wear rings on their fingers and ears; they wear sunglasses and even keep them on indoors. The third year they wear certain clothes, the glossy kind—"

"What do you mean, glossy?"

"The colors shine. Under lamplight, they cast a reflection."

"To catch attention?"

"Probably. And in the fourth year, they dye their hair."

"You mean their parents take them to get it done?"

"No! You can buy dye at any supermarket. Four dollars a package."

"Dye the hair blond?"

"No. Right now the fashion is gold at the top, a combination of colors in the middle, and a spot of black at the bottom."

Heavens, it's hard on these kids! Their parents bequeathed them this difference, then left them to cope with it on their own. I finally understood my son. He has more self-restraint than other kids. He has not kept up with the lifestyle normal for kids around here. He is repressed in many ways, the main reason being his mother's disability. He is actually very observant. He feels that I am hard to talk to. He doesn't want to be always asking me for favors, so he keeps his thoughts under lock and key. I had always thought he had too many temptations. Actually, he not only refuses to dye his hair, he doesn't touch drugs, he is quite hazy about sex, and he is careful with his money. As a result of repression, he immerses himself in computer programs and karate and practices the sprint. Actually, he came in second in a school competition, making the hundred-yard dash in eleven seconds, finishing just behind a black boy who made it in ten seconds. If I try to restrict these last few resources left to him, he will fly into a temper. They are his only release. How can a teenage boy not try to release himself in some way? It was I who demanded too much. I had lost my bearings.

The first morning in the new house, I had breakfast together with Fu Li. The sun poured in from the east-facing window, spilling all over the dining table. It was a life we had never lived before. I began to appreciate Chen ShuPing's words: a struggle of three months, and you've finally done it. It was not easy. What is there to hold on to? After all is said and done, there's only home and family.

It is the anniversary of the death of Xu Zhimo.[25] Chen ShuPing sent me clippings of various newspaper articles on the love affair between Xu and Lu Xiaoman. At first I did not understand why she was doing it, and then one day it dawned on me.

Two years ago, when Professor Yu returned from a trip to Taiwan, he told me that many people were inquiring after me. "You must occupy yourself, after all. You can't just give up because of what has happened, can you?"

He would not believe that I had indeed given up, given up on what was left of the so-called elitist in me. Professor Yu told me that if I cultivated myself for a couple of years I'd find myself a new man. Being a historian, he added, "Try to connect spiritually with the superior people in history." I realize that Professor Yu was trying to lead me out of confusion and make me see that a man can only lift himself out of adversity through spiritual forces, by appealing to the boundless pool of resources accumulated by the ancestors in our culture. This is possible through the Chinese person's power of transcendence,

---

[25]Xu Zhimo (1897–1931), Chinese poet, traveled in Europe and the United States, where he completed his education, returned to China to teach and was celebrated as a leader of the new poetry movement. Sometimes referred to as the "Shelley" of China, Xu divorced his wife and married divorcee Lu Xiaoman, to much publicity.

where it connects to the living essence of humanity. But to someone of my generation, reared in the shadow of "anti-tradition," it is the hardest thing of all.

Chen ShuPing, on the other hand, tried to lead me to see the light by another path. After sending me these clippings commemorating Xu Zhimo, she called me on the phone. "Isn't it interesting?" she said. "Lu Xiaoman's ex-husband Wang Geng was a student at Princeton. His files must still be around somewhere."[26]

She took Fu Li and me to check the university's files on Wang Geng. She felt great pity for Wang and deplored the waste of his talent. She touched something in me that had long been submerged, a glimpse of the soul, a spiritual state.

After Wang Geng, we went on to talk about Lin Huiyin. Chen ShuPing had been Professor Jonathan Spence's assistant when she was at Yale, and she had been very interested in the story of Liang Sicheng and Lin Huiyin.[27] I had also read something about them, and we used to talk animatedly about the famous couple.

[26]In 1924, Wang Geng was the chief of police in Manchuria; when he discovered his wife, Lu Xiaoman, was having an affair with Xu Zhimo, he first threatened to kill his wife's lover but eventually decided to grant her a divorce instead. See Pang-mei Natasha Chang, *Bound Feet and Western Dress* (New York: Doubleday, 1996).

[27]Liang Sicheng, son of renowned historical figure Liang Qichao, reform figure of the late Qing dynasty. Liang Sicheng himself was an architect and professor at Qinghua University. Lin Huiyin

Finally I began running to the library, reading and writing. Chen ShuPing said, "Let me be your supplier while you do the cooking." She also made me read English, saying, "Never mind the words you don't know, just go on reading." Whenever I had a problem, she would go and ask her husband. It seemed that he held the whole of modern Chinese history in his head. No matter how obscure the reference, he was never at a loss for the answer. Sometimes he would go directly to the library to take out a book that he considered useful to me. Thinking that Professor Yu was suddenly interested in the New Writing after May Fourth,[28] the librarian started recommending books in the field.

As we were bustling in this newfound activity, Fu Li remarked, aside, "So you have got a walking encyclopedia."

Chen ShuPing laughed out loud.

She also read my articles as they came out weekly in the *China Times* column. As she talked about what she

(1903–1955), poet and architect, educated in the United States, wife of Liang Sicheng. Xu Zhimo had been in love with her before his romance with Lu Xiaoman. At present there is a renewal of interest in Xu Zhimo. He and his loves are subjects of a popular television series.

[28] May Fourth movement, 1919. Started in 1919 in Tiananmen Square by students as a patriotic movement after World War I, it was also a popular movement of enlightenment against traditional culture and a literary movement for the creation of a new vernacular literature.

read, it seemed that she was leading me back to those years of helplessness and despair. Chen ShuPing often recalled the Fu Li that she knew before the accident. "I never saw anyone from the mainland who could compare to Fu Li, so self-possessed, so down-to-earth, so clear-headed, keeping her distance. She had said that after she got her license as a registered nurse, she would like to work in pediatrics." She added, "For a long time we were watching in helpless suspense; now we feel at ease."

At the time, Chen ShuPing and her husband had been terrified that I could not cope with the disaster and that my helplessness would affect Fu Li and Su Dan. Now that I had emerged from my shell, they relaxed. And they had actually deduced the change in my condition by reading what I had written. Chen's comments and praises were like encouragements to a child taking its first steps. Without realizing it myself, confidence in my writing talent was reawakening in me. This reacquaintance with writing was like reacquaintance with life. Everything started from scratch, as if going through a rebirth. The old Su Xiaokang died in the car crash. Fu Li's and my own good fortune lay in the fact that someone was there to help us connect to a new life.

Step by step we made our way into our new existence. Life and living are worth cherishing. One day Chen ShuPing brought back from Taipei three "longevity peaches" from her father's birthday, one each for Fu Li, Su Dan, and myself. It was her father's ninety-sixth birthday.

Chen said that Fu Li resembled a daughter of her older brother.

"She has a genuine affection for me," Fu Li said.

I had always dreamed of beautiful houses. Now that we had a little place of our own, I was in a flurry of excitement to furnish it. From the sitting room to the kitchen, from the exhaust fan to the cabinets, I took pleasure in overseeing every detail, dashing off to Home Depot again and again for spare parts. I had never tasted such pleasure before.

Just installing the sitting-room curtains had been an unprecedented treat. At first I was unsure of the color, only feeling that it was unique. After hanging them up, I knew I had hit on the right choice. They shimmered like emerald-green silk against the background of the little pond framed within the window. Perfect. Fu Li also liked them.

This commercialism is really a tangible force that draws you on from one thing to the next. I became captivated by the idea of furniture. After several trips to Ikea, I had my eye on several sets of light varnished wood for the sitting room, the bedroom, and the kitchen, and some wicker chairs for the deck. The sofa, of course, should be leather. I reveled in daydreams of material delights, not at all concerned that in rejecting "plain living" I might lose sight of "high thinking."

Taking Fu Li to look at furniture, my mind went back to the time when we first moved to Beijing and furnished an apartment. Now, as then, Fu Li's taste was good. The dazzling array of furniture on display would at first over-power her and make her dizzy. But in one quick glance she would manage to seize on the best in terms of quality and style. The price, of course, was also top notch. I was thrilled that she was with me in the spirit of the thing, and then shocked when she turned on me and said, "There you go again, ready to throw money away at the drop of a hat! Is it worth it?"

It is true, spending was a pleasure in itself, a release, like feeding an addiction. I began to understand what is meant by American consumerism. The directions of man's desires and energies are defined by culture and civ-ilization. Ancient China was steeped in hedonism, in practical life as well as in aesthetic taste. During times of peace and prosperity, "rice glistened like pearls, as men in fashionable garb parade in gaudy chariots."[29] But follow-ing a period of indulgence, the breakdown of that civi-lization was deplorable: "Of four hundred and eighty monasteries of the Southern Dynasties/ How many tow-ers and terraces loom in the misty rain?"[30] And now under the onslaught of American-style "modernization," the pattern was being repeated.

People say that the state of contentment is the hard-

[29]From a poem by Du Fu (712–770).
[30]From a poem by Du Mu (c. 803–852). Translation supplied by Kang-i Sun Chang.

est to achieve—a state of being happy with what you have and not asking for more, a state in which you cease to crave possessions, achievements, fame and gain, longevity, and so on. I was totally immersed in the daily work of fixing up our new home and experienced a sense of contentment after a job well done. I suppose it is just an ordinary human feeling, but I had never enjoyed it before. Now that I know contentment, I look back and see more clearly the face of calculation and petty-mindedness and all the fears I had gotten rid of. Would I ever be bored? Would I be discontented again? This adjustment of mood must be one of the great human accomplishments. The reverse side of the coin is sinking into pettiness, boredom, fatigue, and meaninglessness. I don't think I will stray in that direction ever again.

As to furniture, we ended up buying nothing. The lovely sitting room is still stocked with sticks of furniture that we picked up here and there—though we did buy a computer table and revolving chair for Su Dan, as he spends so much time on-line and should be comfortable.

The only thing I bought was a king-size mattress and blanket. After Fu Li tried it she said to Chen ShuPing, "How come I never knew that the American blanket is so comfortable?"

"Well, since you have suffered the American nightmare, you should enjoy some American luxury," Chen told her jokingly.

"Yes," Fu Li replied. "From now on, it's just a matter of getting on in daily life."

Hearing Fu Li say this, I was reminded of when she first arrived in the United States. At the time, she did not bring much besides three cotton-padded blankets that she had ordered to be made from newly spun cotton fresh from the countryside and which she had literally shouldered all the way from China. It was an offering from the heart. They were slightly narrow for the beds here, but we made do with them for years, right up to the present.

Our house was on one floor, facing east. In the morning, Fu Li would get up first and sit in the kitchen, totally drenched in the rays of the morning sun as she waited for me.

As the days got warmer, she liked to sit on the deck facing the pond. That little pond was a perfect example of "waxing and waning" with the tide. It was usually dry, but the slightest rain or snow would fill it up. I myself liked to sit on the deck when the sun went down. It would be so quiet everywhere. Although I couldn't exactly "lie down on the mat," as the ancients do, the situation was close to what is described as "the deserted scene strikes the eye, the rippling sound soothes the ears, the carefree playfulness matches the mood, the profound ease suits the heart."[31]

---

[31] From prose by Liu Zongyuan, "On the Little Knoll West of Gu Mu Pond."

At spring planting time, Fu Li began to make sugges-
tions. "String beans can run over the deck, and grapes
too. And we can grow some melons or vegetables on the
outer rim. I'll write to my sister for some seeds."

I smiled but said nothing.

All the Fu girls had a gift for gardening, not because of
their experience in being sent down to the countryside,
but because their mother loved growing things. After the
Cultural Revolution, before the girls were married off,
they moved with their mother into a house with a court-
yard where every inch of ground was planted with flowers
or vegetables according to the season. There was even a
little plot of wheat. I still remember that time when I was
just going out with Fu Li. I went to the back garden and
exclaimed, "What glorious chives!" All the Fu sisters
burst out laughing and Fu Li blushed. "Go away! It's
wheat, for heaven's sake!" And thus I was left with the
reputation of being a perfect ignoramus on the basics of
life, and the Fu sisters never stopped kidding me over my
blunder.

I thought to myself that Fu Li must be bored sitting at
home all the time; she must miss the fresh breath of
greenery from the world outside. So I bought a miniature
boxed plant about the size of my palm. It was a pine tree
whose sturdy little branches were quaintly twisted. A few
green leaves clung to the branches. I put the miniature
box plant on the table right before her, but she was not
interested. Several weeks passed and the plant showed

signs of shriveling, so I watered it. Fu Li said uncon-
cernedly, "If you water it, it will die." Indeed, a few days
later the leaves were sere and yellow. I wanted to save it,
so I moved it outside and planted it in the soil, hoping
that it could be saved.

Knowing that Fu Li liked gardening, Chen ShuPing
often passed magazines on gardening along to her. Finally
she passed on to Fu Li something that got her completely
engrossed. She pored over it and kept repeating to herself,
"Tulip, tulip." She called Chen. "Tulips are wonderful,
why don't you grow more?"

"I can't. The deer eat them."

Fu Li was frustrated. All I knew was that she was taken
up by something or other in the magazine.

The rain of late spring kept pitter-pattering all night.
In the morning Fu Li called out from the kitchen, "Come
here, Xiaokang. Aren't they tulips?"

I didn't pay any attention, not knowing the meaning
of the word "tulip." She called to me again. I thought she
must have mistaken them for what she saw in the magazine and again ignored her. She called me for a third time,
stamping her foot in exasperation. I finally went over and
looked out the east-facing window in the direction that
Fu Li pointed. Goodness, a row of brilliantly colored
flowers lined the foot of the wall, with blossoms as big as
lightbulbs, all bursting in bloom. They were red and
pink and yellow. I turned to the magazine, and indeed
there they were, exactly the same flowers.

"They are tulips," she announced.

"Do you mean that tulips are *yujinxiang*?"

"Yes. Seeing them, now I know that what we call *yujinxiang* are tulips."

"You've been harping on tulips the last several days, and here they are!"

The tulips seemed to have descended straight from heaven. Their appearance was probably the only miracle the two of us ever encountered.

One evening, Professor Yu came over softly to look at the tulips. He went back and told his wife, "The curtains are drawn, and the family is sitting down to dinner." Chen ShuPing told this to me later.

The little miniature pine that I planted never showed any signs of picking up, the leaves are still a dismal yellow.

July 17, 1997. Two more days to the fourth anniversary of the accident.

I was totally relaxed. Fu Li told me that twice she saw me smiling in my sleep. Does this mean she often looks at me when I am asleep?

"You laughed out loud," she said.

AFTERWORD

As I was writing this book in the heat of summer, 1997, Fu Li on impulse called her sibling Fu Ling in Beijing. The two sisters chatted for a while. When Fu Li hung up, she told me two pieces of family news.

"Ma told Fu Ling that when she dies, she wants her ashes to be mixed with Father's and scattered in the Yellow River."

"When did she say that?"

"After her visit to the United States. She stopped first in Beijing and left word of this with Fu Ling before setting off for Zhengzhou."

The other piece of news Fu Ling had told her in great confidence: Ma had taken out all her savings to buy an apartment in Zhengzhou that was still under construction and left word that it was for Fu Li. I knew that Ma had no savings; whatever she had was probably what I had sent her after Fu Li's accident, hoping she would live comfortably. It seemed she had not touched any of it but had sunk it all into the apartment.

The news made me thoughtful. In 1994 the old lady, already over seventy, had made that sorrowful trip to the United States to see us. And she had gone back and quietly prepared for the end. How despondent she must have been! Obviously she had given up on life; all she hoped for was to be reunited with her husband, who preceded her thirty years ago. The only thing that tugged at her heart in this world was her daughter Fu Li, paralyzed on the other side of the world. All her life she had never flinched from the worst-case scenario; she had planned for all eventualities. But for her to take this step really tore at my heart. What a wrenching feeling it is to realize that you have let down someone who trusted you!

Thus when I finished my book, I decided to dedicate it to Fu Li's parents, Fu Boling and Wang Jingjuan.

I stumbled through the book somehow. At first it was just scraps of paper torn from notebooks, then a jumble of diskettes. Over the years I managed to put down snatches of thought on a daily basis, sometimes in the lounge of the hospital in Buffalo, sometimes in the streets of Manhattan. I had never been able to get into the habit of writing a diary, even when I was a child. In the first days of my exile in Paris, I bought a notebook, shut myself in the refugee camp, and decided to write a "diary of exile"; I could barely write down those words, my heart was trembling so. For the last couple of years, however, as I kept Fu Li company, I felt the compulsion to write and couldn't let a day pass without putting down something on paper; after putting it down on paper, I never looked at it again. For the first time in my life I was writing without being conscious of what I was doing.

In China we had prided ourselves on being the unique species of the animal kingdom—the animal that "crawls over paper." It was the only activity we deigned to pursue. Some relied on interviews, some on collecting data, some on scholarship, and then there were the superior species who relied on inspiration or imagination, calling it "creative writing." I suppose I had also dabbled in "creative writing." But reduced to my present state, my writing seemed instinctive, a cry for release, an impulse to empty out something on a daily basis. As I "crawled" along, for the first time I did not have a readership in mind, and no desire to turn my crawlings into print.

Later on, when Mr. Yang Ze asked me to write for his column, I started to spell out the feelings that had haunted me all these years and gave no thought as to whether they would interest others. How could I write a column in my condition? I had really lost the knack of writing and had no clue to the fact that people did not realize the state I was in. But having to produce fifteen hundred words per week made me go back to the scraps of writings and diaries scattered on diskettes, as if rereading myself. My own particular version of "wild words scattered on the page, a torrent of heart-broken tears"[1] called up all the minute details and pain without giving me relief. On the contrary, I was plunged into a more acute cycle of emptying out.

With no planning, no trimming, no concern about style, least of all any pretensions to preach, my only desire was to make sense of those details, as if I were piecing together someone who had been lost in the darkness, and that someone happened to be myself. My diary thus became the material to reread myself. Facing my chilling old self, which had lost its bearings, my inspiration and imagination (which had never been abundant) shriveled up further and was driven helter-skelter by my old self. I am not certain whether the feelings recorded in my diary are reliable, but this I know by intuition: They had been caught in the flash of the moment and if I let them go, they would forever remain a chaotic mass. I thought to myself that if I still had the power of language, this was the time to make the best of it. As for the "crawling on paper" of the past and the uncertain prospects of "creative writing" in the future, they are of no account anymore.

I had never exposed myself so nakedly in writing. If I were "stronger," I might not have felt the urge to make notes and this book would not have come into being.

[1] A well-known phrase from the Chinese classical novel *Dream of the Red Chamber.*

Writing the self, the space could have been expanded if I resorted to fiction, but I was not in the mood. The disasters that overtook me—Fu Li without a memory, Su Dan without a mother—seemed the stuff of fiction, an unreal reality. The feeling of being suspended in a timeless spaceless existence, the shock of life being sliced into half, one a previous existence and one present, the intense hopes and disappointments of looking for a miracle—I had never had any such life experiences, nor did I have the experience of writing on such matters. I just let intuition and feelings drive me on. Now that I am writing this afterword and look back to what I have written, I find that there was some planning, trimming, and cutting, but at an unconscious level. Any highlights and evasions were unconscious, but it still is a kind of editing. Thus by editing diaries and letters, I may have concocted something neither fish nor fowl. I may even have lost some of the original flavors and failed to package the whole into passable literature.

Writings thus put together reveal purely private feelings and should not be made public. I doubt if one's personal life experiences, however unusual, are worth sharing with others. Of course if you have packaged it in exquisite literary form, that is another matter. Readers can at least enjoy your verbal skills. But in my own case, I discover as I write this afterword that I am bad at packaging and have no desire to do it. But can I just spill everything out so bluntly? Nowadays in the United States, it seems to be the thing. In nonfiction some people expose their private lives and are applauded for it. But what I am spilling out is not only myself but Fu Li—all that she went through in her pitiful unconscious state—it is her privacy; does she want me to write it out? One day when she is totally conscious and sees how I described her, she may blame me; it is hard to tell. And then there is Su Dan, who was a minor at the time. I have made public his unbalanced state when he lost his mother. Will he accept this version of his terrible adolescence? I have no answers to these questions and feel that I should make a note of them in an afterword.

Even in describing the realm of the private, there is no way to avoid mentioning other people. During the writing, I never asked myself what would be the consequences if some of the details I describe were made public. At the time, I had no taboos and just let myself go. It was only when the book was to be published that I asked myself the question of propriety. When I was writing for the *China Times* column, I did consider sifting and cutting. But so many people and so many events are so closely intertwined with our despair that I could not have extricated them if I had wanted to. So I just let it go. Now that it is in book form, I begin to wonder what passages may be offensive to certain quarters. For instance, I may have been disrespectful of religion and Qigong circles. Now that I have calmed down, I realize it is unfair to blame others when you are crying to heaven and earth in despair. Besides, in spiritual matters, how can you tell that you have not benefited? I wrote a whole chapter on Fu Li's "Noble Dames" as if they were the only ones who helped, which was not true. When we were struck by disaster, many, many people, more than I can count, gave us help, support, and silent concern. A hospital visit, a phone call, a prayer, a postcard—these things warmed my heart just as much as the occasions I recorded. But even as I was describing our suffering and despair, in my heart I knew there were many people more unfortunate than I was who have never received the sympathy that was showered on us, and if we still complain it will be a lack of appreciation of these goodhearted people. I want to extend my belated thanks to all the friends who expressed concern for Fu Li and Su Dan.

I also wish to express my thanks again to Mr. Yang Ze and Mr. Liu Kerang. They conceived the idea for this book and are its first editors. Ms. Ji Ji was a reader of the column the minute it appeared and later encouraged me to turn it into book form. She was like a fellow traveler with me as I "crawled" my way through the "squares" in that icy region. Professor David Der-wei Wang wrote an introduction. He and I had never met, and yet he actually took two weeks off from his busy schedule to read the book and introduce it. He read into the book so many nuances that I am embarrassed. Fu Li also read the introduction and is very pleased. We are both deeply obligated to him for his goodwill.

Last I must reiterate that, as Professor Wang has pointed out, this book, for me and Fu Li and Su Dan, is not just a book but a testimony of disaster. We were not alone; many people helped us through, first and foremost Professor YingShih Yu and his wife, Chen ShuPing. Chen was like a surrogate mother to Fu Li, helping to care for her and standing by my side. After the book was finished, I thought of many titles, none of which seemed to the point. Professor Yu casually suggested "*Li Hun Li Jie Zi Xu*" and personally made the inscription. He remarked that the "self-record" is the perfect form for recording family history as the ancients used to do. I thought to myself that for the Chinese autobiographical style, no title could be more appropriate than "self-record." And anyway, nothing could please me more than the fact of Professor Yu suggesting a title and making an inscription for the book.

Years have passed, but the pain is still there. A couple of days ago, Fu Li suddenly remarked over breakfast, "The thought is frightful. Suppose you were to commit suicide. Isn't that running away?"

"Why do you bring this up again?"

"I remember once, before we moved here, I had wanted to grasp a live wire and electrocute myself. But then I thought if you were to grab me, wouldn't you be electrocuted too?"

"You thought of suicide?"

"Yes. Practicing to walk was so hard, I couldn't stand it anymore. Being alive was meaningless."

It was the first time Fu Li had said this. I was shocked. I had never realized there was this kind of struggle going on in her heart. All I knew was that her mind was in a muddle or that, according to her temperament, she would be obsessed with recovery. Obviously there are secrets that the human heart keeps tightly wrapped and will never make known to others. Strange, why should she mention it on that particular day? Are her psychological defenses breaking down? Is her mind clear again, or is this a sign of deeper depression? Perhaps both. She will never tell. But nowadays she spends more time alone with her own thoughts.

We have a long way to go.

PERMISSION ACKNOWLEDGMENTS

Grateful acknowledgment is made to the following for permission to reprint previously published material:

HarperCollins Publishers Inc. and *Faber and Faber Ltd.:* Excerpts from *Testaments Betrayed* by Milan Kundera, translated by Linda Asher. *Les Testaments Trahis,* copyright © 1993 by Milan Kundera. Rights in the United Kingdom administered for *Les Testaments Trahis* by Faber and Faber Ltd., London. Reprinted by permission of HarperCollins Publishers Inc. and Faber and Faber Ltd.

Time, Inc.: Excerpt from article about the MTV generation (*Time*, 9 June 1997, p. 58), copyright © 1997 by Time Inc. Reprinted by permission of Time Inc.

ZHU HONG THANKS THE DEPARTMENT OF FOREIGN LANGUAGES
AND LITERATURES AT BOSTON UNIVERSITY FOR GENEROUS
SUPPORT DURING THE TRANSLATION OF THIS BOOK.

THE DIVING BELL AND THE BUTTERFLY
by Jean-Dominique Bauby

In 1995, Jean-Dominique Bauby, the editor of French *Elle*, suffered a stroke to the brain stem. Bauby spent twenty days in a coma and awoke into a body that had all but stopped working: only his left eye functioned, allowing him to see and, by blinking it, to indicate that his mind was unimpaired. Almost miraculously, he learned to express himself by dictating a word at a time, blinking to select each letter as the alphabet was recited to him. In this painstaking fashion he communicated with others and wrote this extraordinary book.

Memoir/Inspiration/0-375-70121-4

LIFE AS WE KNOW IT
by Michael Bérubé

When Jamie Bérubé was born with Down syndrome, he was subjected to the medical procedures, insurance guidelines, and cultural representations that surround every child that society designates as "disabled." In this wrenching yet ultimately inspiring book, Jamie's father, literary scholar Michael Bérubé, describes what it is like to bring up this lively, loving, mischievous boy, and shows how such an exceptional child can change our vision of our society and ourselves.

Parenting/Family/0-679-75866-6

WHERE IS THE MANGO PRINCESS?
by Cathy Crimmins

Cathy Crimmins's life changes forever when her husband Alan is run over by a speedboat. The accident severely damages the frontal lobes of his brain, the area that controls speech, memory, movement, and personality. As her husband recovers, Crimmins realizes that the brilliant man who loved foreign cinema and wry humor is gone, and in his place is a childlike replica who laughs at cartoons. Candid, astonishing, and witty, *Where Is the Mango Princess?* is an unforgettable chronicle of transformation and a moving tale of personal triumph.

Memoir/Medicine/0-375-70442-6

VINTAGE BOOKS
Available at your local bookstore or call toll-free to order:
1-800-793-2665 (credit cards only).